THE OFFICIAL INVESTORS GUIDE

BUYING • SELLING

GOLD SILVER DIAMONDS

BY
MARC HUDGEONS

FIRST EDITION

HOUSE OF COLLECTIBLES, INC., ORLANDO, FLORIDA 32809

Published by: The House of Collectibles, Inc.
Orlando Central Park
1900 Premier Row
Orlando, FL 32809
Phone: (305) 857-9095

Printed in the United States of America

Library of Congress Catalog Card Number: 80-85067

ISBN: 0-87637-171-3 / Paperback

ISBN: 0-87637-235-3 / Hardcover

TABLE OF CONTENTS

GOLD

SILVER

DIAMONDS

AUTHOR'S NOTE

Dear Collector/Investor,

Times have changed. Long gone are the days when gold, silver and diamonds were a concern of only the wealthy. Today, the average person has the chance to own these things — as adornments, collectors' items, or financial investments. Most people already do own them, in one form or another. Unfortunately, they know very little about them. Their lack of knowledge often leads them to pay too much when they buy, get too little when they sell, or sell at the wrong time, to the wrong buyer. Additionally, lack of knowledge stops many persons from taking advantage of the great investment potential in precious metals and fine gems.

You must become an expert to buy and sell intelligently. Everything you need to know can be learned in a surprisingly short period of time, by reading this book.

Until now, no single book has existed that provides the facts and sound advice on buying and selling in language that everyone can understand.

This book has been designed to provide the consumer with the basic information that is needed to trade successfully in the precious metals and gem markets. ***Knowing what to buy, how to buy and how much to pay is vital*** . . . but you must also know when to buy . . . and when to sell . . . because timing is critical when values can soar overnight.

No matter what kind of gold, silver or diamond you may already own, old or new, handsome looking or fit for the smelter's furnace, you are shown exactly how to determine their value. Not an arbitrary value that you and a buyer might haggle over, but a specific dollars and cents value in terms of intrinsic worth and the present market. You are shown how to tell real diamonds from fake . . . to determine if gold and silver articles are plated or solid . . . and how you can easily, to the fraction of an ounce, calculate how much precious metal ***ANY*** object contains.

Let's not kid anybody. The market in gold, silver and diamonds is highly competitive. While essentially ethical, these trades have always attracted large numbers of gypsters and fast-buck artists. This book shows you how to choose your dealers, and how to spot any questionable actions on the part of others with whom you may buy or sell. Most of all, it will prevent you from *cheating yourself.* Everyday the public loses millions of dollars buying valuables for more than they're worth, and selling others for less than their value . . . just because they don't know any better.

If you thought that a jewelry store was the best place to buy diamonds; if you thought that sterling was the finest grade of silver; if you believed that "solid" gold was always 24K pure . . . you'll learn differently in this book.

The secret to making money trading in the precious metals and gems market is knowledge.

MARC HUDGEONS

GOLD

GOLD THROUGH THE AGES

How did it all begin, this lust after and fascination with gold?

Historians don't really know. But the ancient world has yielded up ample evidence of the homage paid to gold thousands of years ago, in the form of references in literature and art and, best of all, archaeological discoveries of ancient goldwork.

If any doubt existed about the reverence in which gold was held by ancient civilizations, it was dispelled in 1922 when Howard Carter and Lord Carnarvan, two spunky young English archaeologists, opened the long-sealed tomb of Egypt's King Tutankhamen — better known as Tut. There lay the fabled old pharaoh's bones, vastly overshadowed by an array of artworks that staggered the imagination. There were gold statues, gold rings, gold bracelets, gold urns, gold everything, some of it so heavy it could hardly be lifted. Millions upon millions of dollars worth of gold (even then), wrought into objects designed to satisfy the pharaoh's spirit.

It could logically be adduced that the worship of gold was directly connected to its scarcity, just as that of diamonds and other precious stones. But that was probably not the case. More likely, its lofty position was attained because of its physical properties. It was handsomer than other metals. It was softer and could be fashioned into all sorts of baubles and amulets and other trinkets, not to mention large-scale statuary. Its uncanny malleability allowed just a teensy drop to be beaten out into a big sheet, as thin as a moth's wing. And yet it was strong. It could be engraved on. It could be made into crowns or great blocks for the walls of temples. And not even the Biblical Flood could tarnish it. Sink gold beneath the sea, and no matter how salty the waters or how long you leave it submerged, it suffers not at all.

Quite a bit of ancient gold ore did, in fact, come from the sea. A famous Egyptian bas-relief dating to about 2,900 B.C. pictures gold prospectors panning a stream. This not only tells us that the panning technique was known 4,900 years ago, it additionally tells us that gold was of sufficient importance and value to break one's back looking for. The Egyptians were not dull-witted folk, even in 2,900 B.C. They would not have fooled with panning if some decent reward did not await their efforts.

What do we mean by "value"?

A good question, because obviously "money" as we know it did not exist. How could anyone get paid for the gold they found, when there was no money to pay them with? They did in fact get paid. Not in coins or currency notes but in goods. They could take their gold into the marketplace and swap it for a cow or several sacks of millet or enough dried reeds to build a new roof on their house. If it were a huge amount, they could give it over to a "banker," who would issue a note for it, in the form of a clay cylinder impressed with hieroglyphic writing. The note could then be cashed in at some later date, or spent as money.

There is also the very strong probability that most gold panning in ancient Egypt was not carried on by wide-eyed seekers of riches but by the state. Quite likely, the panner in that bas-relief is not a private citizen amusing himself but a slave laborer, who is doing his duty because directly behind him (though not shown in the picture) stands a slave-driver with a poised whip. It is doubtful that the enormous quantities of bullion consumed by art and industry in Egypt could have derived entirely from chance discoveries by freelancers.

The legends of the treasuries of Egypt's pharaohs, and the riches in gold and other objects they contained, are well-known. Rameses II, the pharaoh plagued by dental problems, is believed to have been — chiefly on strength of his gold ownership — the wealthiest human to ever live. Translated into modern terms, his gold reserves would have a value in the trillions of dollars. What were they worth then? Sadly, we don't really know. We can only say how much gold was worth after it started getting coined into money, which did not occur until the first millennium B.C. Estimates have been made, but they amount to little more than wild guesses.

The Egyptians were not the only peoples of the classical age to place a lofty regard on gold. So did Assyrians, their close neighbors, the Babylonians, the Mesopotamians, and just about everybody else. The only places where gold was not thought much of were those not reached by civilization, or by the kind of highly-polished civilization that flourished through the Mid East. The brutish Cro-Magnons of central Europe could not have rated gold too highly, as it could not contribute much to their way of life. But it should not be overlooked that in 15th century A.D. Nigeria, the Benin natives — who technically were not civilized because they had no written language — made extensive use of gold in their craft works.

Gold succeeded in working its way deep into myth and legend. It could not be otherwise, as all things that were greatest or biggest or most awe-inspiring became ingrained with the tales of the gods. Perhaps the best remembered among Greek mythology was the saga of Jason and the Argonauts who, along with Hercules (or Herakles, if you collect coins), searched long and hard for the Golden Fleece. Exactly what the Golden Fleece was, we are not privileged to know. No explanation of it was made in the myth. It was either some immense deposit of raw bullion or an object made of gold. Some historians have conjectured it to have been a book bound in solid gold, but this is impossible as books with bindings (gold or otherwise) did not exist then. Others believe it refers to deposits washed from river sands in the area now known as Armenia. Sheepskin was used for gold washing in those days, which could very likely be how the word fleece got into Golden Fleece.

King Midas of Phrygia also comes to mind, on the subject of Greek mythology. It has been established beyond reasonable doubt that a King Midas, of genuine flesh and blood, did indeed live and did indeed rule over Phrygia (as for the existence of Jason and Hercules, the authorities are not so sure). But whether the noted events which enshrined his name in history really occurred is doubtful. In any case they make good reading and contribute much to our knowledge of ancient attitudes toward gold. King Midas, it seemed, had a thing for gold, above and beyond that of the average king. It was the passion of his life. The royal presence quivered at the sight of gold. Sparks ran up his spine when he touched gold. He enjoyed nothing more than looking for endless hours upon his accumulations of it, which were tidy. But no matter how much gold Midas collected, his appetite was not satisfied. So he pleaded with Zeus, the chief god, to impart upon him the ability to turn into gold whatever he touched. Wise old Zeus, the thrower of thunderbolts, apparently figured Midas needed to be taught a lesson.

He granted the wish.

Midas was beside himself with glee. He touched a terra-cotta vase; suddenly it was gold. He did the same with a wooden chair; with a silver platter; and with a piece of scrap leather. All turned to gold! Real gold, 24 shiny golden luscious karats! The king dropped to his knees to give his thanks to Zeus. As he did so, the marble floor of his palace turned to gold. He quickly ran and touched the walls. He climbed up to touch the ceiling. Now he was totally surrounded by gold! It was beyond his wildest dream.

But the awakening was soon to come.

That night, a Midas in better spirits than his subjects ever saw him sat down to the royal banqueting table. He would eat hearty for sure, they said. But they were wrong. As he reached for a leg of delicately dressed poultry, it turned instantly to gold. He gave a weak grin and picked up a loaf of bread. It too became gold, and he meekly placed it aside. The same thing happened no matter what he touched. When wine met his lips, it froze into a golden mass in the glass.

So the king went hungry. But he was not totally discouraged. Surely there was some way around that vexing little problem. After all, you had to pay some price for the extraordinary gift he received. As he climbed into bed and laid a royal kiss upon the lips of his queen, the spoils of his greed became evident. In a flash she was transformed into several tons of solid gold.

Seeing now that enough was enough, Midas called upon Zeus to remove the gift that had been a curse in disguise. Zeus complied, accompanying it with a warning to get gold off the royal brain in the future.

Literary historians are convinced that the legend of Midas inspired Charles Dickens to compose "A Christmas Carol." Ebenezer Scrooge seems to have been based on Midas.

As far as Biblical references to gold are concerned, there are many. Gold is repeatedly spoken of in the Old Testament, when reference is made to riches and splendor and things that lead men from the straight and narrow. The worshipping of false idols, written into the commandments given to Moses, was without question an allusion to the homage paid to gold. It should be remembered that the Israelites, while waiting for Moses to return from the mount and becoming increasingly doubtful they would ever see him again, built a golden calf and were in the process of worshipping it when an extremely startled Moses reappeared. Not a wooden calf or a bronze calf or a silver calf, but a golden one, described precisely as such in the scriptures. And we are dealing here not with people accustomed like the pharaohs to riches and luxuries, but a nomadic tribe that was lucky to have robes on its back. It is not stated where this gold came from, but such details are not pertinent to the story. Moses is said to have rent the calf asunder. This may seem hard to take, as no mortal could destroy a solid gold statue bare-handed. But possibly the golden calf was assembled from a number of different pieces, which had not been soldered into place, and therefore could be dismantled without superhuman effort.

Another familiar reference to gold in the Old Testament (there are plenty in the New, too) is the mines of Solomon. This fabled hoard of gold was without doubt located in Africa, but just where in Africa was never revealed. There is speculation that Solomon might, even in that ages-old time, have tapped the gold deposits in what later became the city of Johannesburg. If so, the extent of Biblical-era gold mining was extensive, to say the least.

By the 8th century B.C. gold was being fashioned into coinage. It was not pure gold but a mixture of gold and silver known as electrum, found in great abundance along the river beds near Sardis in Lydia (Grecian Asia Minor).

To the Lydians belongs the distinction — so far as we know — of striking the first coinage and, of course, it was quite appropriate that it should contain gold. These were not beauty contest winners as far as their designs were concerned. The metal was roughly shaped into small lumps, with no attempt made to hammer it flat. Into the soft lumps were pressed designs, picturing various kinds of animals. There was no attempt at this early date to provide coins with a face value or state the issuing government's name. Apparently a coin picturing half a bull (which was the most usual design) equaled the market value of half a bull.

The age of the conquistadors opened a new chapter in gold's history. Columbus, seeking a westward route to the Indies and coming upon the Americas, was more than satisfied to have found a new continent. Later explorers, mostly from Spain, discovered that this much-publicized new land did not only boast tobacco and parrots and strange-speaking natives, it contained something of which they had long been fond in their native country: gold, and plenty of it. American gold did not come from North America but chiefly Peru and Colombia, of which the Spaniards made a clean sweep in their travels. The gold hoards of the Incas bedazzled them. They brought back as much as possible to Spain, and the Spanish government, quick to seize the opportunity of gold for the taking, dispatched fleets of ships to recover the remainder. During the 16th century — which, it has to be kept in mind, was before the pilgrims landed at Plymouth Rock or much of anything was occurring in North America — more than eight million ounces of gold were transported from Central and South America to Europe. By the 17th century, when full-scale mining operations had gotten into swing, the Americas were accounting for 61% of the world's gold production. During the 18th century the mind-bending total of 80% of world gold production came from this source — more than three out of every four ounces.

ALCHEMISTS AND ARTISTS

When Rome fell, in 476 A.D., most of its traditions and glories fell with it. Never would its achievements in the arts be approached again. But successive civilizations made whatever use they could of what the Romans left behind. One was an ample supply of gold and the knowledge of how it could be refined and made into objects of diverse sorts.

Throughout the middle or "dark" ages (roughly 500-1500 A.D.), gold was just as highly prized as it had been by the pharaohs and the Greek kings and the Roman emperors. It was a bit scarcer now, because Europe no longer had access to the rich deposits in Asia Minor or certain other areas of the Graeco-Roman world. But some raw bullion was being mined in Saxony and Austria, and this was supplemented by melting down whatever gold could be rescued from Roman rubbish heaps. Plenty of it was there for the taking in ruined temples, and probably elsewhere as well.

Artisans of the middle ages worked wonders with gold. They did not perhaps churn out as much as their predecessors in better times, but what they lacked in quantity they compensated for with quality. A good deal of this work was performed in the craft shops of monasteries in northern and western Europe, and resulted in splendorous articles for use in church services. From the earliest middle ages, richly decorated manuscript books were occasionally bound in covers of gold. Some of these (or the covers at any rate) have survived and bear ample testimony to the artistic accomplishments of that time.

Wooden boards, usually hollowed out in the centers, served as the core for such bindings. Over them was laid sheets of beaten gold, fairly thick, which were nailed into place. Mountings were then attached to the covers and precious or semi-precious jewels set into the mountings. The bindings could be further embellished by working up engraved designs in the gold or setting large golden crucifixes or other statuary into the recessed portions of the covers. These books must have been worth enormous sums of money even when new. The labor they involved, over and above the expense of raw materials, was considerable. New York's Pierpont Morgan Library owns examples of a few medieval golden bindings. But very few were created, compared to the numbers of books produced as a whole, and of them only a fraction have managed to survive.

It may be wondered why goldwork, whether books or chalices or reliquaries, should have perished at such a high rate, when its very value ought to have encouraged careful protection. The problem, then as now, was that valuable merchandise of any kind was the first to be plundered when a city was sacked or a monastery invaded. There was wholesale invasion of monasteries, often with government sanction, such as occurred as late as the 16th century in England as the result of Henry VIII's quarrels with Rome. As far as goldwork owned by kings and princes was concerned, it fared little better than that in ecclesiastical hands. Often the owners were the worst offenders. In times of pressing financial need, jewels would be pried from jeweled bookbindings and other valuables collected for sale, to bail the king out of a royal mess.

Some gold coinage was struck during the Middle Ages but very little compared to that of Rome and practically nothing in comparison to the bounteous gold coinage of ancient Greece. Silver took its place and even that was frequently debased or hammered so thin that a weakling could bend the coin with nothing but his fingers.

The Scandinavians did some artful work in gold during the Middle Ages. They were perhaps the chief or at any rate the most inventive users of it, from about the 8th century A.D. up to the 12th. The full extent of their productions has yet to be learned, because of the slowness of archaeological work in that part of the world. Some brilliant finds have been turned up, leading to expectations that more might follow.

A notable figure during the Middle Ages was the alchemist, immortalized in a play of that name by Ben Johnson. Alchemists were known to all parts of Europe; they did not exist in America simply because this land had not become sufficiently inhabited in their day. By the time of our colonization, the alchemy trade had disappeared.

Alchemists, as the name implies, were chemists of a sort, or at least they fancied themselves to be chemists. They labored usually in dungeon-like laboratories, surrounded by vials of odd-looking and even odder smelling potions and over flaming hot ovens. What they accomplished was very little, but their purpose was noble. Scientific knowledge being at a low ebb then, it was not known just how gold came to be. There were various theories, one of the popular ones (to which alchemists clung) being that gold resulted from copper or other metal being heated up by the earth's molten gases and turning, through natural transformation, into gold. It was believable in a way, if you look at things from the standpoint of someone uninformed about physics or metallurgy but just going by what he observes with his eyes. Gold is very similar in color to copper. Yet it's softer and heavier. Could not these changes occur as a result of the heating process, which would do something to the color, and probably the softness, and maybe even the weight?

It sounded good. So good that generations of alchemists wasted untold time and perspiration putting copper into furnaces and heating it up, waiting for it to become gold.

Sadly, it always came out copper. No matter how they heated it, or soaked it in boiling water, or pounded it, or squeezed it, or cajoled it, they could not induce it to turn into anything but what it already was.

But they kept trying. Their lack of success, they were convinced, was not because the task was impossible, but rather because they had not yet struck on the correct formula. Perhaps if it were a few degrees hotter, or left in the oven a couple hours longer, or a smaller piece were used, or a handful of chicken feathers thrown atop it for good luck . . .

It was no use. Nothing ever happened. But who cared? Not the alchemists, who were not depending upon production of gold to earn their livings. They were already well provided for. Most of them worked in the employ of wealthy patrons, each of whom wanted *his* alchemist to win the artificial gold making sweepstakes.

By late in the 16th century, after this had been going on several hundred years, it was admitted that a dead horse was being beaten. The alchemists and their sponsors threw in the towel.

MAJOR GOLD STRIKES

Prior to the 19th century most of the world's gold came from Central and South America. During the era of colonization and well into the 19th century, it was not believed that the North American continent contained significant gold deposits. Until then only the eastern half of the nation had been thoroughly explored and assumptions were that metallic and mineral deposits of the west would prove similar. Then came the celebrate "strike" at Sutter's Mill, near what is now Sacramento, California, setting off the biggest gold rush in history.

John A. Sutter was having a sawmill constructed in the winter of 1847-1848 by the Sacramento River. When gold nuggets were found on the property, Sutter tried — in vain — to keep this information secret. It was quickly circulated and triggered wholesale immigration to the area. Not only Californians came to search for the precious bullion, but fortune hunters from Missouri and Kansas and as far east as Boston. They came in droves, by Conestoga wagon or whatever means of travel they could find (rail was out, as the lines of the Northern Pacific had not yet been laid — in fact it was California's growth, due to gold fever, that encouraged establishment of rail service). Many were down-on-their-luck souls who would grasp at any straws. But some men quit lucrative jobs in the east and trundled across the prairie, spurred on by the lure of great riches.

Chaos reigned. News filtering back across the Mississippi amounted to a pastiche of fact and fiction. Strikes were reported that never occurred. When a few hundred ounces of gold were found, it became a few hundred pounds by the time word got to St. Louis and Chicago. Prospectors who sold their bullion for a couple of thousand were referred to as millionaires. So excessively rosy was the picture painted that everyone assumed you just went to California, loaded golden nuggets as big as boulders into wagons, and cashed them in. So they went west, at all costs, abandoning everything if necessary, giving no thought to family or starvation or the perils posed by less-than-friendly Indians. If there were a Golden Fleece by the shores of the Pacific, they wanted their piece of the pie. And they kept going, even after stragglers began returning empty-handed with tales of frustration and hardship. Obviously, *they* didn't know where to look.

Most of those who made it safely to California — which not, by a very long shot, all did — found no gold whatsoever. Claims had quickly been staked on the major deposit locations and late-comers had no choice but to seek elsewhere. Either that, or risk a barrage of buckshot by working claimed land. Considerable quantities of gold were taken by claim jumpers, who ended up either in court or (the legal system not being too finely honed in the west back then) a pine box.

The rest simply looked. And looked. And looked. They fell to their knees, as if confronted by the Divine Presence, at the sight of every yellow-colored pebble in the ground. They took pans and worked the streams around the Sacramento River for days, and weeks, and months, until the sun turned their skin to leather. They grasped at flakes the size of gnats in the bottoms of their pans. And many gradually went a little soft in the head. Men who had held jobs as accountants and attorneys and bank officers found themselves penniless in the desert, with no friends, and frequently with no clear idea any longer of where they were or what they were doing.

The average "strike" in California's gold fields, at the very height of the gold rush, was about *one half ounce per man per day,* or less than $10 worth at that time. But if you take the total, it came to plenty of the magic metal. In a single 12-month period, 2,500,000 ounces were found, or 150,000 pounds — more than would ever again be mined in the U.S. in any one year. That was fact, but it just created more fantasy. Everyone believed that just the iceberg's tip had been hit. Why, with a little more effort, 10 million ounces a year should be possible. Or 20. Or a zillion. There were individuals firmly convinced that the whole state of California lay upon a bed of gold, stretching from the northern woodland to Mexico.

Cities began springing up where the deer and the antelope had played. One of these was, of course, Sacramento — still the state's capital. But there were numerous others, dotted across country previously inhabited by cacti and the bleached bones of bison. They started as frontier trading posts, where donkeys and boots and Colt revolvers were swapped for nuggets or gold dust. As the trading posts attracted so much traffic, enterprising individuals were encouraged to open up barber shops and saloons and various places where the nouveau rich prospectors could disgorge some of their wealth. Hotels began appearing. So did post offices. Pretty soon these were thriving communities served by regular coach lines. But as soon as they came, many of them went. When the gold in a region ran dry, these makeshift towns wheezed and gasped and finally suffocated. There was no other source of revenue.

The effects of the Great Rush of '49 were many and far-reaching. Beneath the facts and figures, the red ink and the black ink, this little episode in mankind's history told more about human psychology than all the writings of Freud and Spinoza: that this most intelligent of all creatures, man, will risk his very existence for scraps of colored rocks.

So much raw gold was being traded in California that things got far out of hand. Nearly everybody who walked into a shop or other place of business presented nuggets or dust instead of coins. This meant it had to be weighed, while other customers waited and fumed; and rarely did the quantity of gold match the amount of the purchase. Pleas to Washington for greater supplies of coinage could not be answered fast enough. Private entrepreneurs stepped in to fill the void, striking their own gold pieces. These, known as "territorial gold tokens," have become sought-after collectors' items. But even they proved insufficient to satisfy the need. Finally the Treasury Department decided to begin striking gold coins of the value of $20 — and that was how the much-revered Double Eagle came to be.

Well, that solved one problem. But it created another. Banks were going crazy counting out Double Eagles — not to mention gold coins of lesser denominations. They petitioned the government for the right to issue paper notes for gold coinage. This proposal was unprecedented in the nation's history. The Treasury Department mused a while and then decided it wasn't a bad idea. So nine California banking institutions were granted the privilege of issuing gold certificates, redeemable for coins on demand — as well as one lone eastern bank, the Kidder Bank of Boston. As late as the 1890's, California was still operating on a chiefly gold economy. And, despite the fact that the Rush was over for 40 years, many a grizzled old prospector still panned the streams amid hopes and dreams of one more find.

Nor has this activity ever totally ceased. Today it's done more as a hobby or a lark, but you will still find people panning for gold in California streams. They find some, too, occasionally.

Naturally, a good deal of bullion from the '49 Rush went into coinage. It was sold by traders to banks, who in turn sold it to the government, which in turn decided that San Francisco might be a good location for a mint, rather than dragging all that gold across hazardous land. So the Rush was responsible for getting that mint, second in importance only to Philadelphia, into business.

After '49, the next big strike was eagerly awaited, chiefly by those unable to cash in on that one. Everybody was certain another would come soon. If there were so much gold in California, there ought to at least be a little in Colorado or Wyoming or some place near California. They waited and wished and hoped. When rail links opened to the west in the 1850's, cash registers jangled in their heads. As soon as word of a strike came, they need only buy a train ticket and be on the road to fame and luxury.

For 10 long years they waited. Then word was received of newly discovered gold fields. They were in Colorado, at a place known as Pike's Peak. Nobody in the East knew from beans about Pike or his Peak, and half could not have found Colorado on a map without assistance. But no matter where gold was, the hopeful and the adventurous would go. They went, in almost the same numbers as they went to Sutter's Mill. This time, many went by rail. But others still traveled by wagon, or horse, or pack mule. The slogan "Pike's Peak or Bust" was scrawled in paint across the canvas sides of numerous wagons, and became the common battle cry of this new band of prospectors. Clever dance hall chorus girls of the time had the slogan elegantly embroidered across the bosoms of their outfits.

Pike's Peak was no Sutter's Mill. In fact the words used to describe it, by those who got there without busting, were largely unprintable. There were vultures. There were snakes. There was drinking water foul enough to paralyze an elephant with one drop. There were insects and diseases as yet unknown to medical science. There were Indians who had hobbies like taking the tops of heads off strangers who ventured into their territories. But there was no gold.

Pike's Peak was, truly, a Bust.

Apparently, either the whole thing was somebody's idea of a practical joke, or some infinitesimal quantity of gold was found there and nothing more. There was no motherlode, no mines, no goldfields. The streams refused to yield up even the tiniest grains.

No towns sprung up. No new rail lines were laid. Nobody got rich. But some of the weary and weak decided to remain in Colorado, either because they were too tired or too ashamed to go home. It had good clean air, they commented. Denver's growth occurred largely thanks to the busted Pike's Peakers and their progeny.

You would think, given that kind of scorching, seekers after gold would not so willingly place their fingers in the fire again. But you would be vastly overestimating human nature. Ambition, especially ambition glittered with the glint of bullion, dies hard. These same men, or others of their like, needed only fresh news or rumors or the scent of gold in their nostrils to fly to the four corners of the globe.

The next gold rush was the last to occur on this continent. It did not prove as big as Sutter's Mill but it was no hoax either. In 1898 reports filtered down through Canada of gold being found in Alaska. Not bitsy nuggets or dust but chunks the size of baseballs or larger. It was there for the taking, except that the taking was no easy task. Getting to the Klondike proved more rigorous than reaching the West, even though this was nearly the 20th century. The Industrial Age had not been visited upon most of the Canadian wilderness, and Alaska was, even then, in about as primeval a state as when inhabited by woolly mastodons. Nor had these relics of lost ages entirely disappeared. Many a prospector, when placing his spade into frozen ground, turned up the soggy carcasses of these prehistoric beasts, who had lain in their icy graves 10,000 years or more.

Now, instead of Pike's Peak or Bust, the slogan was North to Alaska. Once again they used wagons, because they had no choice. But even that did not entirely do the trick. After getting into Alaska and encountering vast expanses of snow and ice, the wagons were useless. They had to be abandoned in favor of sleds, pulled by either horses (as in Siberia) or teams of dogs. It was rugged. Most of those who came were unprepared for the climate's bitterness. They took the kind of winter clothing that sufficed for a January day in New York or Boston, and discovered that 30 below feels a bit differently than 30 above. Many suffered frostbite and sought in vain for medical aid. No doctors could be found, or telephones, or wireless operators, or people or food or anything. Just snow, that fell endlessly and piled so high it seemed it would drown the earth. But they battled on.

The lucky ones did find gold. It had to be mined under unbearable conditions, but it was mined. The unlucky ones returned in various degrees of ill health, and some were not heard of again. But, all in all, it was a colorful era, out of which came much legend and folklore. It was the era of the Face on the Barroom Floor, and the Sawing of Blasphemous Bill (frozen so solid that his body required sawing to fit into the coffin). Nobody realized then that eventually a commodity more valuable than gold, fuel oil, would bring another "rush" to Alaska.

Such were the strikes of North America: two decent ones and a flop, in the space of nearly five centuries of civilized habitation. All told, the bullion taken from them paled before that mined in Africa and the Soviet Union.

But this country did not, by any means, hold a monopoly on gold rushes or on the kind of mentality that created them. Some pretty fair ones occurred on the other side of the world, in Australia for example. In the 19th century Australia was one of Queen Victoria's proud dominions, part of a British Empire on which the sun never set. It was largely unexplored, even though Captain Cook had discovered it a century prior and the British had wasted no time installing the Union Jack on its soil. But being so far away from civilization, it was not visited by too many people. Stories came back about kangaroos and cute little koala bears and natives who threw boomerangs, but not a whole lot was known about the topography or mineral elements of which its crust was composed. Charles Darwin, a scientist of no small reputation, visited the island; but he was looking for birds and bugs and various things besides gold.

News of gold being found in Australia came in 1851, just two years after the California panic. Whether any relation exists between the two, remains open to speculation. Quite likely, the California strikes put gold on the world's mind, and people were looking who would not have otherwise looked, or known what to look for. In any case, the Australian strike was the McCoy. Gold of prodigious size was being turned up. So huge were the nuggets, and so much did they dazzle eye and imagination, that names were bestowed upon the better ones, just in the fashion of gemstones. The so-called Sierra Sands nugget tipped the scales at more than 93 pounds. Then there was a Lady Hotham nugget of 1,177 ounces and a Welcome Stranger nugget (I am not aware of the derivation of that name) weighing in beyond 2,000 ounces. The prize whopper was the Holtermann nugget, with a weight of more than 200 pounds. That was over $32,000 worth, even at the modest trading prices then in effect (multiply that figure about 25 times to get the present equivalent). When you consider that a cubic foot of gold weighs more than 1,000 pounds, a 200-pound hunk may not seem unduly impressive. But nuggets of that bulk occur extremely infrequently. Nature seldom puts gold in such big lumps. In fact, she has a very exasperating habit of intermixing it with all kinds of mineral garbage, to the utter frustration of refiners, or sprinkling grains of it the size of table salt into streams. A 200-pound nugget is as much a freak as a diamond the size of an apricot.

Needless to state, these reports encouraged the hopeful from far and wide to descend upon Australia. Some of them did extremely well, and gold is still mined to this day in Australia, though it is not the biggest gold producer of the world.

That distinction belongs to South Africa, whose mining operations have continued over the past several years despite deep political troubles. Gold was discovered much later in South Africa than elsewhere in the world, but it proved well worth waiting for. (It is possible that the ancient Greeks or Hebrews knew about South African gold mines, and that the secret of their locations went to the grave with them; but this point remains unproven.) It was because of diamond mining that South Africa's gold lode was uncovered, and quite by happenstance. During the 1870's and '80's, numerous fortune hunters were probing around the Dark Continent's tip for salable stones. Sophisticated mining was going on, but this failed to deter the private individual with his spade and pickaxe from getting into the act. It happened that on a historic day in 1886 one George Harrison — unrelated to a later George Harrison, though both were British and both became famous for rock — was doing as he had done on most other days, sweating and slapping at mosquitoes and looking for diamonds. He was on a farm owned by a woman named Oosthuizen, a Dutch immigrant to the area. As usual, Harrison found no diamonds. Poor Harrison never found diamonds. But he possessed sufficient presence of mind to stop and make a close inspection of some yellow colored stones that chanced to be in his path. They looked like gold nuggets. He was, despite his lack of metallurgical expertise, convinced they were gold nuggets.

Unfortunately, his lack of business acumen allowed a very tidy fortune to slip through his fingers.

Harrison staked a claim on the property, which Mrs. Oosthuizen was more than willing to relinquish as she considered it worthless. When he showed the golden nuggets to persons in the neighborhood, he was quickly offered the princely sum of 10 pounds sterling (then $50) for his claim. Not being one to turn aside a profit, Harrison blithely took the 10 quid and disappeared.

He had opened one of history's biggest Pandora's Boxes.

Before the year's end, gold in awesome quantities was being taken from the Oosthuizen/Harrison plot. And more was to follow. Prospectors flooded in, cutting through brush and braving the advances of lions and rhinos. Whole expeditions, complete with caravans of natives toting steamer trunks, moved toward the Hallowed Ground. Africa had not witnessed such activity since the days of Alexander the Great. Very soon a village was established, upon which the name of Johannesburg was bestowed. The little village became a metropolitan center with a population over 1,000,000. And most of its industry was connected with the mining or refining of gold.

Not all remained rosy. Four years after the first discovery, gloom descended. After taking tons upon tons of top-grade bullion from the mines, it was found that miners were starting to bring up less appealing stuff. After getting beyond the initial layers, those beneath proved to contain high proportions of pyrite. Today, with the modern refining machinery now in use, this would not cause any ruffling of feathers. But in 1890 it meant disaster. It was simply too costly, with the techniques then in use, to refine out the pyrite. The mines began shutting down and the boom appeared over. However, in 1892 the cyanide process of refining — which melts the gold and removes it from unwanted minerals — was developed. Once again, Africa's mines went full throttle ahead.

Since then no serious difficulties have been encountered, except World War II and the African Civil War of recent date. Today about two million ounces of gold are extracted annually from the still-fertile South African lodes, far and away the most contributed by any nation to the world's supply.

GOLD RESERVES OF MAJOR WORLD NATIONS

Every industrialized nation of the world holds gold reserves. These can be in the form of coins, bars, ingots or other forms of gold, but are nearly always in bars. Today, when gold is acquired by governments for deposit in their treasuries (as opposed to industrial or other use), it is generally in the form of "Good Delivery" bars, weighing 400 ounces each. However, as the concept of the Good Delivery bar is of fairly recent origin, it has been the practice of governments not to convert their old stocks of bars into 400 ounce units but keep them as is and merely acquire Good Delivery bars when new transactions are made.

WHY DO COUNTRIES KEEP GOLD? Why do governments maintain gold supplies any longer? A very good question.

Originally they did so because the bullion was needed for conversion into coinage. But not many nations of the world are striking gold coinage any longer. When gold coinage was abandoned, nations kept gold supplies to exchange against "demand notes," or currency bills which the bearer could turn in and receive the face value in gold. But this has likewise become a thing of the past. Today the common rule is "paper economy," which means notes that are not redeemable for anything — except what can be purchased for them in the marketplace.

So why have stockpiles of gold?

Basically, gold in the possession of world governments is held for the purpose of stabilizing its currency when and if necessary. Should the value of the U.S. dollar (for example) sink drastically on foreign monetary exchanges, our government can support it by using some of its gold to buy up dollars. If it buys enough dollars, the price will stabilize — at least temporarily. At the same time, the price of gold may temporarily decline. This is preferred over "devaluing" the currency, or officially reducing its trading value against that of other currencies, which can upset the domestic economy.

The following figures show gold reserves from 1963 to 1980. It should be noted that of all the countries listed here that Japan was the only one to show an increase since 1976 in their reserve, while the other's including the U.S. have declined markedly.

WORLD GOLD RESERVES 1963-1980 (OUNCES)

CANADA		OUNCES
	1963 —	23,350,000
	1964 —	29,310,000
	1965 —	32,880,000
	1966 —	29,870,000
	1967 —	29,000,000
	1968 —	24,660,000
	1969 —	24,920,000
	1970 —	22,590,000
	1971 —	22,690,000
	1972 —	21,950,000
	1973 —	21,950,000
	1974 —	21,950,000
	1975 —	21,950,000
	1976 —	21,620,000
	1977 —	22,010,000
	1978 —	22,130,000
	1979 —	22,000,000
As of July	1980 —	21,300,000

FRANCE		OUNCES
	1963 —	90,710,000
	1964 —	106,540,000
	1965 —	134,460,000
	1966 —	149,660,000
	1967 —	149,540,000
	1968 —	110,770,000
	1969 —	101,340,000
	1970 —	100,910,000
	1971 —	100,660,000
	1972 —	100,690,000
	1973 —	100,910,000
	1974 —	100,930,000
	1975 —	100,930,000
	1976 —	101,020,000
	1977 —	101,670,000
	1978 —	101,990,000
	1979 —	81,900,000
As of July	1980 —	81,880,000

GREAT BRITAIN

	Year		Ounces
	1963	—	70,960,000
	1964	—	61,040,000
	1965	—	64,720,000
	1966	—	55,440,000
	1967	—	36,890,000
	1968	—	42,100,000
	1969	—	42,030,000
	1970	—	38,540,000
	1971	—	22,150,000
	1972	—	21,050,000
	1973	—	21,030,000
	1974	—	21,030,000
	1975	—	21,030,000
	1976	—	21,030,000
	1977	—	22,220,000
	1978	—	22,820,000
	1979	—	18,300,000
As of July	1980	—	18,860,000

ITALY

	Year		Ounces
	1963	—	66,940,000
	1964	—	60,190,000
	1965	—	68,680,000
	1966	—	68,970,000
	1967	—	68,570,000
	1968	—	83,520,000
	1969	—	84,460,000
	1970	—	82,480,000
	1971	—	82,400,000
	1972	—	82,370,000
	1973	—	82,480,000
	1974	—	82,480,000
	1975	—	82,480,000
	1976	—	82,480,000
	1977	—	82,910,000
	1978	—	83,120,000
	1979	—	66,700,000
As of July	1980	—	66,670,000

JAPAN

	Year		Ounces
	1963	—	8,260,000
	1964	—	8,690,000
	1965	—	9,370,000
	1966	—	9,400,000
	1967	—	9,660,000
	1968	—	10,170,000
	1969	—	11,800,000
	1970	—	15,200,000
	1971	—	19,430,000
	1972	—	21,110,000
	1973	—	21,110,000
	1974	—	21,110,000
	1975	—	21,110,000
	1976	—	21,110,000
	1977	—	21,620,000
	1978	—	23,970,000
	1979	—	24,000,000
As of July	1980	—	24,230,000

NETHERLANDS

	Year		Ounces
	1963	—	45,770,000
	1964	—	48,230,000
	1965	—	50,190,000
	1966	—	49,450,000
	1967	—	48,910,000
	1968	—	48,510,000
	1969	—	49,160,000
	1970	—	51,060,000
	1971	—	54,530,000
	1972	—	54,170,000
	1973	—	54,330,000
	1974	—	54,330,000
	1975	—	54,330,000
	1976	—	54,330,000
	1977	—	54,630,000
	1978	—	54,780,000
	1979	—	43,800,000
As of July	1980	—	43,940,000

UNITED STATES

	Year		Ounces
	1963	—	445,600,000
	1964	—	442,030,000
	1965	—	401,860,000
	1966	—	378,140,000
	1967	—	344,710,000
	1968	—	311,200,000
	1969	—	338,830,000
	1970	—	316,340,000
	1971	—	291,600,000
	1972	—	275,970,000
	1973	—	275,970,000
	1974	—	275,970,000
	1975	—	274,710,000
	1976	—	274,680,000
	1977	—	277,550,000
	1978	—	276,410,000
	1979	—	265,300,000
As of July	1980	—	264,600,000

WEST GERMANY

	Year		Ounces
	1963	—	109,820,000
	1964	—	121,370,000
	1965	—	126,000,000
	1966	—	122,620,000
	1967	—	120,790,000
	1968	—	129,690,000
	1969	—	116,560,000
	1970	—	113,700,000
	1971	—	116,470,000
	1972	—	117,360,000
	1973	—	117,610,000
	1974	—	117,610,000
	1975	—	117,610,000
	1976	—	117,610,000
	1977	—	118,300,000
	1978	—	118,640,000
	1979	—	95,300,000
As of July	1980	—	95,180,000

PHYSICAL PROPERTIES OF GOLD

Atomic Number — 79	Hardness (Mohs) — 2½-3
Atomic weight — 196.967	Melting point — 2,063F
Boiling point — 2,970F	Specific gravity (24K Pure) — 19.32
Crystal system — face-centered cube	Symbol — Au
	Tensile strength, psi — 19,000

WHITE GOLD

White gold does not come out of the ground white. It isn't a product of nature but the clever skills of mankind, who has learned that odd things happen to metals when alloyed with other metals. White gold is made by taking ordinary yellow gold and alloying it with one of the white metals, in sufficient quantity to change its color and at the same time provide stability and toughness. Nickel or palladium are generally chosen, sometimes a combination of the two. White gold can, just like yellow, be of high or low grade, depending upon the degrees of alloying. This can only be determined via testing.

White gold is chiefly used for jewelry, into which diamonds are set. Yellow gold gives diamonds a yellowish tint. The belief that it is stronger and more longer wearing than yellow gold is often advanced, especially in the advertisements of jewelry retailers. This is true only in cases where palladium has been used as the alloy; nickel does not provide any greater durability than copper. White gold also sees service for dental work.

THE ALLOYING OF METALS

Alloying is the blending together of one metal with one or more of another kind. As all metals can be melted by intense heating, there is virtually no limitation to the variety of alloys that can be produced by varying the recipes.

The motives behind alloying are several. The desire may be (as in the case of gold and silver) to give the metal greater durability by introducing a proportion of stronger metal. It could be to "stretch" a valuable metal and use less of it in manufacture than would be necessary if unalloyed or lightly alloyed. These are the two chief goals of alloying, in coinage and bullion intended for use in manufacturing. A further desire might be to increase its electrical conductivity, or to give magnetic attraction to a non-magnetic metal (or the reverse). Metals are sometimes alloyed just to alter their color.

DURABILITY. In their pure states, 24K gold and .999+ silver are too soft for use in manufacturing and are hardly ever employed in that state, except in instances where a very minute quantity is needed or the metal can be beaten very thin into sheets. An example of the use of 24K gold is in the "gold tissue" used by bookbinders, by which the spines of leather bindings are imprinted with the book title, author, etc., and the covers worked with elegant "gold tooled" designs. But for any articles intended to be handled a great deal and withstand use, gold and silver must be alloyed. Even for coinage an alloy is necessary. When the U.S. struck coins in gold and silver, they were of approximately 90% bullion, the remaining 10% generally made up of copper. As this small an introduction of copper does not alter the appearance, yet provides considerable ruggedness, it is considered an ideal formula. But a 9-to-1 ratio is not suitable for jewelry, where additional hardness is needed. Sterling silver tableware is softer than most silver coins, containing 92.5% silver against only 7.5% copper.

HOW ALLOYING IS DONE. Alloying is accomplished in the refineries. The process requires much care and attention, as the metals must be measured out in exact proportions and blended thoroughly together. If the blending is not thorough, the resulting product will show streaks, as no two metals are of precisely the same color or surface appearance. This occurs once in a great while in the minting of coinage, and yields specimens of much interest to the numismatist.

STRETCHING OR "WATERING DOWN." Economic and commercial considerations often lead to alloying, so that an article may have the appearance and general quality of bullion but can circulate more cheaply than otherwise. Jewelry makers use gold alloyed down sometimes to less than 50%; such pieces may still be advertised as gold, but they will react positively when tested by nitric acid because of their high copper content. Coinage, when heavily alloyed, is called "debased." Debasement of coinage has taken place from the ancient world to modern times, the most noteworthy example in our era being the U.S. government's switch from silver to clad dimes, quarters and half dollars in 1965. Roman coinage began to be seriously debased in the 2nd century A.D.; by the 4th its silver pieces contained virtually no silver at all. The chief difference between that era and ours is that the public, in early times, was not officially informed of debasement and discovered it only when coins were tested or the outer coating began to wear down (producing such coinage as the "red nose" pieces of Henry VIII, on which the copper showed through).

GOLD PURITY BY KARAT

When used in the manufacture of jewelry and decorative objects, and sometimes for other merchandise as well, the fineness or grade of gold is stated upon the item by a karat mark. These karat marks should not be taken at face value in some cases, because

(1) In the jewelry trade it is legal to mark gold one full karat higher than it actually is, if solder has been used in making the article.

(2) The mark could refer merely to an outer covering or plating, which would have to be determined by chemical test or specific gravity.

KARAT	CONTAINS % PURE GOLD	
24K		This is the highest degree of purity. It denotes gold unalloyed with any other material. However, when expressed in decimal terms, 24K is not indicated as 1.000 — which would be absolute purity — but as .999 fine, because it is not possible to refine out every trace of adhering metal. Gold of 24K is extremely soft and weak. It cannot be used in the making of jewelry. Nor is it suitable for coinage. 24K gold is generally seen only in the form of bars and ingots or as gold plating. For plating it is quite useful as strength is supplied by the core metal.
23½K	97.92	The very small proportion of alloying still does not permit use in manufacturing.
23K	95.83	

Karat	Percent	Notes
22½K	93.75	
22K	92.67	Some coin gold, though not that of the U.S., is 22K.
21½K	89.58	Here the alloy becomes greater than 10%. U.S. coins are approximately 21½K.
21K	87.50	
20½K	85.42	
20K	83.33	Still too soft for jewelry, despite the addition of nearly 17% alloy.
19½K	81.25	
19K	79.17	Will still show negative with nitric acid — that is, that proportion of copper, though more than 20%, is not high enough to react with the acid.
18½K	77.08	
18K	75	The highest grade of gold used in the jewelry industry, consisting of three parts bullion to one part copper. Will not react to nitric acid, whether applied on the surface or to a filed notch.
17½K	72.92	
17K	70.83	
16½K	68.75	The gold now contains more than 30% base metal (copper), but even at this level will react the same to nitric acid as pure 24K.
16K	66.67	Exactly two parts of gold to one part copper. No reaction when tested by nitric acid. Usually most dental gold is 16K.
15½K	64.58	
15K	62.50	
14½K	60.42	
14K	58.33	The composition is more than 40% copper, but still will not react to acid testing. One of the most widely used grades of gold for jewelry in the medium price range.
13½K	56.25	
13K	54.17	
12½K	52.08	The proportion of copper is now almost as high as the proportion of gold. Neverthelmss, nitric acid will show the same reaction as with higher grades.
12K	50	Exactly one-half gold and one-half copper. Very extensively used in the manufacture of low-priced jewelry. Will show brownish tinge when tested with nitric acid.
11½K	47.92	Now the percentage of copper exceeds that of gold.
11K	45.83	
10½K	43.75	
10K	41.67	Sometimes used in jewelry. Shows a more marked reaction to nitric acid than 12K. Almost all class rings are 10K.
9½K	39.58	
9K	37.50	Not much more than one-third gold.

TESTING METHODS FOR GOLD

There are two matters to be determined in testing objects believed to be made of gold:

1. Whether the item is gold or something of similar appearance.

2. The fineness, because gold ranges from pure (24K) to heavily alloyed, such as 10K.

Determination that the exterior is gold means little, as the article could be copper or brass with a gold plating. Even if the plating is very high quality bullion, it will be of only minimal value.

Nitric acid is the standard test for gold. It has no effect on gold but reacts to the basemetal alloys, if the item has been made from heavily alloyed gold. It will not react to gold of 10K or higher. Therefore, nitric acid is useless in determining the karat fineness of gold between 14K and 24K. For this, the touchstone method is used.

NITRIC ACID TEST. A notch is filed on the object, in an inconspicuous place if possible. This is done because of the possibility of plating. It need not be very deep — about 1/32nd of an inch will do on most items. A drop of nitric acid is placed on the file mark. If no change in color is noted, the item is 10K gold or higher. If a very light brownish tinge appears, it is lower than 10K. When the acid turns green, this indicates that the object contains no gold whatsoever.

The acid should be wiped away as soon as results are obtained.

TOUCHSTONE TESTING. If the article has not reacted to nitric acid, we know it to be 10K or better. To determine the exact karat, a "streak" is made by rubbing it firmly across a touchplate (these are available from dealers in jewelry supplies). Streaks are then made on either side of the test streak, using gold-testing needles of different karats. These needles are sold in sets and carry a tiny drop of gold at the tip. Each needle is marked by karat. Normally you would begin by streaking 10K and 18K alongside the test streak. A drop or two of aqua regia is then spread across the streaks. If the test streak is either 10K or 18K, its reaction will be the same as that of the 10K or 18K needle streak. If the test streak dissolves faster than the 10K needle streak but slower than the 18K, it is most likely 14K. This can be proved by making a new test and streaking the item plus the 14K needle side by side. Their reactions to aqua regia should be identical or very close. A slight variation could mean that the test object is an odd karat, such as 15K or 17K, or that the streaks were not made with equal pressure.

Aqua regia can be made by combining 8 drops of water with 2 drops hydrochloric acid. Ten drops of nitric acid is then added. Do not inhale more of the fumes than is absolutely necessary and keep the bottle stoppered when not in use.

Nitric acid has long been the chief chemical for testing precious metal. It is volatile and should be handled and stored with cautton. It is, as the name denotes, an *acid,* which will seriously burn human skin should it be accidentally splashed upon it. A sensible precaution is to wear a long-sleeved shirt and heavy gloves while using nitric acid. Rubber gloves are not recommended because this acid can burn through them very rapidly. Canvas laborers' gloves, or gloves of good heavy leather, are better. Do not attempt to store a sizable quantity of nitric acid in the home, because of the hazard it presents in case of fire or other accident. When using it, take care not to inhale its fumes at closer range than is necessary. Nitric acid should be used in a well ventilated room, not in cellars or attics. Pets and children should be removed from the area. Do not smoke while using it, or allow others to do so. Always use the glass "dipper rod" attached to the bottle stopper, rather than attempting to use brushes or other devices. Brushes are *not safe* for working with nitric acid as they can cause tiny droplets of the liquid to fly about.

SPECIFIC GRAVITY. As the specific gravity method is a highly reliable test for determining the nature of metals and mineral substances, everyone who buys or intends to buy gold, silver, jewels, etc. ought to become familiar with it.

This is an extremely delicate test which, if not performed to precise standards, will not yield correct results. On the other hand its accuracy when properly carried out is far above that of almost all other methods of testing, including those employing more costly apparatus.

If one plans on trading commercially or handling a great deal of valuables, it would be wise to purchase a specific gravity testing device. Otherwise, a "homemade" substitute can be used, whose reliability will be fairly close to that of professsional models.

Specific gravity is the ratio at which a material displaces water in relation to its bulk. We all know that lead sinks while cork floats on water. This tells us nothing beyond the fact that some materials are heavier than others, which could as easily be learned by weighing on an oridnary scale. Specific gravity goes much deeper than the mere difference between sink-or-float. It gives the weight of an object in relation to its *exact* size, as water fully encompasses whatever is submerged in it and therefore measures far better than rulers or calipers. As every object of the *same material* gives the *same specific gravity reading,* regardless of size, the specific gravity reading easily distinguishes between (for example) gold and copper, silver and copper, or alloys of these metals, as well as helping to identify precious gems.

A specific gravity scale may be concocted from an ordinary pan scale calibrated in grams. If the calibration is higher than grams it will not be suitable. In other words you cannot use a postal scale or something of that nature. Remove the pan and tie a length of string (thin nylon is good) from the pan holder, at the extreme southeast edge as the scale faces you. The string should not be long enough to touch the desk on which the scale rests. A glass tumbler about 3/4ths filled with water is then positioned beneath the string. It may be necessary to rest the tumbler upon a low platform to arrive at the proper height. It will need to be positioned so that the article to be tested, when tied to the string and dropped into the glass, is fully submerged but *does not touch the bottom of the glass.* If it rests upon the bottom, or even touches slightly, the test is spoiled.

As the object dangles in the glass, a reading is taken of the weight indicated on the scale. This is called the "weight in water." It does not determine the specific gravity but is the chief step in arriving at that figure. To get the specific gravity reading, the object must then be weighed on the scale in the ordinary manner, or "in air." Subtract the weight in water from the weight in air (the latter will always be a higher number), then divide the weight in air by the *loss of weight in water.* The answer will be the item's specific gravity.

Example:

Weight in water, 55.5 grams

Weight in air, 60 grams
Loss of weight in water, 4.5 grams
4.5 divided into 60 = 13.33 (specific gravity of the item)

The item tested in this sampling, with a specific gravity reading of 13.33 was 14K yellow gold.

Depending on the accuracy of your scale you will probably only be able to get very close approximations rather than precise readings. In the previous example we got a specific gravity of 13.33 and called it 14K gold. This is because 13.33 is the closest in the following table to our answer. As in all of these tests and formulas there is always "visual inspection" involved and in this case the item appeared to be 14K gold, so the conclusion reached after testing was obvious.

SPECIFIC GRAVITIES OF METALS

Metal	Specific gravity
Brass	8.52
Bronze	8.82
Copper	8.93
24K Gold	19.32
22K Gold	17.72
18K Gold	15.47
14K Gold	13.55
10K Gold	11.75
Iron	7.81
German silver	8.74
.999 silver	10.50
.925 sterling silver	10.31
Stainless steel	7.8
Platinum	21.45
Tin	7.31

METHODS OF WEIGHING GOLD

You don't put gold ingots or Double Eagles on a bathroom scale. Techniques employed for weighing precious metals are highly sophisticated, because a slight difference in weight can mean a big difference in value. Unfortunately there isn't as yet any single universally agreed-upon method, though several are reliable if performed correctly.

The weight of gold may be given in troy ounces, pennyweight, or by metric division. Troy is the most common and most universally understood by jewelers and bullion dealers. Pennyweight, an invention of the British and later adopted here, is somewhat archaic but its adherents die hard. It has convenience on its side. The metric system, now becoming international, has not yet penetrated into the bullion market to a very major extent and probably will not do so for a number of years.

As statements of weight are likely to be given in grains by one dealer, grams by another, and dwt (pennyweight) by a third, it is important that anyone buying or selling gold become familiar with the different weight systems.

It may be of interest to note that equipment used for weighing precious metal is today identical in design and function to that of the ancient world, as the balance principle is relied upon rather than scales with springs.

AVOIRDUPOIS WEIGHT. Like troy weight, the avoirdupois system also uses pounds and ounces, but these are not equal. Avoirdupois is the common method by which just about everything — except precious metals — is weighed. Your bathroom scale is an avoirdupois scale. Unlike troy scales, avoirdupois scales may be equipped with springs.

PENNYWEIGHT. Abbreviated as DWT. ("D" stands for penny, in British coinage, and "WT" for weight.) The system of weighing by pennyweight was and innovation of English merchants of the distant past, who used pennies as counterweights on their scales. The American penny weighs two pennyweight, which equals 48 grains. The important point is that a pennyweight, used as a measure of weight, is 24 grains. So it is readily apparent that pennyweight is an extremely small proportion of gold — or of anything else. A Pennyweight is considerably less than one full ounce. But this is a very useful method of measuring, as gold is frequently bought and sold in quantitites well below a full ounce. When the price of gold is $500 per troy ounce, you should divide it by 20 (because ther are 20 dwt per troy ounce) to get the price per dwt, which is $25.

TROY WEIGHT. This is a standard system by which the weights of precious metals are figured all over the world. Its basic unit is the grain. Scales (using balances, not springs) for weighing items in troy measure are available and are usually referred to as jewelers' or gemologists' scales.

WEIGHTS AND MEASURES

APOTHECARIES' WEIGHT

one grain	=	.01666 dram
20 grains	=	.33 dram
60 grains	=	one dram
480 grains	=	one apothecary ounce (8 drams)

AVOIRDUPOIS WEIGHT

.0625 ounce	=	1.7719 grams
one ounce	=	28.350 grams
16 ounces	=	one pound (453.59 grams)

TROY WEIGHT

one grain	=	.0416666 pennyweight or .648 grams
24 grains	=	one pennyweight
480 grains	=	20 pennyweights, or one troy ounce
5760 grains	=	240 pennyweights, or 12 troy ounces, or one troy pound

FORMULAS OF CONVERSIONS

To change . . .

grams to pennyweights, mulitply grams by .643
pennyweights to grams, multiply pennyweights by 1.555
grams to troy ounces, multiply grams by .032
troy ounces to grams, multiply troy ounces by 31.103
pennyweights to troy ounces, divide pennyweights by 20
troy ounces to pennyweights, multiply troy ounces by 20
grains to grams, multiply grains by .0648
grams to grains, multiply grams by 15.432
avoirdupois ounces to troy ounces, multiply avoirdupois ounces by .912
troy ounces to avoirdupois ounces, multiply troy ounces by 1.097
avoirdupois ounces to grams, multiply avoirdupois ounces by 28.35
grams to avoirdupois ounces, multiply grams by .035
avoirdupois pounds to kilograms, multiply avoirdupois pounds by .454
kilograms to avoirdupois pounds, multiply kilograms by 2.205

avoirdupois pounds to grains, multiply avoirdupois pounds by 7000
grains to avoirdupois pounds, multiply grains by .00014

DETERMINING THE VALUE OF GOLD

As the weight of gold is often given in pennyweights rather than grains, grams or ounces, anyone handling gold will face the challenge of translating the daily "spot" price (always stated in troy ounces) into pennyweight value.

After determining the karat and weight of the item, the following formula can be used to find its price per pennyweight at spot value on any given day. At this point you will need to determine the karat fineness of the gold item in question. Our "Gold Purity by Karat" chapter will provide this information. If you've determined the item's karat to be 14K, then you will see on the chart that this translates into 58.33% pure gold. In other words, the gold content is 58.33% pure gold and the remainder is nongold alloy. This percentage of fineness is necessary to have in order to calculate price per pennyweight.

Next you have to use the following formula:

Spot ÷ 20 = price per dwt
Price per dwt × fineness = melt value per dwt

Example: Let's assume we have a 14K item which we now know is 58.33% pure and spot was $600 that day. The figures would be:

$600 ÷ 20 = $30 per dwt
$30 × 58.33 = $17.50 melt value per dwt

This formula can be used whether spot is $100 or $1,000 or anywhere in between. Just use the formula exactly.

Now let's take an example through all the steps we've discussed.

We'll say you have a bracelet and want to determine its value. First you would have used one of the gold test formulas and determined its karat at 14K. Now you must find out its weight. If you don't have access to a gram scale, any regular (avoirdupois) scale will do, if it gives readings by the ounce. A bathroom scale obviously isn't suitable, but a postal scale is satisfactory. If the bracelet weighs 2 ounces, you would then proceed to the following formula:

ounces x 28.35 = grams
grams x .643 = dwt (pennyweights)
dwt x melt value per dwt = market melt value
With this item it would be:
2 ounces x 28.35 = 56.70 grams
56.70 grams x .643 = 36.46 dwts
36.46 dwts x 17.50 = $638.05 market value

In this case the market melt value of your 14K bracelet would be $638.05. It weighs two ounces, yet the value is just slightly more than the spot price for one ounce. The reason, of course, is the fineness — 14K — which means nearly half the content is basemetal.

Now remember, when you sell to a dealer he will be buying at 10-25% less than this figure. The discount is fair because he must recover refining costs, pay freight or postage to the refinery and leave himself a reasonable profit.

So, keeping this in mind, you should be able to sell your 14K bracelet to a dealer for roughly $475 to $575. This should be a fair transaction for both parties. If the offer you get varies a great deal from this — on the low side, naturally — you should definitely shop around for another offer.

HOW TO SELL GOLD

The first rule in selling scrap gold is: be certain it's scrap!

"Scrap gold" is the term applied to gold objects that have no value over and above their value as bullion. They're weighed on a scale and paid for by weight, then sent to a refinery for smelting. Anything which might come under the heading of a collector's item should not be sold for scrap, because a higher price could be obtained for it elsewhere. Gold coins are in this category. They should always be sold to a dealer in coins, or a broker who specializes in coin gold, rather than a scrap buyer.

Scrap gold includes nearly all forms of gold jewelry, except antique. You could sell gold jewelry to a jeweler — but you won't be paid any more than a scrap buyer would give. Assuming, of course, that there are no precious stones involved.

Just about every advertisement for scrap gold includes an offer to purchase "old class rings." They are generally big and brawny and mostly of 10K gold; they nearly always carry a karat stamp or mark. As scrap gold their value, based on a spot price of $500 per troy ounce, ranges from $25 to $100 — it all depends upon the size and weight. Womens' are generally worth half as much. If the ring contains a stone you needn't give this much attention as it will not be of any substantial value. Don't worry if there are scratches or abrasions. When a scrap dealer buys this kind of item its fate is the smelter's pot, so looks count for very little.

Numerous manufacturers sold imitations of gold class rings, mostly for persons wishing to masquerade as collegians. These imitations are of approximately the same size and design, but are either gold plated or contain no gold at all.

Most scrap dealers advertise to buy dental gold — gold fillings from teeth and gold bridgework.

The use of solid gold in dental work has greatly declined. It was commonplace from about 1870-1920. At that time gold was comparatively inexpensive and considered desirable for dental work because it can be easily shaped. Not much thought was given to the cosmetic disadvantages of a solid gold smile. In fact many persons took pride in carrying real gold in their teeth, even though it provided glaring proof of their neglect of dental care. Later, substitutes were sought for yellow gold. White gold was used — when used at all — for fillings in molars or other out-of-view teeth. For fillings in front teeth, enamel-like substitutes have taken gold's place.

Yellow dental gold is mostly 16K. It is not entirely pure, which would be 24K, but of high bullion content compared to many other kinds of gold. However, the gold is extremely small in quantity. It is not used by itself but constructed around basemetal, or a composition of heavily alloyed gold, to provide strength and stability. It may be held in palce by a network of tiny basemetal pins. All of this non-gold must be removed in refining. Therefore prices paid for dental gold aren't very high.

Because dental gold isn't marked, many buyers of scrap bullion classify it automatically as 16K and set their prices accordingly.

Choose your scrap buyer carefully. Sell to a well established dealer or broker with a shop or office rather than an itinerant located in a hotel or motel. Do not sell to dealers at flea markets, shows and conventions. Sell to someone who's been at his address for a substantial length of time. These individuals are less prone to cheat because they can easily be found.

It is of course normal and traditional, whenever anything is presented for sale, for the prospective buyer to seek out its shortcomings and obtain the price most favorable to him. There is nothing illegal in this. But when selling scrap or melt items by weight, where condition is not important, bargaining should not be necessary if the dealer is ethical. He will have an advertised price per pennyweight, gram or ounce for bullion, and he will pay this price based upon the weight of your merchandise.

Unfortunately, that is not always the case.

There are many scrap buyers, mostly in the "fly by night" category, who are expert at inventing reasons why they cannot pay the full advertised sum. By shaving just a few dollars off each transaction they can gain considerable extra profits. And sometimes the shaving is not a few dollars but hundreds, depending on the item's value and the buyer's estimate of its owner's gullibility.

A few of the more common techniques are described here. This should not be considered a comprehensive guide; tricksters' imaginations know no bounds.

SHORT WEIGHTING. Probably the most prevalent infraction is short weighting, or informing sellers that their material weighs less than it actually does. This can be accomplished by keeping scales out of public sight (which is illegal in itself, even if the scales are accurate), or fixing them to give low readings. The weight is not usually grossly misrepresented, for fear of detection; but even the difference of a few pennyweights, in a gold object, can mean a big difference in pride.

There is another, more devious, way in which short weighting can be done. This is practiced by many unscrupulous dealers because it can later be attributed to human error. The weight may be taken on an accurate scale, calibrated in ounces and grams. It is then translated on paper into pennyweight, by using a formula that does not give the correct pennyweight equivalent. Very few customers know how to convert standard measures into pennyweights and do not detect the deception. If they do, the dealer merely apoligizes for his "error."

MISSTATEMENT OF CONTENT. An unscrupulous dealer will often claim, after testing, that an article contains less bullion than it actually does. He may run a nitric acid test on goldware, assuming a sour expression and shaking his head at the result, when in fact the test indicates a high proportion of gold content. This is followed by the pronouncement that "I can only pay you X for this, because it's mostly copper . . ." This can be avoided by carrying out tests yourself before offering material for sale or, if that is inconvenient, learning enough about testing procedures to be able to interpret results. Always ask that tests be done where you can observe them.

The question is sometimes asked: can unscrupulous buyers use some chemical for testing, other than nitric acid, which will turn good gold green (or brown) and thereby claim a high alloy content? The answer is: no. There is no known chemical which will do this. If the test is carried out in your presence, you can trust the reaction obtained just the same as if you were performing it. If the treated area turns light brown, it is usually less than 10K. If it turns green, there is substantial (probably 100%) copper content.

FALSE SPECIFIC GRAVITY READING. There are a number of ways in which specific gravity tests can be "fixed." Some involve rigging the scale. A more devious approach is to mix another liquid — a heavier one — with the water, so that less water displacement occurs and a lower reading is obtained. Therefore you should not put great faith in such readings even if taken in your presence.

"THIS IS REALLY PLATED . . ." The claim is sometimes advanced, by dishonest dealers, that a gold object is actually plated or gold filled. This is usually announced after weighing or using the file-and-acid procedure. An offer of 20% or 30% of the actual value is then made.

MISCELLANEOUS HOCUS-POCUS. A dealer may weigh and test your items accurately, tell you their true content and weight, and still cheat you. In fact, cheating of this kind is the most common of all. "The scrap market isn't what it was a couple of months ago," the dealer may explain. "A lot of refiners aren't buying any more, so we have to buy at a bigger discount than before." The uninformed seller acceptes stories of this type and may sell his material for considerably less than could be had from an honest trader. The best way is to calucalate the weight and value yourself. Before selling and as suggested in the chapter "Determining Value" A 10% to 25% discount is thoroughly acceptable.

GOLD THAT SHOULDN'T BE MELTED

Not all articles made of gold should be looked upon as "bullion." Some have value over and above the price that could be obtained by selling them to a bullion dealer.

COINS. If we take gold coins as a whole, from their beginnings in the ancient world down to modern times, we will discover that the *vast majority* boast a numismatic or collector value in excess of their bullion value. Generally speaking — though this does not apply in all cases — it is only gold pieces of the 20th century and the late 19th century that are sufficiently common to qualify as bullion items. Though their values are based upon the daily spot prices of gold, the fact is that these coins are *rarely* melted down to obtain the gold.

United States gold coins dating before 1840 *usually* have a numismatic value, because of their scarcity. Many of later vintages are also numismatically valuable, and it should be needless to advise anyone to check the collector value before disposing of any gold coins — whether U.S. or foreign — to a bullion merchant. A coin such as the South African Krugerrand can, of course, safely be traded as bullion without investigation.

COLLECTORS' ITEMS IN GENERAL. Whenever gold has been fashioned into a work of art or craft, whether very old or comparatively modern, the possibility exists that it could be of collector value. This is true regardless of the grade of gold and even, sometimes, the state of preservation. The advice of an authority on collectors' items should be sought before selling, preferably one whose opinion can be expressed without regard to personal gain. Any articles of gold dating from the ancient world, Middle Ages, Renaissance or baroque eras will inevitably carry some collector value or premium over the bullion content, and later pieces could as well.

MEDALS. Commemorative medals made of gold are invariably more valuable than their bullion content, except perhaps those of very recent origin. These were struck in much smaller quantities than coins and, thanks to the numbers of collectors specializing in medals, a strong demand exists for them.

HOW TO VALUE ANTIQUE GOLD

By and large, antiques made of or containing gold are not used in refining, because their value as collectors' items exceeds their value as bullion. There are exceptions to this, however.

Simply because of the above stated situation — that most gold antiques are worth more than their bullion value — dealers in scrap gold have been making a very neat "sideline" profit. Unless extremely scrupulous, they pay the bullion value (less commission, etc.) for whatever is brought to them. If the item should be an antique, it is paid for at the same rate as a non-antique containing that amount of gold. But instead of reselling it to a smelter, the scrap dealer resells it to an antique dealer, thereby realizing a considerably greater sum. The unfortunate original seller is none the wiser, unless he sees it reappear in a shop down the street.

The word "antique" has been much misused and probably has no really definable meaning where precious metal is concerned. As far as U.S. customs is concerned, an antique (to escape import duty) must be 100 years old or more. However, there are many gold objects of a much more recent date whose artistry or other appeal lends value over and above their metallic worth. Moreover, the value of antique gold or "old gold" or whatever one wishes to call it does not depend on age. It is a matter of scarcity, skill in designing, preservation, place of origin and a number of other details.

The value as a collectors' item can sometimes vastly exceed bullion value. A good example is ancient goldware. Goldwork of ancient Rome is not common on the antique market but it can be found, particularly at the large auction sales in New York, London and Paris. A hairpin containing perhaps $200 worth of gold may sell for $750-1,000. Gold finger rings of the 1st-3rd centuries B.C., which rarely contain more than an ounce of gold, are not easily purchasable under $2,000. Here the origin is of more importance to buyers than the material. There are collectors specializing in ancient jewelry who will compete vigorously for whatever comes on the market — no matter if gold is up, down or sideways. They couldn't care less about the daily "spot." Where gold has been used as an adjunct or decorative touch in items made largely of other materials this situation can also prevail. The gold fixtures on firearms of the 17th and 18th centuries are an example. There may be three ounces of gold, with a bullion value of $1,500. But the item is rare and desirable, and its overall value can be $35,000, $50,000 or more.

As a general rule: if you have gold items which appear, on strength of their age or design or unusualness, to have the potential of appealing to collectors, *do not sell them to scrap merchants.* Take them instead to antique dealers.

Certain categories of old gold objects are, despite their age, of comparatively little interest to collectors and may be disposed of as scrap. Spectacle frames, even if very old, are not a viable collectors' item and can be safely sold as bullion. Watch cases are a borderline item; some of those manufactured around 1900 had very handsome designs and will bring a slight premium as antiques. Many, however, are plain and have value only as bullion.

BUYING PRICES FOR GOLD WATCHES

These are approximate dealer buying prices for fine watches in VF external condition and perfect running condition, calculated at a spot price of $600 per ounce for gold.

POCKET WATCHES

A. LANGE, calendar watch	$3,500.00
A. LANGE, gold closed case	1,200.00
A. LANGE, open face gold case	950.00
A. LANGE, repeater	17,000.00
A. LANGE, stop watch	2,500.00
AUDEMARS, calendar watch	1,500.00
AUDEMARS, gold closed case	600.00
AUDEMARS, open face gold case	400.00
AUDEMARS, repeater	3,500.00
AUDEMARS, stop watch	1,250.00
C. FRODSHAM, calendar watch	4,000.00
C. FRODSHAM, gold closed case	850.00
C. FRODSHAM, open face gold case	700.00
C. FRODSHAM, repeater	7,500.00
C. FRODSHAM, stop watch	2,500.00
EKEGREN, calendar watch	2,500.00
EKEGREN, gold closed case	600.00
EKEGREN, open face gold case	450.00
EKEGREN, repeater	3,000.00
EKEGREN, stop watch	1,500.00
HENRY CAPT, calendar watch	1,500.00
HENRY CAPT, gold closed case	900.00
HENRY CAPT, open face gold case	650.00
HENRY CAPT, repeater	2,500.00
HENRY CAPT, stop watch	1,000.00
J. ASSMANN, calendar watch	3,500.00
J. ASSMANN, gold closed case	1,200.00
J. ASSMANN, open face gold case	950.00
J. ASSMANN, repeater	17,000.00
J. ASSMANN, stop watch	2,500.00
JULES JURGENSEN, calendar watch	1,500.00
JULES JURGENSEN, gold closed case	850.00
JULES JURGENSEN, open face gold case	700.00
JULES JURGENSEN, repeater	5,000.00
JULES JURGENSEN, stop watch	1,500.00
K. GROSSMAN, calendar watch	3,500.00
K. GROSSMAN, gold closed case	1,200.00
K. GROSSMAN, open face gold case	950.00
K. GROSSMAN, repeater	17,000.00
K. GROSSMAN, stop watch	2,500.00
PATEK PHILIPPE, calendar watch	1,500.00
PATEK PHILIPPE, gold closed case	900.00
PATEK PHILIPPE, open face gold case	600.00
PATEK PHILIPPE, repeater	5,000.00
PATEK PHILIPPE, stop watch	1,500.00

WRIST WATCHES

Patek Calendar/Moonphase	4,500.00
Patek Ladies', gold case	200.00
Patek Repeater	12,500.00
Patek Round, gold case	500.00
Patek Square, gold case	600.00
Patek Stop Watch	1,500.00

Rolex Chronometer, gold $750.00
Rolex Datejust, gold 750.00
Rolex 18K Ladies' President 3,000.00
Rolex 18K President 3,500.00
Universal Calendar 500.00

MISCELLANEOUS WATCH BUYING PRICES

Columbus, 25 jewel 750.00
Edward Howard Freespring 2,000.00
Gruen 50th Anniversary 750.00
Hamilton 947, 23 jewel hunting 600.00
Hamilton 951 .... 500.00
Illinois Ben Franklin, 25 jewel 1,000.00
Illinois Bunn Special, 24 jewel 250.00
Illinois Bunn Special, 26 jewel 1,000.00
Rockford, 24 jewel 500.00
Rockford, 25 jewel 3,000.00
Seth Thomas Maiden Lane, 25 jewel 1,000.00
Waltham Premier Maximus, 23 jewel with winding indicator in original case 2,000.00

BUYING GOLD BARS

When the ban was lifted on private ownership of gold by American citizens on January 1, 1975, gold bars were publicly offered for sale for the first time in more than 40 years. Today their sales volume has reached astronomical proportions.

Gold bars are made of .999 pure gold, meaning 24K or the highest possible grade (the designation .999 is used instead of 1.000, the theory being that it is impossible, even with the most sophisticated refining procedures, to guarantee that no trace of base metal remains). They are sold in sizes beginning at one ounce which, of course, is an extremely small size physically because of gold's heavy weight, and ranging up to 27.4 pounds. The largest size, 27.4 pounds is known as the "Good Delivery Bar." If the spot price of gold is $600 per ounce, these bars have the following bullion value:

one ounce —	$ 600.00
one pound —	7,200.00
10 pounds —	72,000.00
27.4 pounds —	197,280.00

Gold bars are made by refineries, using either raw gold as it comes from the mines or scrap gold from which the alloying material has been refined out. In either case the result is 24K and it makes no difference where the gold came from. Each bar carries a mark of fineness and most (but not all) bear the refiner's name. Investors prefer bars marked with a well-known refiner's name as this serves as assurance of purity and actual weight.

ADVANTAGES OF BUYING BARS. Probably the chief advantage for investors in buying gold bars over other forms of gold is that the value is very easily calculated. You have an object of stated weight, and the weight will always be in full ounces; therefore, its current market price can be tabulated without difficulty using daily spot quotations. Bars are no less easily salable than other forms of gold. Larger bars usually take a little longer to liquidate due to the large amount of money involved.

The price charged for bars varies somewhat but averages from 3% to 5% above gold's spot price on the day of sale. This covers the dealer's commission as well as the cost of refining the gold and shaping it into bars. When sold, a small percentage will be deducted from the spot price. It is still an attractive percentage margin compared to those encountered in buying and selling many other forms of gold.

VALUES OF U.S. GOLD COINS

When you say "what's the value" of a certain gold coin, this is a difficult question to answer unless you know why someone wants to know. As an example, a coin's value is different when you sell than when you buy. The same is true regarding condition: is it uncirculated or is it damaged or severely worn?

Let's take the latter example first. When you have a damaged gold coin the value of it relates directly to that of bullion. That's why we call it the "bullion value" (or "melt value") of a gold coin. This means that its value relates directly to the spot price of gold on that day.

The following formula enables you to figure the bullion value of any U.S. gold coin, whatever the spot price is on any given day. Simply multiply spot that day by the net weight in gold of each coin. This will give you the melt value in dollars of each coin. You will need the following chart of net weights to assist you with your calculations.

Gold Coin Denominations	Amount of Pure Gold it Contains (in fractions of an ounce)
$ 1.00	.04837
2.50	.12094
3.00	.14512
4.00 (proofs only, extremely rare)	
5.00	.24187
10.00	.48375
20.00	.96750

Examples:
A. $20 gold piece. If spot was $577.50: 577.50 X .96750 = $558.73
B. $10 gold piece. If spot was $429.75: 429.75 X .48375 = $207.89
C. $5 gold piece. If spot was $719.00: 719.00 X .24187 = $173.90
D. $3 gold piece. If spot was $900: 900 X .14512 = $130.61
E. $2.50 gold piece. If spot was $1,020.00: 1,020.00 X .12094 = $123.36
F. $1 gold piece. If spot was $837.00: 837.00 X .04837 = $40.49

The other values given to gold coins are those that range from fine to uncirculated condition. First, exact condition must be determined. The following grading rules will assist you on this:

GOLD $1, LIBERTY HEAD.

MINT STATE, MS-60. (Uncirculated). A strictly Uncirculated coin with no trace of wear, but with blemishes more obvious than for MS-65. May lack full mint luster and brilliance. Checkpoints for signs of abrasion: hair near coronet; tips of leaves.

EXTREMELY FINE, EF-40. *OBVERSE:* Slight wear shows on highest wave of hair, hairline and below ear. All major details are sharp. Beads at top of coronet are well defined. *REVERSE:* Leaves show visible wear at tips but

OBVERSE

REVERSE

central details are clearly defined. Traces of mint luster will show.

FINE, F-12. *OBVERSE:* LIBERTY is complete but weak.Earlobe is visible. Hairlines and beads on coronet are worn smooth. Stars are clearly outlined but centers are flat. *REVERSE:* Legend within wreath is worn and weak in spots. Leaves and wreath are well outlined. Rim is full and edge beveled.

GOLD $2.50, LIBERTY HEAD.

MINT STATE, MS-60. (Uncirculated.) A strictly Uncirculated coin with no trace of wear, but with blemishes more obvious than for MS-65. May lack full mint luster and brilliance. Checkpoints for signs of abrasion: tip of coronet, hair, wings, claws.

OBVERSE

REVERSE

EXTREMELY FINE, EF-40. *OBVERSE:* Light wear shows on coronet, hair above ear and eye, on forelocks, and on cheek. All major details sharp. *REVERSE:* Light wear shows on edges and tips of wings, on neck, below eye, on feathers and claws. Shield well defined. Traces of mint luster will show.

FINE, F-12. *OBVERSE:* Hair and cheek smooth. Stars outlined with no visible details. LIBERTY worn but readable. *REVERSE:* Wings show very little detail. Head and one claw outlined only, with no details visible. Neck almost smooth. Most of shield lines merge.

GOLD $2.50, INDIAN HEAD

MINT STATE, MS-60 (Uncirculated). A strictly Uncirculated coin with no trace of wear, but with blemishes more obvious than for MS-65. May lack full mint luster and brilliance. Checkpoints for signs of abrasion: cheekbone, headdress, headband feathers, shoulder of eagle's left wing.

OBVERSE

REVERSE

EXTREMELY FINE, EF-40. *OBVERSE:* Light wear shows on cheekbone, jaw and headband. Slight wear visible on feathers of headdress. Stars sharp. *REVERSE:* Light wear shows on wing, head, neck and breast. Leg has full feather detail. Traces of mint luster will show.

FINE, F-12. *OBVERSE:* Cheekbone worn; all feathers worn with very little detail visible. Stars outlined with no details visible. Hair cord knot is worn but visible. *REVERSE:* Wing worn, with only partial feathers at bottom visible. All lettering worn but visible.

GOLD $5, LIBERTY HEAD

MINT STATE, MS-60. (Uncirculated). A strictly Uncirculated coin with no trace of wear, but with blemishes more obvious than for MS-65. Has full mint luster but may lack brilliance. Surface may be lightly marred by minor bag marks and abrasions. Checkpoints for signs for wear: hair, coronet; wings.

OBVERSE

REVERSE

EXTREMELY FINE, EF-40. *OBVERSE:* Light wear shows on coronet, on hair above ear and eye, on the forelock, on top of head and on cheek. All major details are sharp. *REVERSE:* Light wear visible on edges and tips of wings, on neck, below eye, on feathers and claws. Shield is well defined. Traces of mint luster will show.

FINE, F-12. *OBVERSE:* Hair and cheekbone smooth. Top line of coronet worn. LIBERTY worn but visible. *REVERSE:* Wings show very little detail. Head and one claw outlined only, with no details visible. Neck almost smooth. Most of shield lines merge. (For the 1866 through 1908 group, the motto is worn but readable.)

GOLD $5, INDIAN HEAD

MINT STATE, MS-60 (Uncirculated). A strictly Uncirculated coin with no trace of wear, but with blemishes more obvious than for MS-65. Has full mint luster but may lack brilliance. Surface may be lightly marred by minor bag marks and abrasions. Checkpoints for signs of wear: cheekbone, headdress, headband feathers; shoulders of eagle's left wing.

OBVERSE

REVERSE

EXTREMELY FINE, EF-40. *OBVERSE:* Light wear shows on cheekbone, jaw and headband. Slight wear visible on feathers of headdress. Stars are sharp. *REVERSE:* Light wear shows on wing, head, neck and breast. Leg has full feather detail. Traces of mint luster will show.

FINE, F-12. *OBVERSE:* Cheekbone worn; all feathers worn with very little detail visible. Stars outlined, with no details visible. Hair cord know is worn but visible. *REVERSE:* Wing worn, with only partial feathers at bottom visible. All lettering worn but visible.

GOLD $10, LIBERTY HEAD

MINT STATE, MS-60. (Uncirculated). A strictly Uncirculated coin with no trace of wear, but with blemishes more obvious than for MS-65. Has full mint luster but may lack brilliance. Surface may be lightly marred by minor bag marks and abrasions. Checkpoints for signs of wear: hair, coronet; wings.

OBVERSE

REVERSE

EXTREMELY FINE, EF-40. *OBVERSE:* Light wear shows on coronet, hair, cheek and stars. All major details sharp. *REVERSE:* Light wear visible on wings, head, neck and claws. Shield is well defined. Traces of mint luster will show.

FINE, F-12. *OBVERSE:* Hair and cheekbones smooth. Top line of coronet worn. Some details show in stars. LIBERTY worn but visible. *REVERSE:* Wings show very little detail. Head and one claw outlined only, with no details visible. Neck is almost smooth. Most of shield lines merge. (In the 1866 through 1907 group, the motto is worn but readable.)

GOLD $10, INDIAN HEAD

MINT STATE, MS-60. (Uncirculated). A strictly Uncirculated coin with no trace of wear, but with blemishes more obvious than for MS-65. Has full mint luster but may lack brilliance. Surface may be lightly marred by minor bag marks and abrasions. Checkpoints for signs of wear: above eye, cheek, wing.

OBVERSE

REVERSE

EXTREMELY FINE, EF-40. *OBVERSE:* Light wear shows on hair, cheekbone and feathers. *REVERSE:* Light wear visible on wing and head. Traces of mint luster will show.

FINE, F-12. *OBVERSE:* Hair smooth with no details; cheekbone almost smooth. No feathers touch headband but most feather details visible. *REVERSE:* Left wing top and head are worn smooth. Lettering worn but visible.

GOLD $20, LIBERTY HEAD

MINT STATE, MS-60. (Uncirculated). A strictly Uncirculated coin with no trace of wear, but with blemishes more obvious than for MS-65. Has full mint luster but may lack brilliance. Surface is usually lightly marred by minor bag marks and abrasions. Checkpoints for signs of wear: hair, coronet; eagle's neck and wing, top of shield.

OBVERSE

REVERSE

EXTREMELY FINE, EF-40. *OBVERSE:* Light wear shows on hair, coronet prongs and cheek. *REVERSE:* Light wear visible on wings, head, neck, horizontal shield lines and tail. Traces of mint luster will show.

FINE, F-12. *OBVERSE:* All hairlines are well worn with very little detail visible. About one-quarter of details within coronet visible. Stars show little detail. LIBERTY readable. *REVERSE:* Wings show very little detail. Head and neck smooth. Eye visible. Tail and top of shield smooth.

GOLD $20, SAINT-GAUDENS

MINT STATE, MS-60. (Uncirculated). A strictly Uncirculated coin with no trace of wear, but with blemishes more obvious than for MS-65. Has full mint luster but may lack brilliance. Surface is usually lightly marred by minor bag marks and abrasions. Checkpoints for signs of wear: forehead, breast, knee, nose; eagle's wings and breast.

OBVERSE **REVERSE**

EXTREMELY FINE, EF-40. *OBVERSE:* Light wear shows on forehead, nose breast, knee and just below left knee. Drapery lines on chest visible. *REVERSE:* Light wear visible on wings and breast but all feathers bold. Traces of mint luster will show.

FINE, F-112. *OBVERSE:* Forehead and garment smooth; breast flat. Both legs worn with right bottom missing. *REVERSE:* Less than half the wing details are visible. Only a little breast detail is visible.

Now you have an idea of the grade. The following values are for properly graded coins. As dealers usually only buy Fine or better grade coins at higher prices than "bullion value" these are the prices that are given. The reason is that gold coins are seldom collected in grades lower than fine. The A.B.P. at the top of the first column means Average Buying Price. This is the price most dealers will pay for that particular coin in Fine condition. The other columns represent the retail value, or in other words the price that the average dealer would sell these coins for in his shop. Keep in mine that buying prices vary just as much as selling prices. When the selling price is up the buying price should be up as well.

The following prices are for common-date gold coins. Better dates are worth more. For values on these as well as more statistical information we recommend **"THE OFFICIAL BLACKBOOK OF U.S. COINS,"** the annual publication relied on by buyers and sellers of coins. It is available for only $2.50 plus $1 postage and handling from The House of Collectibles, Inc., 1900 Premier Row, Orlando, Florida 32809.

The following prices are based on a "spot" price of $565 and were current as of February, 1981. As spot price changes regularly you should check the up-to-the-minute figure (normally in the financial section of your daily newspaper).

	A.B.P. in Fine F-12	Fine F-12	Extra Fine EF-40	Uncirculated MS-60
Gold $1, Liberty Head I	$200.00	$250.00	$315.00	$825.00
Gold $2.50, Liberty Head	100.00	130.00	220.00	545.00
Gold $2.50, Indian Head	110.00	140.00	175.00	420.00
Gold $5, Liberty with Motto	100.00	130.00	170.00	285.00
Gold $5, Indian Head	120.00	150.00	200.00	825.00
Gold $10, Liberty with Motto	225.00	29.00	350.00	435.00
Gold $10, Indian Head	300.00	375.00	465.00	825.00
Gold $20, Liberty Head III	460.00	575.00	615.00	725.00
Gold $20, St. Gaudens	485.00	600.00	650.00	775.00

NOTE: With motto means "IN GOD WE TRUST" inscribed on reverse.

VALUES OF POPULAR FOREIGN GOLD COINS

The following are dealer buying prices and retail prices for the more popular foreign gold coins. Values are figured against a spot price of $565. Refer to the previous chapter for an explanation of A.B.P. (Average Buying Price) and retail price.

	Uncirculated A.B.P. MS-60	Retail Price Uncirculated
Austria 1 Ducat	$55.00	$68.00
Austria 4 Ducat	200.00	260.00
Austria 20 Corona	95.00	120.00
Austria 200 Corona	450.00	565.00
Mexico 50 Peso	585.00	725.00
Mexico 20 Peso	235.00	295.00
Mexico 10 Peso	115.00	145.00
Mexico 5 Peso	60.00	75.00
Mexico 2½ Peso	32.00	40.00
Mexico 2 Peso	26.00	32.00
South African Krugerrand	475.00	595.00
Germany 20 Mark	120.00	150.00
Belgium 20 Franc	100.00	125.00
Netherlands 10 Guilders	100.00	125.00
Russia 5 Rubles	60.00	75.00
Colombia 5 Peso	110.00	135.00

KRUGGERANDS — NEW DEVELOPMENTS

From 1967, when it was introduced, until 1980, South Africa's "Krugerrand" served as the chief gold bullion investment coin of the world. Named after a hero of the 1898 Boer War, the Krugerrand was for many years the only available bullion coin that contained precisely one Troy ounce of gold (plus an additional amount of copper, yielding a total weight of 1.0909 Troy ounces). As long as the demand for bullion gold remained fairly constant, as it did prior to 1979, the South African government met investor needs simply by producing additional quantities of the Krugerrand. During the "gold rush" of late, '79', it became apparent that this single denomination was insufficient to satisfy worldwide demand.

In September 1980, divisionals of the Krugerrand were announced. Their purpose is to meet the needs of smaller bullion investors, whose budgets do not allow for purchase of one full ounce of gold. Three fractional denominations were to be struck:

One-half Krugerrand, containing ½ ounce 24K gold
One-quarter Krugerrand, containing .250 ounce 24K
One-tenth Krugerrand, containing .100 ounce 24K

With a $600 spot price of gold, these coins would have the following bullion values:

One-half Krugerrand, $300
One-quarter Krugerrand, $150
One-tenth Krugerrand, $60

The actual prices at which they will sell can be figured at about 10% or slightly more above the face values. Figures on extent of initial production were not available as this book went to press. Early reaction from investors and investment counselors was positive. The obvious advantage of these coins over other low-denomination gold pieces is that bullion content is fixed at precise divisions of a Troy ounce, thereby rendering calculations vs. the daily spot very uncomplicated.

U.S. COMMEMORATIVE GOLD COINS

The gold commemorative series began not long after the silver, in 1903. Far fewer gold commemoratives were issued, as the large physical size necessary for impressive designing resulted in a coin of very high face value. Experiments were made with $1 gold commemoratives, which some critics called puny, and goliaths of $50 denomination, which were indeed eye-catching but well beyond the budgets of most citizens in those days. The final gold commemorative was coined for the 1926 Sesquicentennial or 150th anniversary of American freedom from Britain.

These are not suitable pieces for bullion investment because they carry a rather substantial collector value.

The Panama-Pacific $50 commemorative, containing nearly two and one-half ounces of gold, was not the world's largest gold piece but by far the most substantial coin of that metal struck by the U.S. government. To give some indication of changes in the market from its time of issue in 1915 to now: The issue value was $50, now the present value in uncirculated MS-60 condition is between $35,000-$50,000.

GOLD COMMEMORATIVE MEDALS — PRIVATE ISSUES

The term "private commemorative medal" refers to medals issued by non-government corporations and societies. The majority of these, in recent years at any rate, have been struck for the purpose of public sale. The pages of every numismatic publication reveal many advertisements for gold commemorative medals of all kinds.

Should the investor buy these medals?

What is the metallic quality?

How much is charged, in relation to bullion value?

Are they likely to appreciate in value as collectors' items?

It is obvious, to anyone with even elementary knowledge of medals or numismatics, that the majority of such productions are neither skillfully designed or of much aesthetic appeal. A great number of them are made for sale to persons who will order anything to which the magic word "gold" is attached. Unfortunately, increased media attention on the bullion market has spawned a whole new class of "marks" for manufacturers of low-quality merchandise. These are well-intentioned people who believe they are getting their full money's worth.

Such medals can have value either for bullion content or as collectors' items or both. But they may have very little of either. If the retail price is well above that of their bullion content — and frequently it exceeds it by 50% or more — the investment potential is generally nil. Quite often this is impossible to determine from the advertisement, which is worded in such a way as to give the impression of heavy bullion content but does not actually state specifics. For example, a medal may be advertised as 18K gold, accompanied by a photo blown up several times the actual size. The ad copy states it to be "fully as large as a U.S. quarter." This tells only half the story. The medal may be equal in diameter to a quarter; but the ads fail to mention its thickness. It may be paper thin. Or the ad may give the medal's weight, without stating that this is the *overall* weight, of which its gold content is only a portion. It is uncommon for ads for private commemorative medals to give the full specifics of the item: so much weight of such-and-such quality gold for X price. The reason this is not done, of course, is that the prices charged for such medals are much higher than the same quantity of bullion could be obtained for in buying gold quarter eagles, half eagles or other gold coins. If the truth were plainly stated, not many amateur investors would place an order. The medal would have to depend for its sale on collectors.

What sort of potential lies in *that* direction?

Medals struck by the more respected companies such as Franklin Mint do appreciate in value, because there are collectors specializing in Franklin Mint issues. If the firm is little-known and little-collected, it is quite likely that any medal it strikes will have a difficult time becoming a sought-after collector's piece. Scarcity alone will not accomplish this, even if the edition is limited to 100 or some other conservative figure. Who really cares about a medal honoring some obscure cause or event, poorly designed, and containing only a medium amount of gold, when much better medals are on the market?

Take care when you buy and don't be misled by advertising jargon.

ALL ABOUT GOLD INVESTMENT

Investing in gold is simpler than investing in stocks. There's less red tape and you can start with a smaller amount of money. With gold it's very easy to calculate what your investment is worth at any given time. It isn't difficult to sell, when the time comes. But you must remember that, unlike stocks, gold pays no dividends as you hold it. It makes money only when it's sold. Therefore, the object in owning it is to eventually sell it — when the market is right.

GOLD AS AN INVESTMENT. Gold is a potentially volatile investment. It can leap upward in price very rapidly; during the last several months of 1979 and the first month of 1980 its value more than tripled. Because of this it has earned a reputation as a gambler's investment. This is not entirely deserved. The gamble occurs mostly in the manner in which gold investment

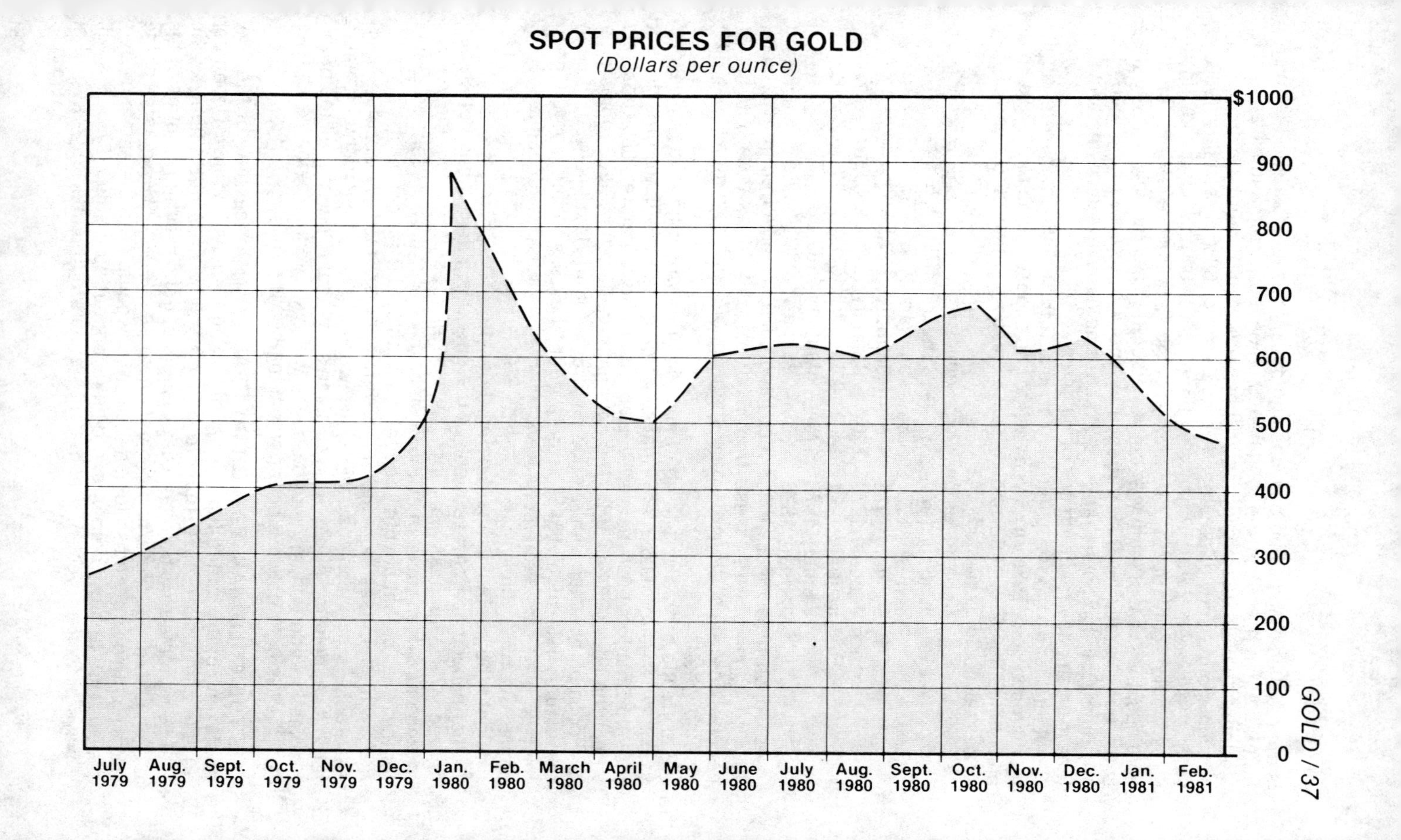
SPOT PRICES FOR GOLD
(Dollars per ounce)
$1000
900
800
700
600
500
400
300
200
100
0
July 1979
Aug. 1979
Sept. 1979
Oct. 1979
Nov. 1979
Dec. 1979
Jan. 1980
Feb. 1980
March 1980
April 1980
May 1980
June 1980
July 1980
Aug. 1980
Sept. 1980
Oct. 1980
Nov. 1980
Dec. 1980
Jan. 1981
Feb. 1981

is approached. Those who buy when gold is high, seeking a short-term profit, take some risk. Over the long haul, bullion (both gold and silver — and platinum as well) has proved safer than most Wall Street blue chips. True enough, gold's spot price dipped from a high of $850 in January 1980, to $475 a few weeks later. Those who bought at $700 or $800, believing the price would soon top $1,000, took a gamble. If they've cashed in their holdings, they've lost money — quite a bit of it. If they haven't sold yet, they could be rewarded for their patience by another upswing in the market at any time. Gold isn't perishable, and there's no danger — as with stocks — that the company might go out of business.

But let's look at the long haul, which is how the intelligent investor ought to approach gold. Take any 5-year period you choose during the 1970's up to and including 1980. Gold showed an increase in price during any 5-year span that could be named:

Spot prices per 1 troy ounce

January 1970	$ 32	—	January 1975	$175
January 1971	38	—	January 1976	125
January 1972	43	—	January 1977	100
January 1973	60	—	January 1978	175
January 1974	140	—	January 1979	200
January 1975	175	—	January 1980	850
January 1976	125	—	January 1981	600

As will be seen, the lowest proportion of increase occurred from January 1974 to January 1979, a rise from $140 to $200. In all the other 5-year periods, the price did no worse than double and sometimes did considerably better.

For trends of this sort to continue, the price would have to get beyond $1,000 by January 1985. Many analysts predict that it will; they feel in fact that the magic $1,000 barrier will be broken long before 1985, possibly within the coming year. If that should happen, $2,000 by 1985 looms as a real possibility. After all, the price quadrupled in the last five years, taking the January 1980 high of $850 as our working figure. Another quadrupling in the next five years, even if one works with a price of $850 for January 1980, comes out to $3,400.

Is gold the best investment going these days?

That depends on how you look at it. Some things have done better, percentage-wise, such as paintings by master artists. Their value on the average has risen more than 300% since 1977. But they present problems for the investor that are not encountered with gold. They cost a great deal of money to purchase, for one thing. For another, there is absolutely no assurance how much they will bring when sold. Occasionally, art sales fetch disappointing prices — even some sales that occur at the "top of the market." In addition, an auction house will take a commission as high as 20%. Art is definitely a bigger gamble than gold.

IS THE GOLD MARKET A GRAVY TRAIN? A lot of people got the very mistaken notion, during that month of spiraling prices from mid-December 1979 to mid-January 1980, that big money in gold was as sure a thing as the sun rising tomorrow morning. They thought of gold investing in terms of the old chain-letter racket. As more and more people buy, they reasoned, the price has to go up. And so long as the price is going up, more and more people are sure to buy. Of course, it didn't work out quite that way. There will always be *sellers,* too, and sometimes sellers outnumber buyers. In that event the price has to go down. There is no way the gold market — or any other commodity market — can regulate the flow of buyers and sellers. It cannot maintain an even pace. It must sell to those who want to buy, and buy from those who wish to sell. And there is no certain way of forecasting when one group will outnumber the other. Obviously, when gold was advancing by $35 and $50 per day, buyers vastly outnumbered sellers. But gold holders were watching the daily spot. Those who had bought at $200 — and many had bought at even less — decided that a price of $800-$850 per ounce was too attractive to miss. They poured tons of gold back into the market. Naturally, as prices began to slip, buyers got discouraged and held off. They feared a total collapse of prices. Whether this same situation would prevail in the event of another quick upward climb is hard to say. There might be greater confidence next time, because investors saw that the bottom did not totally fall out in January 1980. Gold went through a period of adjustment, but even with that adjustment the price ended up twice as high as a year earlier. Those are fairly good odds — even for a gambler.

GOLD PRICES VS. VALUE OF ARTICLES CONTAINING GOLD. It can be stated flatly and unarguably that any object made of gold, or containing gold, of any grade or weight, is worth more when the spot price advances and less when it declines. But there is a great difference between the price at which a Krugerrand (weighing slightly more than one ounce, and containing an exact ounce of gold) can be sold, and the price of a pocketwatch case of the same weight. Some gold articles are *worth much more than others,* for any or all of the following reasons:

1. The gold is a higher grade or karat.

2. The item does not require refining.

3. If refining is required, it is simple refining, not the difficulty faced with plated material and dental gold.

Simply stated, the investor's goal should be to acquire types of gold whose resale value is closely in line with the spot price. The rise or fall in price of bullion gold can be easily calculated based on the daily spot prices of gold. With collectors' items there will of course be some flucuation according to spot prices but these might be balanced out or at least influenced by trends in the collector market — trends the investor is likely to be unaware of unless he has knowledge of that particular market or has aid of an advisor. Gold collectors' items are apt to rise more sharply in value during a time of "gold fever" than raw bullion. But they could also prove more difficult to find buyers for, or to find buyers willing to pay the full market price. Bullion items can, on the other hand, generally be sold across-the-counter at a standard rate of discount, making it very easy to know what you'll be getting before you sell.

Coins are a good example. There is no guesswork involved with coins; the purity of every gold coin is well-established and does not call for weighing or testing. Gold bars and ingots are another. Poor investment material includes most kinds of gold jewelry and novelties or miscellaneous items made of gold. The retail price of gold jewelry is considerably higher than its bullion value, because of the long chain of profits involved in its manufacture and sale. A ring which could be sold for scrap at $200 will carry a retail price of $750 to $1,000. This obviously is not an attractive investment. The only worthwhile bullion investments are those in which purchasing can be done at a minimal advance over the bullion value, and selling accomplished at the smallest possible discount. Of course, there is no way to sell without incurring some discount. The dealers or agents to whom you sell are in business to make money,and if they bought bullion for its actual value and sold it for its actual value they would make nothing. Even on "tight" material, such as Krugerrands, you must expect to pay a reasonable commission. This is discussed in detail below.

Bars and ingots are convenient and relatively safe gold investments — convenient because their weight is in full ounces and their value can be figured easily against the daily spot, safe because the fineness is marked upon them and there is no argument over karat or weight. You should always try to buy a bar or ingot with a well-known hallmark, (Englehard, Handy and Harmen, etc) as these are generally easier to sell when the time comes. Gold coins are somewhat more popular than bars or ingots, however, because of the greater ease with which they can be disposed of; coin dealers can be found just about everywhere. It should be noted, however, that an increasing number of coin dealers are now buying bars and ingots, and paying the same prices as gold brokers. They are able to do this because they do not resell to the gold brokers — if that were the case they would have to discount. Instead they sell to their own customers, at the same prices gold brokers charge, or keep them themselves.

When buying gold coins as bullion investments, the proportion of gold vs. the coin's weight must be taken into consideration. Not all gold coins from every part of the world have the same fineness. US. gold coins are standard at 90% gold and 10% copper. Those issued by foreign governments are sometimes of higher grade, sometimes lower. Because the Krugerrand contains exactly one ounce of 24K gold, it is considered by many investment specialists as the perfect bullion coin. When gold is trading at a spot price of $600, the Krugerrand's gold content is worth $600 — no more or less.

HOW INVESTMENT GOLD IS BOUGHT AND SOLD. As we said, buying gold is less of a fuss than buying corporate stocks. With gold there is no registration required, and no broker touting questionable stocks in which he has a personal interest. You simply buy, as you would buy any other kind of merchandise. In the case of gold bars, ingots and Krugerrands, you will be charged the spot price on *that day* plus a percentage of commission. Unless the transaction occurs early in the morning, before the London gold exchange has closed for the day (London is from six to nine hours ahead of us in time, depending on what part of the country you live in), the price will be based on the London closing as this is the world barometer. Should you buy in New York — or Boston, or Philadelphia, or somewhere else in the East — at 9:00 in the morning, while the London exchange is still open, the price will usually be calculated on the London opening. Here it's a matter of the individual dealer's practice. He could use the previous day's London close as his price. Or he could get hour-by-hour spot figures from the teletype and change his prices accordingly. This is all quite legal to do, as long as he follows the same method at all times and does not choose one price arbitrarily because it's lower or higher than another price. By law the dealer is required to use the same figure for buying as for selling. When his selling price changes, he must change the buying price, too. And these prices should be clearly posted. Dealers who specialize in "gold brokerage" normally flash the current buy/sell price in their shop windows.

The commission when buying depends upon the type of gold purchased and the dealer's practice. There is no law regulating such commissions. A dealer is free to charge whatever commission he chooses in buying or selling, because technically he's selling "merchandise" and there are no price controls on merchandise. Obviously, this leaves the door ajar for profiteering; but few gold dealers attempt to gouge, because competition in the industry is strong. Prices are advertised and the public will not patronize a dealer whose commissions are higher than those of his competitors.

When buying straight bullion material — Krugerrands, bars and ingots — the usual commission is 5% to 8%. This means that if gold is selling at $600 spot, a Krugerrand will cost from $630 to $650. At times of very heavy buying or selling the commission could get slightly higher; the dealer will explain that this is necessary because he's required to hire extra personnel, do additional paperwork, etc. The real reason, of course, is that dealers seek to discourage heavy volume selling when gold is falling in price, and the only way they can do this (aside from refusing to buy) is to raise commissions. But commissions never vary too greatly and this is nothing to be concerned about.

If you buy U.S. gold coins, or foreign coins other than Krugerrands, there may not be a flat commission charged. It all depends upon the dealer. Some dealers price the old Liberty "Double Eagles" a touch lower than the St. Gaudens, though both contain the same amount of gold and are of the same purity. There might seem to be some numismatic reason behind this but the dealers deny it. Their explanation is that the newer $20 gold pieces have been handled less and consequently can be figured, on average, to contain a slight extra fraction of gold than the older ones. In fact, St. Gaudens Double Eagles did practically no circulating at all. Their use was almost strictly as banking pieces. But as a whole a St. Gaudens $20 gold piece will and does commend a slightly higher price on the selling end as well as the buying end.

On the whole you will *pay more* for the gold in coins (other than Krugerrands) than for the gold in bars or ingots. This does not, however, render them any less attractive an investment. U.S. coin gold is a high grade: 90% pure. Coins are unquestionably the best kind of gold to be holding if the market should slip. When gold goes down appreciably, numismatists who simply want these coins for their collections start buying. Of course, their prices fall, but not usually as rapidly as the price of gold bars, ingots or Krugerrands.

HOW MUCH SHOULD YOU INVEST? The amount to be invested should be determined by the sum you can safely and comfortably put aside for a while, possibly an extended period of time if necessary. It is foolish to follow the course taken by some persons during the Gold Rush of last year, who sold their cars, homes, insurance policies and everything else of value to buy gold. When all your eggs are placed in one basket, investing can be a nightmare. The smart investor plays it cool. The beginner is best advised to invest gradually, putting in a portion of his available investment capital at first and holding the remainder for future purchases. These can be made on a regular schedule, depending upon the market.

SHOULD YOU BUY "HIGH" OR "LOW"? Should you wait until gold is down and take advantage of the favorable price — or wait to buy until it's showing upward movement? Investment analysts are not in agreement on this point, but generally the following advice is given. The *riskier* times to buy are when gold has been making strong advances over a period of weeks or months and the spot price is near or exceeding the all-time record high.

When announcements are made day to day in the media of "new records set," this encourages many holders to go out and sell. Also risky is a period when gold is sharply declining, because this sets off a mini-panic and there is no way of telling how low it might get before rebounding. The events of January 1980 should provide ample evidence of this. When the price reached $850 and then slid back to $750, that figure might have looked like a bargain. That is, if you were confident enough to think in terms of a temporary adjustment that would right itself in a few days. But the price did not rebound from $750. Nor did it hold steady. It slipped below $700, then, very rapidly, below $600, and was under $500 before the levelling off started. If you bought at $750, thinking you were taking advantage of a $100 price-break, you suddenly discovered that your investment had lost about 30%. When the price is bounding around wildly, *be careful.* Under the normal conditions of day to day trading, the price does not fluctuate by more than $10 per day and generally much less. When prices are changing by $20, $30 or more daily, this is an indication that the market is out of whack and is reaching an unpredictable point. People who do not normally buy or sell gold are trading in it, and in large quantities. The big investors have sufficient punch to upset the whole world market, if they all buy or sell at the same time. They trample small investors underfoot, and by the time the dust has settled these small investors could be in a very bad position.

Probably the best time to buy is when gold has been advancing pretty steadily, though not dramatically, for at least two months — yet is far from its record high. If the spot were $475 — 60 days ago and $575 today, that would be considered a favorable time for investment. These small steady advances are usually followed by larger advances, more often than by declines. And even if a decline should occur, declines following steady advances are generally not of the panic variety. They can be regarded as a natural adjustment which will lead to further price climbs in the near future. One thing is certain. Whenever the price of gold (or just about anything else) soars upward in a short period of time, it is going to come down again — not necessarily to the level it held before the buying rush started, but it will come down. It cannot be otherwise, because leaps of 100% or 200% within a month are proof positive indications that many investors seeking short-term gains are playing the market. These people cannot be depended upon to hold for a long period of time. They buy with the intent of selling fast and nine times in 10 they do sell fast, upsetting the market as they do so. *On the other hand,* there is no logical reason why steady increases of even as much as 50% annually cannot be maintained. They could be, and would, if they did not encourage bandwagon buying. Just left to itself, taking short-term investors out of the picture, gold would inevitably go up — and by a healthy percentage. Its use in industry, coupled with the dwindling world supply, would account for part of its growth; the rest would be made up for by long-term investors who are willing to hold gold for three, four or five years. But the market cannot be regulated that way. You cannot keep the gamblers and quick-buck profiteers out. And they, unfortunately, are often the heaviest buyers and sellers.

UNCLE SAM CAN DO SOMETHING ABOUT IT. Yes, the U.S. government does have the power to regulate gold prices. Not in the old-fashioned sense of fixing "official trading prices," but by becoming a buyer and seller. This nation owns more gold bullion — more than 275 million ounces of it — than any other nation or investor in the world. At a spot price of $600 per ounce, it owns more than $165,000,000,000 worth of gold. Yes, 165 *billion* dollars. It could, very simply and legally, sell some of its reserves when the international price starts going up too rapidly. And it would profit handsomely by doing so. The market would be kept in line and most investors would welcome the move — so long as the government did not sell so much gold that its price was seriously hurt.

Why doesn't the Treasury Department do this?

Well, it does. But only occasionally and in small amounts. During the early 1970's, it sold large quantities of gold to protect the value of our dollar abroad. But now that currencies are traded freely, without the backing of bullion, it takes other measures to strengthen the dollar — such as import quotas on Arab oil. The likelihood of wholesale gold selling by Fort Knox is very remote. Apparently this country has taken the position of allowing gold to find its own watermark in free trading without making any interference.

WHEN TO SELL. In deciding when to sell there are a number of considerations. First, of course, you must figure up exactly how much you would be getting versus the price *paid* — not the value of gold at the time you purchased, but the final price you paid including commissions. The amount you would receive has to be calculated not on the daily spot, but the spot price *less* commissions or dealer margins. If you bought $10,000 worth of Krugerrands and paid $10,800 for them, and they have now advanced to a spot value of $15,000, you can expect to receive around $14,800 when selling. This means you have a profit of $4,000. But the actual profit should be examined in light of inflation. Say you held those Krugerrands for two years, and in that time the inflation rate increased by 20%. Take 20% from your $14,800 and the yield is $11,640, a relatively small advance over your investment of $10,800. Whether it is worthwhile to sell at such a profit is a matter for you to decide. If the market appears healthy and likely to show further gains, it would be reasonable to wait, or to liquidate only a portion of your holdings if necessary. Investing is always a waiting game, and generally those with greatest patience do best. After all, what do you do with the money after selling? Put it in a savings account? The rate of return on a savings account is likely to be less than the rate of inflation. Stocks? Bonds? Certificates of Deposit? Something else? Unless the money is needed for a specific purpose, you are probably much better off leaving it in gold and awaiting further market developments.

SHOULD I BE PREPARED TO TAKE A LOSS? The approach of many investors in corporate stocks is to set an amount at which they will sell, if the stock is declining, even if this means taking a loss. This is called "stop-loss." In other words, putting a stop to the loss before it becomes bigger and bigger. The figure may be 20% under their cost price, or 30% or more, based upon the speed of decline and general market opinion about stocks of that class. This philosophy can, of course, be applied to precious metals as well. But if used it should be used cautiously. If buying has been done at a favorable time, not in a period of panic, there should be no need for "stop-loss." In fact it would be very inadvisable to sell during a period when the market has been reasonably steady, simply because the price is down $30 or $40 per ounce from your cost. The odds are greatly in favor of an upward swing in the future. The only logical time to sell gold at a loss is when you've made the mistake of buying at the top of the market, when spot is at or exceeding the record high. In that event it is probably wise to sell at the first sign of market weakness, as a sharp price drop is likely to follow.

SILVER

SILVER IN THE ANCIENT WORLD

As far as can be determined, silver was not employed in arts and crafts as early as gold, and probably not as early as copper. Just why this should have been is difficult to understand; but the fact is that silver objects have not yet been archaeologically discovered which can be dated as early as some preserved goldwork.

The oldest we yet have are specimens from the tombs of Egypt's pharaohs, which cannot be placed before 3,000 B.C. This indicates that silver have been worked for 5,000 years at least; how much earlier than this its use might have begun, is not possible to estimate. Certainly the prehistoric races of as long ago as 10,000 B.C. had the knowledge and equipment necessary for smelting silver, and had access to supplies of it. The possibility that it might have proved unappealing to them because of its color have been suggested. This is believable, as the yellow metals were undoubtedly regarded as related to the sun in some way.

The fact that relatively modest quantities of silverwork have been recovered from Egyptian tombs is not regarded as indication of low production. For the burial of pharaohs, objects of the richest materials were usually selected, and even then gold was in much higher esteem than silver. A good deal of silverwork was manufactured in Egypt and elsewhere in the ancient world.

There is not much information on the comparative values between gold and silver until the era of coined money. But apparently silver was, at least in the 4th millennium B.C., more valuable than it subsequently became, for we have a decree in the Code of Menes (c. 3,100 B.C.) that "one part of gold equals two and a half parts of silver in value." This was, of course, long prior to the striking of coinage, which did not take place in Egypt until after that nation was conquered by Carthage.

That the ancients respected silver and did much investigation into its potential uses, there is no question. By the time of Pliny the historian, in the 1st century A.D., the Romans were refining silver by cupellation, or oxidizing the ore's lead content into lead oxide. Long before this, statues were being cast in silver or mixtures of gold and silver. Silver served as a favorite alloying material for gold. It provided little additional strength (unlike copper alloy), but was deemed more suitable for works of art because of the brilliance of silver.

Silversmithing was a flourishing occupation in Greece. We do not know how far back it dates, but as there is considerable mention of silver in Greek mythology, and as these legends originated around 1,200 B.C., it can be safely presumed that the silversmiths were active by then. Their method of operation is not believed to have differed greatly from that of Roman smiths a thousand and more years later. The archaeological remains of a number of Graeco-Roman silversmith shops are known and have provided much evidence into the trade's development.

The typical silversmith establishment of the ancient world was not enclosed. It had no roof because the chimney has not been invented, and the furnace smoke would otherwise have been able to exit only from windows. It might occasionally have sported a makeshift covering of wooden slats laid across beams, with sufficient airspace to allow for smoke escape. The furnace was not constructed of brick or iron but hewn from solid stone, and recessed somewhat into the ground. It was, by all odds, a very primitive affair, but it got the job done. Recovered tools tell us that ancient smiths worked with tongs of various sizes, iron hammers, and used anvils not very different in design from those of modern date.

In addition to these small shops there were also, especially at Rome beginning in the Republican era, extensive silver factories that performed the equivalent of mass production and employed mostly slaves as laborers. Coins were not among the articles produced by these factories, as they were struck in regular mints set up for the purpose. But all sorts of military equipment was, including sword and dagger blades and shields. Though bronze and brass were preferred for breastplates, because of their durability and cheaper cost, the Romans did sometimes fashion gear of this sort from silver; very likely it was intended for officers, who could thus set themselves apart from common soldiers. In Athens, military breastplates of silver were made extensively.

BULLION INVESTMENT AND SPECULATION. Most of the details of silver investment and speculation in the ancient world are lost to history. What little we know is not very informative. Obviously, bullion investment did occur, and was without question more extensive than in our time, simply because most ot the modern means of investment did not then exist. Investment generally meant hoarding coins. It is established that the poorer and middle classes of society did a great deal of coin hoarding, and that their hoards consisted at least 80% of silver. Gold coinage did not frequently come into their possession, while that manufactured of base metal was (apparently) looked upon as too insignificant to put away. The "savings account" of many a Roman consisted of an old earthen jar with narrow neck, having a capacity between one and two modern quarts, which he buried partially in the soil floor of his dwelling so that only the lip protruded. Into this he deposited such coins as were not of immediate necessity for his survival. As need be, it could be covered over with soil (after stopping the mouth with a stone), or hidden under an object of furniture. That the Romans on the whole were a frugal lot, who denied themselves much to build up savings, there is ample proof, despite tales of their lavishness and waste. This waste was undoubtedly committed chiefly by the wealthier classes. Numerous jars filled with coins have been removed from the sites of Roman communities. Those who eschewed earthen vessels used leather pouches in their place.

It could well be said that these accumulations of coins represented not only savings in the traditional sense but speculation. Debasement of coins occurred frequently, and it was, probably, rumored even more often than it actually occurred. A far-sighted citizen could have salted away multiple specimens of the denarius, or other silver pieces, in lieu of a debasement. This is mere speculation but given the Roman cleverness and the pace at which news traveled in the chief towns, it is not an unreasonable supposition.

Speculation might not be the correct term to apply to another practice, the shaving or clipping of silver coinage. This activity, which had its origins even before the Romans, was not to be discontinued until the change in manufacturing technique to machine milling produced coins with symmetrical edges. In the age of hammering, coins were not quite circular. A bit of metal could be removed from their edge, by the use of sharp shears and exertion of heavy pressure, without the shortage being apparent. The coin could then be spent for its face value, and the "clipper" might in this fashion accumulate many ounces or even pounds of ill-obtained silver.

COMMON ARTICLES. Discussion (and museum exhibition) of ancient silverware usually centers upon lavish works of art or military equipment. But a great deal of what might be termed ordinary commercial ware was likewise made of silver, of various grades. Though it was abundantly available, the average citizen of Rome or Greece was in no position to purchase goldwork. What the privileged classes bought in gold, those in the middle ranks owned in silver or some other material. The poorer classes owned it not at all, or settled for a substitute in baked clay, leather, wood or another cheap substance. During the more prosperous days of Rome, when its markets did business approaching in volume that of our large modern cities, silver objects of every conceivable variety were on sale. These included, of course, selections of jewelry of all description, both of plain silver, engraved, chased, or set with stones. So many examples have been discovered that an almost complete record of Roman silver jewelry making is preserved. We know for a fact that silver jewelry was held in utter contempt by the fashionable citizenry of that time; but that failed to discourage its sale. It was made in a number of grades to suit the budgets of different groups of customers, from totally pure (unalloyed) down to a metallic composition that contained less than 50% silver. The "wonderful patina" frequently observed on ancient jewelry is often the result of heavy alloying with copper. By using a high proportion of copper, it was possible to manufacture such articles extremely cheaply and sell them for next to nothing. Not a great deal of labor went into their design or construction.

One of the more intriguing classes of objects made from silver — though often from other materials, too — was the hand mirror. Vast numbers of mirrors have been pulled from archaeological sites, bearing ample testimony to the narcissism of ancient Romans. The technique of manufacturing mirror glass being unknown to the Romans, they made the best substitute they could, by taking smooth metal plates and affixing them with handles. If kept well-polished, the surfaces had sufficient reflective capabilities to serve as mirrors. And as nothing better had been seen, they were undoubtedly regarded as very adequate. Remarkable as it may appear, some of these 2-millennia-old silver mirrors are still reflective enough, when taken from digs, for the archaeologist to see his likeness in them.

There is no contemporary information on prices but it can be presumed, based on the quantity and fineness of silver employed, that the cost of mirrors ran somewhat above that of most silverware sold as general merchandise. Gold appears not to have been used in mirror making, or possibly we have just not been successful in discovering buried specimens.

Silver tableware was made in ancient Rome. It was not very extensively produced, however, compared to some other articles. Those who could afford gold demanded it, and most other people seem to have been well-contented with pottery dishes and jugs. There was very likely a belief that metal utensils imparted a metallic taste to food and drink, and possibly even a fear that their use could be harmful. This was certainly true in the case of utensils made from metals alloyed with lead. Perhaps lead was at one time employed as an alloy in silver cooking vessels, illness resulted, and a general distrust of all silver utensils followed.

USE OF SILVER AS MONEY BEFORE COINAGE. Prior to the coining of official government money, which began at Lydia around 800 B.C., a variety of substitutes were used in trading, some of them with fixed value but the majority merely exchanged for whatever could be obtained. This was the "bartering" system, whose establishment can, in its rudimentary forms, be traced to palaeolithic man. Certainly, precivilized humans traded and swapped things: food, clothing, tools, perhaps wives. When they did not, they fought over them; but as mankind grew more intelligent, he found it was more to his advantage to swap than to fight, as he could, by the clever use of his wits, gain a profit in the bargain. It remains a matter of conjecture, but quite possibly the Old Testament declaration of "an eye for an eye, a tooth for a tooth" was not intended as encouragement of revenge but a mere reference of things of equal value being exchanged in barter. We know beyond argument that bartering continued long after the introduction of coinage, which, in its earlier stages, was not available in nearly the quantities needed to satisfy day to day trading.

Silver was probably used in bartering earlier than 5,000 B.C., but we cannot prove this. It was certainly used very extensively for that purpose at later dates. There is a wonderful Biblical reference to bartering with silver, though its precise interpretation is open to discussion. Abraham is said to have purchased the cave of Machpelah for 400 shekels of silver. As Abraham lived at approximately 2,300 B.C., these "shekels" could not have been the Hebrew coins of that name used at a considerably later date. They must have been something else. We can assume that the word shekel was a measure of weight, and that the silver could have been in any form — rings, bars, ingots — as long as it measured up to 400 shekels. If a standard weight measure had been evolved for trading with silver by 2,300 B.C., it was very obviously in use for bartering from a much earlier period.

In 1901 an intriguing find was made at Cnossos in Crete, site of many of the supposed events in Grecian mythology. A circular piece of silver was discovered, believed to date from the 13th century B.C., on which was impressed a character resembling an H. It was conjectured that this, while not official government money, could well represent the efforts of a private banker or moneyer to get standardized silver trading pieces into circulation. It would be difficult to explain the manufacture of such an object in any other way. It is presumable that when silver was used in bartering, its value was calculated upon that of livestock, especially the ox, and that pieces of various weights equaled so much proportion of an ox's market price. It is not likely that any silver piece could represent the value of a whole ox, unless very heavy.

MAJOR U.S. SILVER STRIKES AND PRODUCTION FIGURES

In the colonial era there was a general shortage of silver in America. Most of it used by silversmiths came from melted-down secondhand articles. These comprised, chiefly, plate and other household items brought over by immigrants.

The first known use of silver in America dates to 1652, when crude coins were struck at Boston for the Massachusetts settlers. This silver came from the West Indies. At that point no native American source was known.

When the federal government decided to strike silver coins in 1792, it faced a problem of obtaining sufficient bullion. There is a popular story that George Washington, then serving as President, was so enthusiastic over the coinage project that he donated a plate from his kitchen for melting down. While this may or may not be true, the early Mint did obtain supplies of silver from private individuals who turned in scrap articles and foreign silver coins. Much of it came by way of melting down Spanish dollars or 8 reales pieces. The arrangement was that everyone would receive a receipt for his silver, then the alloted value in coins after they were struck.

This proved satisfactory but did not provide a very great supply. Hence, the earliest silver coins were manufactured in small quantitites and became scarce collectors' items.

Purchasing silver from abroad presented obstacles, not only in financial terms but the risks involved. Our ratio of value between silver and gold (15 to 1, as established by Congressional Act of April 2, 1792) was wider than in Europe, making it very expensive for the U.S. to buy silver overseas. Futhermore, there was the danger of ships transporting bullion being overtaken by pirates.

Another problem arose, after the striking of silver coins had been going on for just four or five years. Vast numbers were being shipped out of the country, for sale in Europe. Because of the difference in the gold/silver exchange rate abroad, anyone could profit by taking our silver coins overseas and disposing of them as bullion. By 1802 the quantity of silver coins of all denominations in circulation had dipped to less than 50% of those struck. In 1804 it was decided to halt this rampant profiteering by ceasing to strike dollars in silver. No silver $1 pieces were manufactured from then until the 1830's, and it was not before the 1840's that his denomination returned to genenal circulation.

Obviously the country needed a rich native source of silver, but hope of locating significant deposits waned as the 19th century progressed.

Finally in 1859 a major strike was made, the Comstock Lode in Nevada. This was the most noteworthy silver find in the country's history. It resulted in establishment of a subsidiary Mint at Carson City, Nevada, whose purpose was to manufacture silver coins with bullion from the Comstock Lode. Collectors need not be told of quantities produced; as late as the 1970's there were still storehouses of "CC" silver dollars that had never reached circulation. These were disposed of by the government in a series of public-bid offerings.

The Comstock Lode pushed America into a prominent position among world silver producers. While many foreign countries had local sources, some had been mined for centuries and were on the verge of depletion.

Then, in the 1860's, further exploration in the West brought additional discoveries. Silver mines were found at Butte, Montana; Black Hawk Canyon, Colorado; Cottonwood Canyon, Utah; and Owyhee County, Idaho. The U.S. then became the world leader in silver production, a rank it held until 1938 when Mexico's output surpassed ours.

In 1890 a Congressional Act was passed, authorizing the Treasury to buy 4½ million ounces of silver from privately-owned mines every month. This was known as the Sherman Silver Purchase Act. It was intended to guarantee that the government always have enough bullion on hand for coinage and to meet obligations.

After 1900 the mines were worked at a stepped-up rate, as industry as well as the government required greater and greater supplies of silver. In 1915 the peak of production was reached, with more than 74 million ounces mined. This total was never surpassed. However, production continued strong from then until the present, even during chaotic times such as the Depression and World War II. In the Depression's depths, 1935, more than 45 million ounces were mined in the U.S. Production in 1940 was over 69 million ounces. Today the U.S. silver production averages around 40 million ounces yearly. This country is responsible for about 12% to 15% of world output.

In terms of .999 silver bars, total output of U.S. refiners in November, 1980, was 10,577,904 troy ounces. This figure was about the same as for October, 1980, but about 3% less than the monthly rate for the earlier part of 1980 — indicating that silver supplies are becoming more difficult and expensive for the refineries to secure. The silver used in .999 bars produced in November, 1980, was derived from the following sources:

Freshly mined ore . . . . 2,132,066 troy ounces
Coins . . . . 63,984 troy ounces
Industrial and other scrap . . . . 5,348,309 troy ounces
Refining company scrap . . . . 3,033,545 troy ounces

"Refining company scrap" covers all silver waste generated at the refineries, such as clippings, floor sweepings, etc. Manufacture of bars continually yields a certain amount of this scrap, which is simply recycled.

"Industrial and other scrap" refers to all manufactured objects of silver, except coins, which are bought as bullion by the refineries. It includes jewelry and articles commonly supplied by scrap merchants, who obtain it from the public; but a far greater quantity of scrap comes by way of purchasing used or waste materials from large industrial users, such as used photo film.

Foreign totals are not complete as statistics are not contributed by every foreign refinery. Nevertheless, the following is roughly comprehensive:

.999 silver bars produced in November, 1980 . . . . . 19,197,708 troy ounces.
Which derived from:

Freshly mined ore . . . . 11,419,501 troy ounces
Coins . . . . 708 troy ounces
Industrial scrap . . . . 6,633,617 troy ounces
Refining company scrap 1,113,883

It will be readily noticed that foreign refineries depend on freshly mined ores to a much greater extent than do those of the U.S. This is why the market for scrap or "melt value" objects is so much stronger in this country than anywhere else.

PHYSICAL PROPERTIES OF SILVER

Atomic number - 47
Atomic weight - 107.870
Boiling point - 2,212C
Chemical symbol - Ag
Crystal system - face-centered cubic
Melting point - 2,212C
Specific gravities of:
.999 pure silver - 10.50
.925 sterling silver - 10.31
german silver - 8.74

USES OF SILVER

Extensive use has been made of silver in art, industry, science, and for coinage since very early times. Prior to the Industrial Age (beginning around

1840), silver was employed mainly for articles of personal adornment, objects d'art, coinage, tableware and the like. It was used wherever a fine quality of metal was desired, which would be pleasing to the eye. Thus, the blades of fine swords were invariably made of silver. Throughout the ages, almost any common object or article could be had in deluxe models in silver, including snuffboxes, pill cases, powder horns, walking sticks, haircombs, hand mirrors and numerous other things. Their cost, even though made partially or wholly of silver, was relatively modest because silver was not as expensive as today. The price of these items depended more on the artistry or handwork that went into them, rather than the bullion.

Thus, silversmithing was a flourishing business in just about every age of the civilized world. If the smith was not making things to order, such as personalized items, he was working on contract for a manufacturer of jewelry or what used to be called "fancy goods." In the 1800's every variety shop featured wide selections of notions and novelties made of silver, of various grades, and the prices were extremely low by today's standards. A glance through Sears Roebuck catalogues of the late 1800's and even the early 1900's will show the vast range of personal and household items made in silver, and the negligible prices at which they sold.

When the Industrial Age began, it revoluntionized silversmithing and the silver trade in general. Though the "village smithy" was still to be found in rural areas, most silversmiths now went to work in factories and received salaries rather than running their own businesses. Quality of work declined, because nearly all pieces were now cast in molds. Some finishing work was done to them after leaving the molds, such as surface engraving, but on the whole they were "mass production" items that showed no individuality from one to another. The independent smiths of that era satisfied demands of persons who were not content with factory items. They charged higher prices but they did good business, for a while. By around 1890 mass-production silverware had become so abundant, and generally accepted, that their trade gradually fell away. It was claimed that only about one customer in ten could tell the difference between a factory and a handmade article; and that only one in ten *of those* really cared.

As silversmithing declined, silver advanced into a kind of Renaissance Era, where demand for it exceeded all precedent. Not only was silver bought up in great quantities by jewelry and novelty makers, it began to be used in scientific instruments and other apparatus invented in the Industrial Age. This era, which saw such men as Edison and Alexander Graham Bell at work, witnessed more important technical and scientific inventions than had occurred in the whole history of the world. Silver, because of its high electrical conductivity, became very important after the harnessing of electricity for industry in the 1870's.

Since then, the special properties of silver have rendered it indispensible for many, many modern industrial uses. Each new invention or discovery — photography, motion pictures, phonographs, the auto, airplanes — made use of silver to one degree or another. In many cases it was just a tiny amount, not even possible to see, but it played a vital role in operation of circuits or machinery. To this day silver continues to be used in photography, in the form of silver bromide for making film plates. The photography industry is one of the chief industrial users of silver. In the 1920's and and 1930's silver was extensively used for bearings in airplanes and diesel locomotives; such bearings had a much more desirable seizure resistance than those made of other substances. So necessary was silver in war production, chiefly for aircraft, that the government placed restrictions on private industrial consumption during World War II. Interestingly enough, though, silver was at this time introduced to the U.S. 5¢ coin as a substitute for nickel — also needed in war production.

New vistas for the use of silver were opened with the Space Age, beginning in the early 1960's. It has also been relied upon for the delicate circuitry of computers and devices operating by transistors. These circuits were printed on very thin sheets of silver which, despite their thinness, can conduct electricity an unlimited distance.

PURE SILVER (.999 FINE)

Pure silver is bullion with all, or nearly all, adhering mineral or other matter (generally known as waste matter) removed. This is done by refiners as the raw silver comes from the mines. In its freshly mined state, silver is very far from pure; it is normally fused with miscellaneous "rock junk." The refining process is costly and this is one reason, though not the principal one, why silver increases in price.

Pure silver is made into bars, ranging in weight from one ounce upward; 30 pound bars are the largest commonly produced. They carry a fineness marking, which will be .999 or .999+. The fineness is never given as 1.000, which would stand for absolute purity, since it cannot be guaranteed that every last trace of adhering matter has been successfully removed. In addition they should carry the refiner's name and a statement of the weight. Often, bars or bricks are encountered that bear a fineness marking and statement of weight but give no indication of the refiner's identity. These are considered suspect by investors, and by purchasers in general, as they could be of private manufacture and contain alloy additives. When such a bar is offered for resale, the prospective purchaser may demand that it be re-assayed, or tested to determine if the statement of fineness is accurate. As a rule, investors are cautioned against buying such bars, unless it is determined beyond doubt that the fineness is as indicated. There are no bargains in buying silver bullion; whenever anyone is offering bars at a discount from the normal spot-plus-commission rate, second thoughts must arise.

Pure silver is rarely made into anything but bars, or ingots (small bars). It isn't sturdy enough for use in manufacturing. Coins made of pure silver would wear down rapidly in circulation. Even with the customary addition of 10% copper, silver coins do not stand up well in circulation. Pure silver could be employed in plating, where only a thin layer of bullion is overlaid on a basemetal core; but this is seldom done, since lightly alloyed silver has the same physical appearance in terms of sheen and brilliance and can be used more inexpensively.

The belief of some beginners, that antique silverware (plates, knives, spoons, etc.) is made of pure silver, is incorrect. All of these items, no matter how splendid or valuable or how old, are made from alloyed silver, usually sterling silver.

BRITANNIA SILVER (.9584 FINE)

This is an industry term for a very high grade of silver, the highest used in manufacturing. It is made in Great Britain and carries an impressed figure of Britannia, a goddess-like female who symbolizes the British Empire. Britannia silver is 95.84% pure, meaning it contains less than 4½% alloy. It is very soft — too soft for most uses but satisfactory for tableware. You will pay more for Britannia silver than for .999+ bars because of the surcharge for workmanship. It is therefore not attractive as a bullion investment. On the other hand, older Britannia ware found in secondhand shops is occasionally priced below the silver market, raising the possibility of quick profit-making. This happens because many proprietors of antiques and secondhand shops, especially in small towns, do not keep up on the spot price of silver or do not bother to weigh their merchandise (or both). They have items bought ages ago when silver was inexpensive, which they continue to offer at the original price or a slight advance.

STERLING SILVER (.925 FINE)

Sterling is the best-known grade of silver in manufacturing, but not the highest grade; its purity is slightly less than that of Britannia, which is 95.84% against 92.5% for sterling. This negligible difference cannot be detected by the naked eye, nor can the difference in weight. However, objects made of sterling are slightly less valuable *as bullion* than those of Britannia. Whether they are less valuable overall depends upon (as stated elsewhere) their merits as possible collectors' items or other circumstances.

Sterling is normally hallmarked and/or stamped "sterling," depending on the place of origin and prevailing regulations in that country. Occasionally the marking .925 is used.

Though sterling is identified with Great Britain, mainly because of the term "pound sterling" to denote the British currency, its manufacture is just about universal. Sterling is made from the Orient to America. While it naturally varies stylistically, the value of all this merchandise is identical *as bullion,* ounce for ounce.

Origin of the word sterling is doubtful. Its use in relation to silver is of great antiquity, going back to the Middle Ages. Apparently, "silver" and "sterling" were interchangeable words at one time. It may have arisen as a means of identifying silver used by smiths in the making of plate, etc., as opposed to the slightly inferior grade used by coiners.

COIN SILVER (.900 FINE)

A misleading term, because silver coins exist with varying proportions of silver content. Coin silver is taken to mean .900, or 90% silver against a 10% basemetal alloy, which nearly always is copper. It is thus a slightly lower grade than sterling and an appreciably lower grade than Britannia. Coin siver, when marked (which it frequently isn't), will usually carry the designation "coin silver" or ".900." Antique objects of coin silver are sometimes marked "DOLLAR" or "D," to indicate their manufacture from melted dollars. Most coin silver used in the U.S. is still obtained from melted coins,all the way from dollars down to pre-clad dimes. Coin silver is attractive for manufacturers to use because it required no refining; the coins used in producing it already have the necessary alloy and need only be melted. It is cheaper to do this, than to refine out the alloy and use silver from coins to make sterling or another higher grade. Since there is no government regula tion against melting and reusing U.S. coins, the practice could conceivably continue until *all* silver coins that have no collector value are depleted. But it is unlikely that this could occur, since continued melting on a large scale would gradually render common coins scarce, and they would acquire a numismatic value over and above the bullion content. How long this might take to happen, at the present rate of absorbtion, is hard to forecast.

GERMAN SILVER

A low grade silver, composed chiefly of nickel and copper and containing a small amount of silver, or an exterior silver wash that accounts for perhaps 3% of the overall weight or less. As German Silver has been manufactured for more than 150 years, the composition has changed many times along the way. It first appeared as a material used in the making of novelties and souvenirs in Bavaria, sold at a very cheap price to tourists and to the import/export trade. The motive was to achieve a substance which could retain a high surface polish and bear the general appearance of silver, or at least sufficiently to be convincing to undiscriminating persons. By around 1850 the world market was being innundated with German Silver trinkets of all descriptions. Quite frequently dealers succeeded in leading customers to believe that they were good silver. After 1890, when the law was passed in the U.S. requiring all imported merchandise to be stamped, the designation "GERMAN SILVER" showed up on countless numbers of articles, as we were then importing more goods from Germany than from any other nation. Still, devious merchants were not discouraged. They now explained to customers that "German Silver" was a special kind of silver made only in Europe and very desirable; in this way they sometimes obtained higher prices for it than for sterling. The so-called Feuchtwanger Cent, proposed for use as a government coin and circulated to some extent as a token in 1837, was made of German Silver. It should not be supposed that the manufacture of German Sivler has been confined to Germany. It is now produced worldwide, and has been for many years. The common reference to it as "low grade" silver is misleading; it should more correctly be called "no grade."

SILVER PLATE

During the 19th century, silver plating began on a large scale. The technique was known earlier but not placed to extensive use. In earlier times, customers who could not afford such articles as silverplates, utensils, and other items settled for the same designs in pewter, which was just as sturdy and not bad-looking. Then, gradually, the social revolution of Europe during the late 1700's changed public buying habits. The middle classes wanted things that the upper classes owned, or as near to them as possible. If they could not have the exact same clothing, furniture, etc., they wanted facsimilies or imitations that could not easily be detected from the real thing. Manufacturers of silverware brought out plated ware, to satisfy the vast demand for silver by persons who could not afford it. The wealthy continued to buy fine silver but for the masses — who, as always, spent a total of considerably more money — plated ware served the purpose. It looked exactly like solid silverware, the difference being only in the weight; and even that was similar enough to deceive everyone but the most astute experts.

Silver plated objects are made of basemetal, to which an exterior of good silver is bonded (generally by electroplating). The bullion invariably accounts for less than 10% of the object's weight, sometimes much less. The layer applied is as thin as practical, to withstand normal wear and tear without the underlying metal showing through. Very frequently, however, the surface will wear down and "dark spots" will appear. If desired, such items can be replated, but are often less expensive and troublesome to simply replace.

Silver plated items are sometimes bought by scrap dealers. The price paid is very low, since the quantity of silver that will be obtained after refining is hard to precisely calculate without performing elaborate tests. Therefore the dealer pays a so-called "tolerance" price, meaning he pays for the lowest quantity of silver that the item could reasonably be expected to contain. He in turn receives a tolerance price from the refinery, and the refinery profits if the article proves to contain somewhat more silver than was paid for.

ALLOYS AND SILVER

Like the other precious metals, silver in its pure state (.999 or .999+) is quite soft and unsuitable for use in art or industry, except in instances where ruggedness is not important. Where *electrical conductivity* is vital, as in circuitry, it is usually desirable not to alloy silver as this reduces its capacity to conduct electricity.

The degree to which silver is alloyed for manufacturing depends largely upon the type of items to be made from it. Durability, appearance, and price are the three chief considerations. Determinations are not easy to make, as the factors go far beyond the simple question of what grade silver is most appropriate. For example, a manufacturer may have the choice of putting out a dinner service in Britannia or sterling. Both are fine grades of silver but Britannia is slightly finer and more costly. He must decide whether the additional cost is likely to reduce sales to a point where Britannia would not be as profitable to use as sterling. There may be greater profit to him on each sale of Britannia, but if fewer customers buy, his overall profit will not be as substantial. There is no "happy medium" to be reached, as some customers want the best and are willing to pay for it, while others think in terms of saving money before any other consideration.

Whether used to a small or great degree in any given article, copper is the standard and universal alloy for silver — just as for gold. It alloys silver splendidly. When used in small ratios it does not materially effect the color or brilliance, and just a minimal quantity lends the necessary durability. Of course, the alloying process is important in itself and must be executed correctly to achieve proper results. Since silver and copper are of very different colors in their natural state, silver being white or grey-white and copper being dark brown or red, *streaking* is inevitable if the blending is not carefully carried out.The silver will show dark streaks or cloudy areas, where the copper has not totally mixed in. Alloying must be done when the ingredients are in absolutely liquid state, and the blending cannot be rushed. Before the modern age, this was done by workers who literally churned the mixture in the manner of cream.

Silver can, of course, be alloyed with metals other than copper. This is done occasionally but is rare in the modern world, as there seems no possibility of improving on the silver/copper combination excepting for an occasional special use. There is nothing to be gained, for example, in alloying silver with brass or bronze, which themselves are largely copper. This was often done in early times, because the foundries used whatever was at hand without really caring one way or another. This is why old coins, especially those of the Romans, are found in the same denomination made from various metals or combinations of metals.

If there is a desire to whiten the color, silver can be alloyed with nickel or zinc; but the resulting product is not (in the opinion of most) as handsome, nor does it consistently polish as well as silver alloyed with copper.

Naturally, the more alloy used, the lower the grade of silver. Britannia silver contains nearly 20 parts of silver for every part of alloy, and is therefore an extremely high grade (the highest used in manufacture). So-called coin silver is .900, which means nine parts silver to one part alloy. Even though the difference between coin silver and Britannia is just .900 to .958, Britannia is *more than twice as pure as coin silver.* This is because it contains less than half as much alloy.

The lowest grade of silver to carry a fineness is .800, which contains 80% silver and 20% alloy. At this point the silver begins taking on a darker color, which could, of course, be mistaken for oxidation or failure to polish it regularly. An experienced silver handler can tell the difference in weight, too, when this much alloy is employed, unless the item is very small.

The important point for the investor or seller of scrap silver to keep in mind is that *the alloy is worthless.* You will not be paid anything for the alloy, but only the quantity of .999+ silver that can be obtained in refining. Therefore, the more alloy in an article, the less its value as bullion in relation to its overall weight. True enough, the refineries obtain a great deal of copper as a result of melting down scrap silver, and you can be sure they dispose of it profitably; but this is not considered in the price when they buy scrap objects from suppliers.

TESTING METHODS FOR SILVER

A good deal of silver is marked and in most cases can be used to determine the exact proportion of pure bullion vs. basemetal. In the case of unmarked articles, tests must be performed to discover this information.

The object in testing silver is to determine one or more of the following:

1. Whether the item contains any silver at all, or is simply an imitation such as German Silver, polished nickel, or some other substance that gives the appearance of silver (there are numerous combinations of metals that look more or less like silver, especially to the untrained eye).

2. If the object is silver plated — that is, coated with silver but containing a core of basemetal.

3. If solid silver, the grade or quality. The "grade" is the degree to which the silver it contains has been alloyed with basemetal. If heavily alloyed, the item may be worth very little in spite of being solid silver. "Solid silver" simply means that it isn't plated; it makes no representation of the fineness.

As a general rule it can be presumed that most, or nearly all, manufactured items intended for commercial sale are not of high grade silver unless marked. It is obviously to the maker's and seller's advantage to mark high-grade items, as this increases their appeal. The only instances in which markings may not occur on good silver are custom made items and, occasionally, antiques and objets d'art fashioned by persons who were not licensed smiths or guild members. Of course, coins are unmarked, but their content is a matter of record (if the specimen is genuine).

WEIGHTED ARTICLES. In addition to the possibility that silver articles may be plated, or contain a silver coating over a basemetal core, the likelihood of *weighting* must also be investigated. In the modern era, and even dating back to the 19th century, commerical manufacturers have been notorious for weighting silver goods to give them the "feel" of being solid silver, when in fact the silver content is quite low. For example the base of a candelabra may be filled with cement, plasticene, gravel bonded with glue, or other substances. The uniformed person, coming upon such an item, places it upon a scale, discovers it to weight 3 or 4 pounds, and believes he has a fortune in silver bullion. The actual melt value, when this stuffing is extracted, will generally amount to less than 1/20th the original weight. Of course the figure varies depending on weight of stuffing material, thickness of silver, type of article and other factors. In instances where the weighting material is totally hidden by the silver exterior, so that it cannot be observed even when the object is turned upside-down, testing by specific gravity will tell if the item is wholly silver.

Table utensils can likewise be deceiving. The handle may be marked and this leads to the conclusion that the whole piece is silver, but very often it has components which are not — such as stainless steel blades on knives.

NITRIC ACID. Nitric acid has traditionally been the popular method of testing silver. It reacts to basemetal differently than to silver. If a positive reaction is obtained, proof is given that the metal is either not silver or silver heavily alloyed. The nitric acid test should be run on any article suspected of being made of low grade silver, or plated in silver. It is improtant to conduct such testing carefully, as laxness can cause incorrect results.

Applying nitric acid to the surface will determine if the object is made wholly of low-grade silver or non-silver, but it does not provide proof of plating. A plated item tested on its surface will give the same reaction as one made entirely of silver because the acid reacts only on the outer layer. It does not "eat in." It is therefore logical to make both tests at once: for silver content and the possibility of plating.

This is easily done on most kinds of articles. A notch or groove must be filed into the surface, down to a depth of about 1/32nd of an inch. In the case of very large or heavy objects, such as punch bowls, where plating might be thick, a deeper notch is called for. The owner's consent must be obtained before doing this. If consent cannot be obtained, and only a surface test can be performed, the item must be regarded as plated. It can, however, be tested by specific gravity, which we'll get into, if you have the equipment to do this.

Choose an inconspicuous place for filing the notch, such as the underside of a plate or the inside of a watch case. If this isn't possible, the notch should at least be placed where it won't interefere with prominent portions of design. A drop of nitric acid is placed in the notch and determination of content will be made by the acid's change in color, which will occur very quickly.

If the object is made of high grade silver, such as sterling, the acid will merely turn a greyish color. In other words it will tone down the metal a bit but not change its basic color. Should there be a high proportion of copper alloying, a green color will appear. Whenever green is obtained you are dealing either with low grade silver or an article made chiefly of copper with the addition of enough nickel or other metal to give an appearance of silver (usually 75% copper/25% nickel).

Be certain to remove the acid as soon as possible after obtaining results, by wiping with a clean cloth. It may cause pitting to the surface or permanent discoloration if this is not done.

Dichromate acid can also be used to test silver. This is a more sophisticated approach because the dichromate solution does not merely tell if the item is silver or non-silver; it indicates the presence of several other metals, depending upon the color to which the acid-treated region turns. But dichromate acid is somewhat more difficult to get. If you can't get it from a chemist or jewelry supply house, it can be prepared in the following manner. Use care in handling ingredients; the fumes are quite toxic and serious burns can result from dichromate acid coming into contact with the skin.

Dissolve an eighth of a teaspoon of potassium dichromate in a quarter ounce of nitric acid. Place the potassium dichromate into the nitric acid, not the other way around. This should be done in a small bottle, not a dish, to contain fumes as much as possible. Stir it around gently with a glass rod until it achieves a rich burgundy color. It is then ready for use. If not to be used immediately, the bottle ought to be tightly stoppered to keep it fresh. Dichromate acid deteriorates rapidly in contact with air. In fact it will deteriorate in a stoppered container but not as quickly.

The same testing procedure outlined above is used: filing a notch and applying a drop of solution. If the article is solid silver of a high grade, the resulting color will be bright red. When applied to an item containing a large proporiton of copper, it turns green — just as does nitric acid alone. If the metal is lead, the color will be yellow. Pewter gives a black color.

BULLION CONTENT OF PLATED ITEMS. It is very difficult to calculate the bullion content in plated items because thickness of plating varies. The *average* plated article contains about 2% of its weight in silver and this figure can be used as a rough guide. You need therefore to weigh it, multiply the weight by .02, and the result will be approximately its weight in bullion — but it will not be exact and a scrap dealer will not pay you on the strenghth of this calculation. A table fork of plated silver, weighing two ounces, would have a silver content of about 1/5th of an ounce. Of course if the article has a bone handle or any non-metallic components this method becomes even less reliable.

SPECIFIC GRAVITY. The specific gravity method is a high reliable test for determining the nature of metals and mineral substances. Everyone who buys or intends to buy gold, silver, jewels and the like should become acquainted with it.

This is a very delicate test which, if not performed to exacting standards, will not yield correct results. On the other hand its accuracy when correctly carried out is far above that of almost all other testing techniques, including those using more costly equipment.

If one plans on trading commercially in silver, it would be wise to purchase a specific gravity testing device. Otherwise a homemade substitute can be used, whose reliability will be fairly close to that of professional models.

Specific gravity is the ratio at which a material displaces water in relation to its bulk. We all know that lead sinks while cork floats in water. This proves nothing except that some substances are lighter than others, which could be determined by weighing on an ordinary (avoirupois) scale. Specific gravity goes beyond the mere difference between sink-or-float. It gives the weight of an object in relation to its *exact* size, as water fully surrounds whatever is submerged in it. It therefore measures much better than rulers or calipers. As every object of the *same material* gives the same specific gravity reading, regardless of size, the specific gravity reading easily distinguishes between (for example) silver and copper, silver and nickel, or alloys of these metals. It also helps in identifying precious stones.

A useful specific gravity scale can be concocted from an ordinary pan scale that gives readings in grams. If it gives readings in larger measures than grams it isn't suitable. In other words you cannot use a postal scale or something of that nature. Remove the pan and tie a length of string, such as thin nylon, from the pan holder, at the extreme southeast corner as the scale faces you. The string must not be long enough to touch the desk on which the scale rests. A glass tumbler about 3/4ths filled with water is then placed beneath the string. It may be necessary to set the tumbler on a low platform to achieve the right height. It has to be positioned so that the item to be tested, when tied to the string and dropped into the glass, is fully submerged but *does not touch the bottom of the glass.* If it rests upon the bottom, or even touches lightly, the test is spoiled.

As the object dangles in the glass, a reading is taken of the weight indicated on the scale. This is called the "weight in water." It does not determine specific gravity but is the main step in arriving at the figure. To get the specific gravity, the object must then be weighed on the scale in the ordinary manner, or "in air." Subtract the weight in water from the weight in air (the latter will always be a higher number), then divide the weight in air by the *loss of weight in water.* The answer will be the item's specific gravity.

Example:
Weight in water, 27.10 grams
Weight in air, 30 grams
Loss of weight in water, 2.9 grams
2.9 divided into 30 (weight in air) = 10.34 (specific gravity of the item)

The item tested in this sample, with a specific gravity reading of 10.34, was.925 sterling silver.

Depending on the accuracy of your scale you will probably only be able to get very close approximations, rather than precise readings. In this example we got a specific gravity of 10.34 and called it .925 sterling silver. This is because 10.34 is the closest on the following table to our answer. As in all of these tests and formulas there is always "visual inspection" involved and in this case the item appeared to be .925 sterling silver, so the conclusion reached after testing was obvious. It also must be kept in mind that, even using advanced equipment, specific gravity readings can vary minutely on the same grade of silver or gold. This is because the alloy material is not always exactly the same. If bronze or brass is used as an alloy instead of pure copper, .925 sterling (or any other grade of silver) made from it will not have the exact same specific gravity reading as .925 alloyed with pure copper.

SPECIFIC GRAVITIES OF METALS

Metal	Specific Gravity
Brass	8.52
Bronze	8.82
Copper	8.93
24K Gold	19.32
22K Gold	17.72
18K Gold	15.47
14K Gold	13.55
10K Gold	11.75
Iron	7.81
German silver	8.74
.999 silver	10.50
.925 sterling silver	10.31
Stainless steel	7.8
Platinum	21.45
Tin	7.31

WEIGHING METHODS FOR SILVER

Silver bars and Morgan Dollars aren't weighed on a bathroom scale. Methods of weighing precious metals are very sophisticated, as a minute difference in weight can mean a big difference in price.

There isn't, as yet, any universally agreed-upon technique. Several are reliable if performed carefully.

The weight of silver may be stated in troy ounces, pennyweight, or by metric division. Troy is the most common and the most universally understood by jewelers and bullion dealers. The daily spot price of silver is always given by the troy ounce. Pennyweight is much more commonly used for gold than for silver, but is included here in the event you may need to make this calculation. The reason why pennyweight is applied to gold more than to silver is that it represents a very small measure of weight; silver, being much less valuable than gold, has little value by pennyweight.

The metric system, now becoming international, has not yet penetrated into the bullion market to a very major extent and probably will not do so for a number of years.

As statements of weight may be given in grains by one dealer, grams by another, and dwt (pennyweight) by a third, it is important that anyone buying or selling silver become familiar with the equivalents, and methods of changing one to another.

AVOIRDUPOIS WEIGHT. Like troy weight, the avoirdupois system also uses pounds and ounces, but these are not equal. Avoirdupois is the common method by which just about everything — except precious metals — is weighed. Bathroom scales are avoirdupois scales. Unlike troy scales, they may be equipped with springs.

PENNYWEIGHT. Abbreviated as DWT. ("D" stands for penny, in British coinage, and "WT" for weight.) The system of weighing by pennyweight originated with English merchants of the distant past, who used pennies as counterweights on their scales. The U.S. penny weighs two pennyweight, equal to 48 grains. So it is readily apparent that pennyweight is an extremely small measure. A pennyweight is considerably less than one full ounce. But this is a useful method of weighing.

TROY WEIGHT. This is a standard system by which weights of precious metals are given all over the world. Its basic unit is the grain. Scales (using balances, not springs) for weighing items in troy measure can be had and are usually referred to as jewelers' or gemologists' scales.

WEIGHTS AND MEASURES

APOTHECARIES' WEIGHT

one grain	=	.01666 dram
20 grains	=	.33 dram
60 grains	=	one dram
480 grains	=	one apothecary ounce (8 drams)

AVOIRDUPOIS WEIGHT

.0625 ounce	=	1.7719 grams
one ounce	=	28.350 grams
16 ounces	=	one pound (453.59 grams)

TROY WEIGHT

one grain	=	.0416666 pennyweight or .648 grams
24 grains	=	one pennyweight
480 grains	=	20 pennyweights, or one troy ounce
5760 grains	=	240 pennyweights, or 12 troy ounces, or one troy pound

FORMULAS OF COVERSIONS

To change . . .
grams to pennyweights, mulitply grams by .643
pennyweights to grams, multiply pennyweights by 1.555
grams to troy ounces, multiply grams by .032
troy ounces to grams, multiply troy ounces by 31.103
pennyweights to troy ounces, divide pennyweights by 20
troy ounces to pennyweights, multiply troy ounces by 20
grains to grams, multiply grains by .0648
grams to grains, multiply grams by 15.432
avoirdupois is ounces to troy ounces, multiply avoirdupois ounces by .912
troy ounces to avoirdupois ounces multiply troy ounces by 1.097
avoirdupois ounces to grams, multiply avoirdupois ounces by 28.35.
grams to avoirdupois is ounces, multiply grams by .035
avoirdupos pounds to kilograms, multiply avoirdupois pounds by .454
kilograms to avoirdupois pounds, multiply kilograms by 2.205
avoirdupois pounds to grains, multiply avoirdupois pounds by 7000
grains to avoirdupois is pounds, multiply grains by .00014

DETERMINING THE VALUE OF SILVER

The value of silver bullion in any given article of silver is somewhat easier to calculate than gold, so long as the fineness is known, since silver prices are nearly always expressed by the troy ounce. This is different than with gold, where ounces are used along with pennyweights and grains. These lesser measures are not very useful with silver because of its lower value.

The daily spot price of silver is always stated in troy ounces (like the daily spot price of gold). Dealers buy and sell silver by the troy ounce. Even when more than a pound is involved, the weight is invariably expressed in troy ounces. Therefore, you need only know the weight and fineness of a silver object, and perform some simple mathematics, to arrive at the "melt value" at any given spot price.

The daily spot price is quoted for one ounce of .999 fine. If you have bars or ingots of .999 or .999 + fine, their value is obvious. You merely multiply the spot price on that day by the number of ounces in your bars or ingots. Of course, when selling you will not receive that sum, as the broker or dealer deducts a percentage of commission. With silver the percentage margin tends to be larger than with gold.

Spot price of $15 per troy ounce.
six .999 silver bars weighing 1 oz. each = 6 ounces
six × $15 = $490.00 (melt value)

If your silver is not .999 fine, it is naturally worth less than spot, but the difference in value is extremely slight if you have fine quality ware such as Britannia or sterling. Britannia is .958 and sterling .925. Since *coin silver* is .900 fine, the calculations for it are very simple — you need only deduct 10% from the weight and then multiply the resulting figure by "spot." Technically, the answer will not be precise, since the 10% of alloy (copper, usually) does not comprise exactly 10% of the weight. This is because silver and copper have slightly different weights. it is, nevertheless, accurate enough for buying and selling purposes.

Before any price calculations can be attempted, it is necessary to learn.

1. How much the article weighs, in ounces.

2. What the fineness is.

Good quality silver, .800 fine and over, will usually carry a marking, stamped on some inconspicuous part of its surface. If there appears to be no marking, study it closer to be certain you have not overlooked it. The marking could be extremely small — so small that a person with sub-par vision might need a magnifier to find it. Or it could be partially or totally hidden by grime, if the item has not been thoroughly cleaned. If the marking is not in numbers and/or letters, but a decorative symbol, it is probably a foreign hallmark or touchmark and suggests that the piece may be very old. As the variety of markings that can be encountered are numerous, and often very similar but with different meanings, the aid of a book on hallmarks or an expert will be needed. *Generally,* though not invariably, hallmarked silver that does not state the fineness is .925. Many dealers will buy it at .925 even if further evidence is lacking. This grade is known as "sterling."

It may be easier to understand fineness and value in the following way. Silver which has been alloyed is like a beverage into which water is added. A few drops of water and little or no difference is noticed in the taste; but as more and more is added, the beverage grows weaker. So it is with silver. The more alloy that is added, the more reduction in quality or fineness.

If you have silver which is *not marked,* tests outlined in the chapter on testing will determine whether the object contains any silver and will provide an approximate indication of the fineness. Generally speaking, though, you are likely to have a difficult time selling silver which is not marked, as many dealers prefer not to handle it. Antique items are another matter. And, of course, coins are not marked — with the notable exception of U.S. Trade Dollars.

Once the fineness is known, the weight must be determined to calculate the article's melt value.

This can be done very easily be weighing it on any scale that gives readings in troy ounces, or on an avoirdupois scale and then converting the weight into troy ounces. To change avoirdupois is ounces to troy ounces, the avoirdupois ounces are multipled by .912 (For additional conversions, see the section on "Methods of Weighing Silver.")

You now have a fineness reading plus a weight. The next step is to multiply the *fineness* by the *weight,* which will tell you the amount of .999 silver the object contains.

For example:

Tray made of coin silver, .900 fine, weighs 5 troy ounces

5 X .900 = 4.500, or 4½ troy ounces of .999 fine

You then multiply the *spot price* by this figure to arrive at the melt value:

Spot price of $15 per troy ounce

$15 X 4½ = $67.50 melt value

Now remember, when you sell to a dealer he will be buying at a discount, usually 10% to 25%. This discount is fair because, as when buying gold, the dealer must recover refining costs, pay freight or postage to the refinery, and leave himself a reasonable profit.

So, keeping this in mind, you should be able to sell your .900 silver tray to a dealer for roughly $50 to $60. This should be a fair transaction for both parties. If the offer you get is substantially lower, you ought to definitely shop around and get another dealer's price.

HOW TO SELL SILVER

There are of course numerous different kinds of silver articles, old and modern, high-grade and low, decorative and plain. To simplify matters we have grouped them into categories as follows. Any type of silver that you might possibly own should fall into one of these classifications.

1. .999 or .999 + fine silver, such as *marked* bars and ingots

2. Items of melt value — meaning the silver they contain is worth as much, or more than, the item could be sold for as merchandise. *Most* things made of silver, new and secondhand, fall in this class: common circulated coins, tableware, toilette articles, old jewelry, etc.

3. Articles of silver which have greater than melt value: uncirculated or scarce-date coins, popular antiques and collectors' items, works of sculpture.

The approach to be taken in selling depends to some extent upon whether you have Category One, Category Two, or Category Three material.

Detailed explanation and information on these different types of silver are given in other chapters.

All of them are salable, and there are many dealers who will gladly purchase any kind of silver you might have to offer, from a few grubby coins to a pharaoh's treasure. But you are likely to do better, in terms of price and fair treatment, if you become a little choosey about selecting a buyer.

.999 or .999 + FINE SILVER. Bars and ingots, bearing a fineness marking and (preferably) the name of a refiner, are the least trouble to sell. You know beforehand exactly what they're worth, based on the day's spot price; and, what may be more important, any prospective buyer *knows that you know* what they're worth. There will not be any haggling over the price. Their value is a matter of record; how much of that value you receive depends upon the dealer's rate of commission and spot price on that day. If the dealer makes a fulltime business of buying and selling precious metals, his handling charges for .999 silver (as well as 24K gold) should be prominently displayed in the show window or posted inside. If the handling charge is not posted, this naturally leads to speculation that no fixed charge exists but that the percentage is changed customer-by-customer depending on how much the dealer feels he can get. You should avoid doing business with buyers of this type. Reputable dealers work off a standard handling charge and are more than content with the profits they realize from it. They treat every seller alike, whether the transaction is large or small or the seller appears to be knowledgeable or uninformed. These dealers do a tremendous volume of business, because of their reputation for fair practices, and do much better than the gypsters. The respectable dealers are just as dedicated to protecting their reputations as the fly-by-nighters are to gouging out unfair profits.

The handling charge for buying silver bullion is greater than for gold. This is true even of .999 fine, where no refining is necessary. A fair commission charge or discount on .999 bars or ingots is anywhere from 10% to 12% off "spot." In other words, if you present $500 worth of silver (according to the spot price on that day), you can expect to be paid $440 to $450. In times of rapidly soaring prices — or rapidly falling ones — dealers might adjust their commissions upward or downward to achieve (or attempt to achieve) a balanced flow of buyers and sellers. There is nothing illegal in this so long as the commission charge is posted and all customers are charged the same rate. When utter chaos occurs, as in the gold/silver stampede of January, 1980, some dealers will temporarily discontinue buying and/or selling. This, too, is their right.

ITEMS OF MELT VALUE. Coin dealers and bullion brokers will sometimes purchase miscellaneous articles of melt value. Coin dealers will obviously purchase common-date circulated coins, and pay you the spot price on that day less their handling fee. For many kinds of melt-value articles, however, you will need to find a dealer who advertises to purchase scrap silver or "anything of melt value." Such individuals were once hard to locate but in the past 1-1½ years they have been appearing in increasing numbers, and no matter where you live there should be one (probably more) very close by. The same advice given above about buying practices applies here, too. The reputable melt-value buyer advertises his prices or calculates according to spot on that day, charging a standard handling fee. There is some leeway here, however, as the scrap buyer might occasionally be purchasing unmarked or other questionable articles, and for these he is not required to pay any announced or posted sum. He takes a certain gamble on such items because the quantity of silver they contain is not positively known; he is therefore justified in making an estimated valuation, and offering a price based on this valuation. The seller is, of course, at liberty to accept or refuse it. He may wish to obtain another offer before reaching a decision. Offers for unmarked or other problem pieces will vary more than for marked silver. (An example of a "problem piece" is something made partly of silver and partly of another material, such as a fork with a bone handle, which is hard to weigh.)

Be prepared to accept a rather substantial discount from the spot price, for the dealer's handling charge. The discount on scrap items is always higher than for .999 bars or ingots, because the refinery to which the dealer resells them will not pay as much. They must go through a refining process to extract the alloy. This is costly and the cost is naturally passed along, as is always the case in business, to the public. A fair commission charge or discount on melt items is 10% to 25% off "spot." Thus, if you sell scrap silver with a bullion melt value of $500, you should receive $375 to $450.

Another reason why discounts are smaller on bars and ingots is that the dealers often do not pass them along to refineries, but simply resell them to investors.

ARTICLES WITH GREATER THAN MELT VALUE. These should not, of course, be sold to a scrap merchant or bullion dealer. If the item is a scarce coin, or a bullion coin in uncirculated condition, it should be sold to a coin dealer. Antiques may be sold to an antiques dealer or put up for acution. More information is given in the chapter on "Silver Antiques."

SILVER — MORE THAN MELT VALUE

It is important, when contemplating the sale of silver as scrap bullion, that the item's overall value be considered in relation to the "melt" value.

When something is sold for melting, whatever it may be, you will be paid the current spot price on that day (if the buyer is reputable) less a discount for the buyer's commission. This is true whether the object is a coin, a silver ingot, or a chalice made in France in the 14th century. The scrap dealer buys it as scrap — nothing more.

Whether he turns around and resells it as scrap is another matter. Dealers, even if they appear totally without knowledge of art or collectors' items, are faily adept at identifying *objects that should not be melted.* They will buy them at the melt value, but will sell them to dealers in antiques or whatever the article happens to be. All scrap merchants have friends in related trades, to whom they dispose of worthwhile items that come in. Quite a few scrap dealers run their own coin and/or antiques businesses, too, and use favorable purchases for their own stock. By buying merchandise for its scrap value, they can get it cheaper, in many instances, than they would be compelled to pay if buying from a collector.

The scrap dealer profits greatly from the simple fact that the public, at large, has a hard time distinguishing *silver that should be melted from silver that shouldn't.* This is especially true of persons who have not personally bought the objects presented, but found them in their attic or acquired them in some other way. In these cases they are likely to have no idea of the value, and may be very happy to get the "spot" price for something worth many, many times more.

There is no point asking the scrap dealer for his opinion of whether the item should be sold for melting. He is not impartial. He wants to make money on your merchandise and cannot be depended on to give a straightforward answer — assuming he has the knowledge to do this in the first place. An antiques dealer may likewise undervalue an item. The temptation to do this is very strong for some dealers (the trade as a whole is ethical — let's not have any misunderstanding) when they see that the owner is totally uninformed. If you must, as a last resort, obtain a price estimate from a dealer, you are more likely to get an accurate one by taking the right manner of approach and by getting estimates *from several dealers for comparison.* When someone goes into a shop, and admits his lack of knowledge by saying, "I have no idea what this is worth . . .," this is a red flag for the dealer to take advantage. Even if you have no idea, don't say so. Conceal your ignorance of the item's value as best as possible. The clever seller will say something like this: "I'd like to get an idea of what this would be worth *to you.*" This implies that he has a good notion of the value but is simply interested in seeing what the dealer will pay. Then when a dealer ask you: "Well, what do you think it's worth?" Don't give him a figure as this will put an absolute ceiling on his offer, simply ask him to make you an offer.

Silver coins are an example of silver items that *can* have greater value than melt value. The vast majority of 20th century silver U.S. coins, in ordinary circulated condition, cannot be sold for more than melt value. However, before selling any, it is certainly smart to check their value against a reliable guide, such as **"THE OFFICIAL BLACKBOOK OF U.S. COINS,"** published by The House of Collectibles, Inc., 1900 Premier Row, Orlando, Florida 32809. This very useful paperback is revised annually, so if you get the current edition there's no danger of it being out of date. It can be had by mail at $2.50 plus $1 postage and handling.

As far as modern manufactured objects are concerned, they can usually be sold for the melt value only. This may seem unfair, especially if you bought a dinner service for $800 and it contained, at the time, $300 worth of silver. You might expect to be paid, when reselling it, the current melt value plus the difference between its original bullion value and retail price ($500). But you won't be, because that $500 represented profits to the manufacturer, wholesaler, shopkeeper and others, and none of it can be reclaimed. It's in their pockets and it's gone forever. What you have now is X amount of silver; the fact that it happens to be in the shape of saucers and forks and other objects is meaningless in most cases.

Antiques and collectors' items are another matter. If something is genuinely old, or for some special reason is out of the ordinary (if it belonged to a famous person, for example, or is a highly collectible limited edition), it could very possibly have greater than melt value. The difference between melt value and collector value cannot be shown on a chart. It all depends on the specific object, and varies from one to another. The 14th century French chalice we mentioned above might contain $2,000 worth of silver and have a collector value of $50,000 or more. Silver bookbindings (which are rare) contain extremely little silver by weight, but are very valuable because of their scarcity and artistry that went into them. A binding with 5 or 6 ounces of silver could sell for $20,000. In general, though, the difference between the melt value and collector value of antiques and art objects is not nearly this extreme. Miscellaneous silverware from the Victorian and Edwardian eras (say 1840-1910), unless very ornate, generally can be sold for about 20% more than the melt value. In other words if you have a snuffbox containing two ounces of .999 + silver (plus alloy), and the spot price is $15, you can expect to be paid about $40 for it. If it had no collector value, you would get only about $25, as the dealer would take his handling charges out. For more detailed information, refer to the following chapter on antique silver articles.

ANTIQUE SILVER ARTICLES

Because of silver's immense popularity in manufacturing and craftwork for centuries and centuries, antiques made of silver (or containing silver components) are abundant.

Their surface appearance may be slightly different than that of modern silver of the identical grade, due to the effects of age. If silver is not regularly cleaned and polished, it can lose its luster and become grimy looking. When exposed for ages to the harshness of nature, such as silver articles from shipboard or decorations from the exteriors of houses, the condition may truly be poor. Any silver item that has been buried underground for a long time (archaeological silver), or brought up from a shipwreck, is sure to show signs of its ordeal.

The melt value of these items, appearance notwithstanding, is the same as for modern silver of the same fineness and weight. It is no more and no less. But, unlike modern silver, which may be flashy and very catching to the eye, these old soldiers frequently have an added *collector value* which removes them from the melt category.

It should not be presumed that anything to which the magic word "antique" attaches is automatically very valuable. An item can be extremely old without exciting great collector interest, either because of commonness, poor workmanship, bad condition or other considerations. Some articles are very "offbeat" and appeal only to highly specialized collectors, of which there may be few in the market at any given time. An antique silver object may only be worth 10% or 20% more than the melt value — but some are worth much more.

It is important to keep in mind that an article need not fall under the definition of "antique," generally taken to mean 100 years old or older, to have *collector* value. Collectors, being unpredictable folk, sometimes value a semi-modern item higher than a very old one, because of its manufacturer, design, topical interest or for various other reasons.

With collectors' items, the quantity of silver they contain is often secondary to other considerations in arriving at a value. An article made of one ounce of .925 fine could outsell something containing three or four ounces of the same grade; it has a much lower melt value but the *other considerations* greatly enhance its price. For example, a decorative table fork made in England in the reign of George I (early 18th century) will generally contain from two to three ounces of .925 fine silver. This would mean $30-$50 worth of silver — approximately — when the spot price is in the $15-$16 category. If the workmanship is really outstanding, as it sometimes was on these specimens, it could easily have a collector value of $150.

You will find, however, that *most* antiques and collectors' items made of silver are valued *primarily for the silver.* In other words, more than 50% of their value is in the bullion. The great majority of silver articles found in ordinary antiques shops, which date no earlier than the mid 1800's and are not remarkable in workmanship, are in that class. So, too, are probably any silver antiques you have in your attic or are preserving as family heirlooms. Unless extremely old, or brilliantly made, they are likely to carry most of their value in bullion content. Obviously, if you have a punch bowl made by Paul Revere, or a salver known to have been owned by George Washington, the collector value is 20 or 30 times the bullion value or more. (But don't jump to conclusions on these things — fakes are very abundant.)

Why should this be so? Why should an object 100 or more years old, which has collector appeal, be worth only a fractional sum above the bullion value?

The answer lies mostly in the fact that bullion prices have advanced much more sharply, since mid 1979, than prices on collectors' items. When silver was $3 an ounce (not really too long ago), miscellaneous Victorian and Edwardiana made of silver was selling at *double* to *triple* the bullion value. But the premium for collector value was still just a few dollars. Today, the collector premium has risen somewhat, but it has been vastly overshadowed by advances in bullion prices.
vances in bullion prices.

The following may help to illustrate this:

Hairbrush containing four ounces of .999 silver (approx.), made c. 1885, sold at $25 in 1973. Silver was $3 per ounce. Item contained $12 worth (approx.) of silver, had $13 collector value — more collector value than bullion value.

Same item sells at $85 in 1981, with spot price of silver at $15. Item now has $60 bullion value, $25 collector value, or 2½ times as much bullion value as collector value. Collector value nearly doubled since 1973 ($13 to $25), bullion value increased more than 5 times.

There are many other factors involved, too, much too numerous to discuss at length.

Unfortunately for the owners of such material, the discount taken by dealers off their buying prices is quite high for antiques and other collectors items. In the chapter on selling silver, we pointed out that the usual discount or handling fee for melt-value objects is 10% to 25%. You receive the full spot price for these objects less 10-25%. With antiques or collectors' items, the same discount is taken from spot (even though there is no intention of shipping off your filigreed pillbox to a refiner), plus another discount — and a bigger one — from the collector value.

It usually works out something like the following.

Say you're selling the aforementioned c. 1885 silver hairbrush, which has a retail value of $125 and contains $100 worth of silver. Ten to 15% will be knocked off the bullion value, bringing that down to $85-90. From the collector value at least 50% will be shaved, making it $12.50 or less. Put them together and you get a price of $97.50-$102.50 — which means an overall discount on the item of about 20%. And you will be lucky to get away that well! Often the collector value is cut down by 75%, depending on the item, the dealer's stock, his class of cutsomers, and, perhaps, the mood he happens to be in that day. There is no standard rate of discount because collectors' items have no standard retail prices. It's all a matter of "What will you pay?"

Some devious dealers — in antiques, secondhand items and related — have reaped windfall profits from the bullion upsurge of recent months. They have devised a variety of what are strictly gimmicks, used in buying from the public, to acquire items at less than reputable dealers pay. Some will pay only the bullion value, less commission, claiming that the high price of silver makes it impossible for them "to make a larger investment." Or they may go so far as to say that old silver is less valuable than modern because of oxidizaton or some such reason, which of course is not true.

PRICES FOR ANTIQUE SILVER

As an aid in evaluating your silver antiques we have provided the following listings of various silver items. Though it is far from complete or extensive it will give you some aid in identifying most antique silver pieces. For a complete listing of all collector silver items you should refer to **"THE OFFICIAL PRICE GUIDE TO AMERICAN SILVER AND SILVER PLATE"** available for only $9.95 plus $1 postage and handling from The House of Collectibles, Inc., 1900 Premier Row, Orlando, Florida 32809.

NOTE: The following prices were obtained mainly from auction sale results during the spring and summer of 1980. Prices asked by dealers are informative but may, in some instances, be higher than the dealer is actually prepared to sell for. Therefore, these price ranges should *only* be used as a guide.

Bread Knives (Silver-Plated)	**Price Range**	
1847 Rogers "Vintage", *bread knife, silver-plated, no monogram, 14½" L., excellent condition*	**$70.00**	**$ 75.00**
(Sterling Silver)		
Gorham "King George", *bread knife, sterling silver, monogram*	**90.00**	**100.00**
Gorham, *bread knife, sterling silver, pattern unknown, monogram*	**90.00**	**100.00**
Coffee Spoons (Coin Silver)		
Kirk "Repousse", *coffee spoon, coin silver, no monogram*	**35.00**	**40.00**

Coffee Spoons (Silver-Plated)	Price Range	
Alvin "Brides Bouquet", *coffee spoon, silver-plated, monogram, excellent condition*	$4.00	$ 5.00
Community "Bird of Paradise", *coffee spoon, silver-plated, no monogram, excellent condition*	7.00	8.00
Community "Bird of Paradise", *coffee spoon, silver-plated, no monogram, fair condition*	2.00	3.00
Gorham "Providence", *coffee spoon, silver-plated, no monogram, excellent condition*	5.00	7.00
Holmes & Edwards "Carolina", *coffee spoon, silver-plated, no monogram, excellent condition*	5.00	6.00
Holmes & Edwards "Spring Garden", *coffee spoon, silver-plated, no monogram,*	3.00	4.00
Holmes & Edwards "Youth", *coffee spoon, silver-plated, no monogram, excellent condition*	6.00	7.00
Oxford "Narcissus", *coffee spoon, silver-plated, no monogram, excellent condition*	7.00	9.00
Stratford "Shakespeare", *coffee spoon, silver-plated, no monogram*	3.00	5.00
Tudor "Royal York", *coffee spoon, silver-plated, no monogram, good condition*	1.00	3.00
Wm. Rogers "Berwick", *coffee spoon, silver-plated, no monogram, good condition*	4.00	6.00
Wm. Rogers "Fairoaks", *coffee spoon, silver-plated, no monogram, excellent condition*	5.00	7.00
1835 R. Wallace "Blossom", *coffee spoon, silver-plated, monogram, excellent condition*	3.00	5.00
1847 Rogers "Old Colony", *coffee spoon, silver-plated, monogram, mint condition*	6.00	7.00

Dinner Forks (Coin Silver)		
Hood & Tobey, *dinner fork, coin silver, c. 1848, monogram*	—	24.00
(Silver-Plated)		
Alvin "Bouquet", *dinner fork, silver-plated, excellent condition*	3.00	4.00
Alvin "Diana", *dinner fork, silver-plated, monogram, excellent condition*	2.00	3.00
Alvin "Molly Stark", *dinner fork, silver-plated, monogram, good condition*	2.00	3.00
American Silver Co. "Corona", *dinner fork, silver-plated, no monogram, excellent condition*	3.00	5.00
American Silver Co. "Wildflower", *dinner fork, silver-plated, no monogram, excellent condition*	5.00	7.00
Benedict Mfg. Co. "Continental", *dinner fork, silver-plated, no monogram, good condition*	3.00	4.00
Community "Adam", *dinner fork, silver-plated, no monogram, excellent condition*	3.00	5.00
Community "Bird of Paradise", *dinner fork, silver-plated, no monogram, excellent condition*	4.00	6.00

Dinner Forks (Silver-Plated)

	Price Range	
Community "Coronation", *dinner fork, silver-plated, no monogram, mint condition*	$ 5.00	$ 7.00
Community "Louis XVI", *dinner fork, silver-plated, no monogram, good condition*	4.00	6.00
Community "Milady", *dinner fork, silver-plated, no monogram, good condition*	4.00	6.00
Community "Morning Rose", *dinner fork, silver-plated, no monogram, excellent condition*	5.00	7.00
Community "Noblesse", *dinner fork, silver-plated, viande style, no monogram, good condition*	4.00	6.00
Community "Patrician", *dinner fork, silver-plated, monogram, excellent condition*	1.00	2.00
Community "Patrician", *dinner fork, silver-plated, no monogram, excellent condition*	5.00	7.00

(Sterling Silver)

Alvin "Chateau Rose", *dinner fork, sterling silver, 7⅞ long, no monogram*	28.00	30.00
Alvin "Majestic", *dinner fork, sterling silver, monogram*	38.00	40.00
Blackington "Scroll & Bead", *dinner fork, sterling silver, no monogram*	52.00	55.00
Dominick & Haff "Louis XIV" , *dinner fork, sterling silver, (old style), no monogram*	28.00	30.00
Dominick & Haff "Renaissance", *dinner fork, sterling silver, monogram*	32.00	34.00
Durgin "Bead", *dinner fork, sterling silver, monogram*	28.00	30.00
Durgin "Chrysanthemum", *dinner fork, sterling silver, no monogram*	72.00	75.00
Durgin "Fairfax", *dinner fork, sterling silver, no monogram, 7⅞ L.*	34.00	36.00
Durgin "Louis XV", *dinner fork, sterling silver, monogram*	32.00	35.00
Frank Smith 'Fiddle Thread", *dinner fork, sterling silver, no monogram*	52.00	55.00
Gorham "Buckingham", *dinner fork, sterling silver, no monogram*	34.00	36.00
Gorham "Cambridge", *dinner fork, sterling silver, no monogram*	30.00	32.00
Gorham "Camellia", *dinner fork, sterling silver, no monogram*	14.00	15.00
Gorham "Chesterfield", *dinner fork, sterling silver, no monogram*	26.00	28.00
Gorham "Fairfax", *dinner fork, sterling silver, no monogram, 7⅞ L.*	34.00	36.00
Gorham "Greenbrier", *dinner fork, sterling silver, no monogram*	26.00	28.00
Gorham "Imperial Chrysanthemum", *dinner fork, sterling silver, no monogram*	28.00	30.00
Gorham "Lancaster Rose", *dinner fork, sterling silver, monogram*	38.00	40.00
Gorham "Marguerite", *dinner fork, sterling silver, no monogram*	36.00	38.00

Dinner Forks (Sterling Silver)	Price Range	
Gorham "Newcastle", *dinner fork, sterling silver, monogram*	$32.00	$34.00
Gorham "Old French", *dinner fork, sterling silver, no monogram*	18.00	20.00
Gorham "Plymouth", *dinner fork, sterling silver, monogram*	30.00	32.00
Gorham "Poppy", *dinner fork, sterling silver, (old), monogram*	32.00	34.00
Gorham "Sovereign", *dinner fork, sterling silver, no monogram*	18.00	20.00
Gorham "Strasbourg", *dinner fork, sterling silver, old and heavy, monogram*	32.00	34.00
Gorham "Tulleries", *dinner fork, sterling silver, monogram, 7⅞ L.*	30.00	32.00
Wallace "Grande Baroque", *dinner fork, sterling silver, no monogram, 7½" L.*	42.00	44.00
Wallace "Grande Colonial", *dinner fork, sterling silver, no monogram*	28.00	30.00
Wallace "Normandie", *dinner fork, sterling silver, monogram*	30.00	32.00
Whiting "Imperial Queen", *dinner fork, sterling silver, monogram*	52.00	55.00
Whiting "Ivy", *dinner fork, sterling silver, monogram, large*	50.00	52.00
Whiting "Louis XV", *dinner fork, sterling silver, monogram*	28.00	32.00

Dinner Knifes (Silver-Plated)		
Alvin "Diana", *dinner knife, silver-plated, monogram, excellent condition*	2.00	3.00
American Silver Company "Moselle", *dinner knife, silver-plated, no monogram, excellent condition*	16.00	20.00
American Silver Company "Moselle", *dinner knife, silver-plated, no monogram, good condition*	10.00	15.00
Benedict Mfg. Co. "Continental", *dinner knife, silver-plated, monogram, poor condition*	2.00	3.00
Community "Adam", *dinner knife, silver-plated, flat-handled, no monogram, excellent condition*	5.00	7.00
Community "Bird of Paradise", *dinner knife, silver-plated, no monogram, good condition*	3.00	5.00
Community "Coronation", *dinner knife, silver-plated, viande style, no monogram, excellent condition*	6.00	8.00
Community "Georgian", *dinner knife, silver-plated, no monogram, fair condition*	1.00	3.00
Community "Grosvenor", *dinner knife, silver-plated, no monogram, excellent condition*	4.00	6.00
Community "King Cedric", *dinner knife, silver-plated, viande style, no monogram, excellent condition*	6.00	8.00
Community "Lady Hamilton", *dinner knife, silver-plated, flat-handled, no monogram, good condition*	2.00	4.00
Reed & Barton, *"Rembrandt"long handled, no monogram, good condition*	5.00	6.00
Reed & Barton "Sierra", *dinner knife, silver-plated, no monogram, excellent condition*	6.00	8.00

Dinner Knifes (Silver-Plated)	**Price Range**	
Reed & Barton "Tiger Lily", *dinner knife, silver-plated, no monogram, excellent condition*	$ 4.00	$ 5.00
Reliance "Briar Rose", *dinner knife, silver-plated, no monogram, excellent condition*	8.00	10.00
Reliance "Bridal Rose", *dinner knife, silver-plated, no monogram, excellent condition*	6.00	8.00
Reliance "Exeter", *dinner knife, silver-plated, flat-handled, no monogram, good condition*	2.00	3.00
Reliance "Wildwood", *dinner knife, silver-plated, flat-handled, no monogram, good condition*	3.00	5.00
Rockford "Fairoaks", *dinner knife, silver-plated, no monogram, excellent condition*	6.00	8.00
Rogers "Alhambra", *dinner knife, silver-plated, no monogram, excellent condition*	9.00	11.00
Rogers "Ambasador", *dinner knife, silver-plated, no monogram, excellent condition*	5.00	7.00
Rogers "Burgundy", *dinner knife, silver-plated, no monogram, good condition*	5.00	7.00
Rogers "Desota", *dinner knife, silver-plated, no monogram, excellent condition*	6.00	8.00
Rogers "Inspiration", *dinner knife, silver-plated, viande style, no monogram, excellent condition*	6.00	8.00
(Sterling Silver)		
Alvin "Maryland", *dinner knife, sterling silver, no monogram, old silver plated blades in good condition*	16.00	18.00
Dominick & Haff "Louis XIV", *dinner knife, sterling silver, old style, no monogram*	22.00	25.00
Durgin "Chrysanthemum", *dinner knife, sterling silver, no monogram*	50.00	55.00
Frank Smith "Fiddle Thread", *dinner knife, sterling silver, no monogram*	40.00	42.00
Frank M. Whiting "Georgian Scroll", *dinner knife, sterling silver, no monogram, 9¼" L.*	18.00	20.00
Gorham "Buckingham", *dinner knife, sterling silver, no monogram*	27.00	29.00
Gorham "Buttercup", *dinner knife, sterling silver, no monogram*	24.00	26.00
Gorham "Cambridge", *dinner knife, sterling silver, silver-plated old style blade, no monogram*	22.00	25.00
Gorham "Camelia", *dinner knife, sterling silver,)no monogram*	22.00	24.00
Gorham "Chantilly", *dinner knife, sterling silver, monogram*	25.00	27.00
Gorham "Chesterfield", *dinner knife, sterling silver, monogram*	16.00	18.00
Gorham "Etruscan", *dinner knife, sterling silver, monogram*	20.00	22.00
Gorham "Fairfax", *dinner knife, sterling silver, stainless blade, no monogram*	18.00	20.00
Gorham "Imperial Chrysanthemum", *dinner knife, sterling silver, silver-plated blade in fair condition*	16.00	18.00
Gorham "Lancaster Rose", *dinner knife, sterling silver, stainless blade, no monogram*	30.00	35.00
Gorham "Versailles", *dinner knife, sterling silver,*	—	35.00

Teaspoons (Silver-Plated)	Price Range	
Alvin "Diana", *teaspoon, silver-plated, no monogram, excellent condition*	$4.00	$6.00
Alvin "Molly Stark", *teaspoon, silver-plated, no monogram, excellent condition*	4.00	6.00
American Silver Co. "Camelot", *teaspoon, silver-plated, no monogram, excellent condition*	2.00	3.00
American Silver Co. "Rosalie", *teaspoon, silver-plated, no monogram, excellent condition*	4.00	6.00
American Silver Co. "Tours", *teaspoon, silver-plated, no monogram, excellent condition*	2.00	4.00
Community "Adam", *teaspoon, silver-plated, no monogram, excellent condition*	2.00	4.00
Community "Ballad", *teaspoon, silver-plated, no monogram, mint condition*	3.00	5.00
Community "Beverly", *teaspoon, silver-plated, no monogram, excellent condition*	4.00	6.00
Community "Bird of Paradise", *teaspoon, silver-plated, no monogram, excellent condition*	4.00	6.00
Community "Coronation", *teaspoon, silver-plated, no monogram, excellent condition*	4.00	6.00
Community "Deauville", *teaspoon, silver-plated, no monogram, excellent condition*	4.00	6.00
Derby "Lily", *teaspoon, silver-plated, no monogram, excellent condition*	4.00	6.00
Embassy "Bouquet", *teaspoon, silver-plated, no monogram, excellent condition*	4.00	6.00
Fortune "Fortune", *teaspoon, silver-plated, no monogram, excellent condition*	4.00	6.00
Gorham "Cavalier", *teaspoon, silver-plated, no monogram, excellent condition*	3.00	4.00
Gorham "Empire", *teaspoon, silver-plated, no monogram, good condition*	3.00	5.00
Gorham "Kings", *teaspoon, silver-plated, no monogram, excellent condition*	4.00	6.00
Gorham "Roman", *teaspoon, silver-plated, monogram, excellent condition*	5.00	7.00
Holmes & Edwards "May Queen", *teaspoon, silver-plated, no monogram, good condition*	3.00	5.00
Holmes & Edwards "Orient", *teaspoon, silver-plated, no monogram, excellent condition*	5.00	7.00
Holmes & Edwards "Pageant", *teaspoon, silver-plated, no monogram, excellent condition*	4.00	6.00
Holmes & Edwards "Queen Anne", *teaspoon, silver-plated, no monogram, fair condition*	2.00	3.00
Holmes & Edwards "Romance II", *teaspoon, silver-plated, no monogram, excellent condition*	2.00	4.00
Holmes & Edwards "Rosemary", *teaspoon, silver-plated, no monogram, excellent condition*	4.00	6.00
Holmes & Edwards "Silver Fashion", *teaspoon, silver-plated, no monogram, excellent condition*	4.00	6.00
Holmes & Edwards "Spring Garden", *teaspoon, silver-plated, no monogram, excellent condition*	2.00	4.00

Teaspoons (Sterling Silver)	Price Range	
Alvin "Chateau Rose", *teaspoon, sterling silver, no monogram*	$18.00	$ 22.00
Gorham "Hunt Club", *teaspoon, sterling silver, no monogram*	16.00	18.00
Gorham "Imperial Chrysanthemum", *teaspoon, sterling silver, no monogram*	15.00	18.00
Gorham "Imperial Chrysanthemum", *teaspoon, sterling silver, monogram*	16.00	18.00
Gorham "Jac Rose", *teaspoon, sterling silver, no monogram*	12.00	13.00
Gorham "LaScala", *teaspoon, sterling silver, no monogram*	22.00	25.00
Gorham "Lancaster", *teaspoon, sterling silver, monogram*	18.00	20.00
Gorham "Lancaster Rose", *teaspoon, sterling silver, no monogram*	20.00	22.00
Gorham "Maryland", *teaspoon, sterling silver, no monogram*	14.00	15.00
Gorham "Medici", *teaspoon, sterling silver, no monogram*	20.00	22.00
Gorham "Newcastle", *teaspoon, sterling silver, monogram*	18.00	20.00
Gorham "Norfolk", *teaspoon, sterling silver, no monogram*	15.00	17.00
Gorham "Plymouth", *teaspoon, sterling silver, monogram*	14.00	15.00
Gorham "Poppy", *teaspoon, sterling silver (old), monogram*	20.00	22.00
Gorham "Raphael", *teaspoon, sterling silver, no monogram*	8.00	10.00
Gorham "Rondo", *teaspoon, sterling silver, no monogram*	18.00	20.00
Gorham "Sovereign", *teaspoon, sterling silver, no monogram*	20.00	22.00
Gorham "Strasbourg", *teaspoon, sterling silver, monogram*	20.00	22.00
Gorham "Tbileries", *teaspoon, sterling silver, no monogram*	16.00	18.00
Gorham "Versailles", *teaspoon, sterling silver, no monogram*	20.00	30.00
Gorham "Willow", *teaspoon, sterling silver, no monogram*	17.00	19.00
Gorham "Zodiac", *teaspoon, sterling silver, no monogram set of 12*	375.00	395.00
International "Abbotsford", *teaspoon, sterling silver, monogram*	16.00	18.00
International "Angelique", *teaspoon, sterling silver, monogram*	17.00	19.00
International "Avalon", *teaspoon, sterling silver, monogram*	28.00	30.00
International "Brandon", *teaspoon, sterling silver, no monogram*	17.00	19.00

Trays (Silver-Plated)		
Reed & Barton, *tray, silver-plated, square, Georgian styling, scrolls and flowers in relief, ribbing on inner rim, excellent condition*	36.00	38.00
Maker unknown, *tray, silver-plated, round, 14" diameter, ornate rim and handles, divided glass insert, excellent condition*	32.00	35.00
Maker unknown, *tray, silver-plated, rectangular, 17" handle to handle, plain design, excellent condition*	36.00	38.00
Maker unknown, *tray, silver-plated, gallery type, 15" x 1¼" H., mint condition*	22.00	24.00

TRAYS (Sterling Silver)	Price Range	
Gorham, *tray, sterling silver, 8½" L., reeded rim, no monogram*	$ 48.00	$ 50.00
Kalo, *tray, sterling silver, c. 1920, plain shape, round, hammered finish, 12" diameter, 21 oz.*	300.00	330.00
Maker unknown, *tray, sterling silver, made for Bailey, Banks & Biddle Co., Philadelphia, c. 1908, rectangular, 24½" L., pierced gallery border, crest and motto in center, 145 oz.*	1,500.00	1,650.00

BUYING AND SELLING SILVER BULLION

Success in silver investment depends upon knowledge of the market, which means not only keeping up with the daily spot prices and events that might have influence on it, but knowing where and how to buy and sell. Though the beginning investor is likely to be unaware of this, small variations in price when buying or selling (which could be nothing more substantial than a few percentage points in the dealer's commission) *add up,* and could mean the difference between a profitable or very marginal investment.

HOW SILVER BULLION IS SOLD TO THE PUBLIC. Silver bullion, being less expensive than gold, can be invested or speculated in by persons in just about every income level — and it is, increasingly. You can start with as small an amount as you wish; there's no minimum. In most instances, however, definite price advantages can be gained by buying as much as you can safely afford at any given time. The dealers normally reduce their commission fees on larger purchases. This is particularly true of .999 bars and ingots, on which the commission drops significantly on substantial purchases. So far as *coins* are concerned, there is often a discount offered on quantity bullion orders. These discounts may not seem impressive, possibly in the range of 1½-2% on $100, but as stated above they add up. In investing, you must take advantage of whatever opportunities there may be to save or make money.

A lot of people have the mistaken notion that buying silver bullion means buying .999 bars or ingots. This is one form of silver bullion and a very attractive one for investors (if you don't pay too high a dealer's commission, which can pretty well ruin things, or buy .999 silver that fails to carry the refiner's identification), but it's certainly not the only one.

Silver bullion is also available via coins, sold in rolls or bags or simply by weight.

Additionally, it can be bought by the contract method — which means no actual silver changes hands. You simply buy a contract or ownership paper, stating that a certain quantity of silver (by troy ounces) is being held in your name through a certain company at the company's bank. Many bullion brokerage firms as well as coin dealers offer this service. Depending upon terms of the contract it may either be sold — still without the silver changing hands — or can be turned in against delivery of the silver. The advertisements for such contracts paint such glowing pictures of their advantages that many novice investors eagerly purchase them. In some instances, the purchaser is allowed to pay off the contract on installments, even if he has no credit history. The brokers take no risk because they hold the bullion and title does not pass until the last payment is made. Another apparent advantage is that the investor is saved all worry about storage, theft, insurance and related matters. He doesn't have the silver, so nobody can steal it from him.

But in fact the contract method is *undesirable* for investors, and should not be seriously contemplated. Despite the need for much more "ready money" when buying outright, despite the problems of transportation and storage, you are in a much better position with *fully owned* silver. "Fully owned" is the investor's term for anything — bullion or otherwise — to which you have title and physical possession. Just having title alone isn't good enough. Complications could arise that prevent you from *ever* taking physical possession, and title by itself is simply a piece of paper. The broker could go out of business without making satisfactory legal arrangements for transferral of his accounts. The silver could get lost — or maybe it never existed in the first place. Would you doubt for an instant that in this day of classic swindles, that dishonest brokers are active, selling contracts on silver that they don't own and probably will never obtain?

Physical possession may be a hazard, security-wise. But it's much less of a hazard, overall, than not having possession.

Silver bullion is sold to the public by the ounce or multiples of ounces. When sold by reputable dealers, including coin dealers, the price is calculated on the basis of *that day's spot,* against the weight and fineness of the items being sold. Dealers who do not use the current daily spot, but base their selling prices on some arbitrary or abstract figures, cannot be considered entirely legitimate. It is not a valid excuse that the dealer does not own a teletype machine, or that the machine is broken, or that for some reason he is unaware of the day's spot price for silver. You can be very certain that he would not be buying, if he was unaware of the current price quotations.

When items are sold as silver bullion, no consideration is made of the value of other materials they might contain (such as alloy), or any additional value they could have either utilitarian or as collectors' items, decorations, etc. You buy this material strictly for its melt value — the amount of silver it contains, or can be extracted from it — and the goal is to resell it for melt value at some future date, when the price of silver has advanced far enough to show you a worthwhile profit (*when* to sell is discussed in the investing chapter).

Occasionally, bullion items acquire a collector value after you buy them. This is not common and it is surely not easy to predict, but it does happen from time to time. In that case, you could realize a higher price when selling than selling merely for the melt value. Bars and ingots, though .999, have no potential of doing this. Coins are the most likely form of bullion silver to acquire collector value with passage of time, but certainly not all coins will. Which ones do — or don't — depends very much on trends in investing, collecting, and the bullion market. During the big Silver Rush of late 1979/early 1980, when Morgan and Peace dollars were being melted in the refineries at a record pace (tens of thousands daily), there was strong speculation that common-date, circulated specimens of these coins would become scarce on the numismatic market if the rate of destruction continued. Since no more are being manufactured, every specimen melted is one less than can possibly be owned by a collector.

When you want to buy *.999 bars or ingots,* look for a dealer or broker who charges a reasonable rate of commission. Commissions vary from one seller to the next, so shop around. The major coin publications, as well as the general press, carry many ads from bar and ingot dealers.

A fair rate of commission on .999 bars or ingots is (approximately) 8-10%

on small purchases, 5-6% on purchases from $100 to $1,000, and around 3% on purchases over $1,000.

In buying bullion coins, you will need to decide whether you want silver dollars, so-called "small silver" (under $1 face value), and the form in which you want it: by the roll or bag. U.S. silver bullion coins are nearly always sold by roll or bag. Unless stated otherwise, rolls and bags contain common-date circulated, *all of the same denomination,* but mixed so far as dates and types are concerned. In other words a bag of bullion dimes can be expected to contain Roosevelts and Mercuries, and a bag of silver dollars will likely have Morgans and Peace dollars. Bags contain $1,000 *face* value, regardless of denomination — in other words, 1,000 dollars, 10,000 dimes, 2,000 half dollars and so forth. Since the coins are all .900 fine, the silver value per bag is the same, no matter if it contains dimes or dollars or any other denomination. This $1,000 face value naturally has nothing to do with the value of the coins as bullion, which, of course, is considerably higher. At the height of the silver price boom (January, 1980), refiners were paying as much as $35,000 for these bags, or about 35 times the face value. This was still considerably below the current spot value at that time, however, since refiners were not anxious to tie up huge sums of money in bullion when the market was behaving so erratically. Very likely this situation will prevail again if silver makes another sudden leap up to $45 or $55. Refiners will fall back upon their on-hand supplies, and await developments. The prices they pay influence prices paid by scrap buyers and other purchasers.

PREMIUM ON BULLION COINS. The dealer's premium over spot varies on silver bullion coins more widely than on bars or ingots. It may run from 5% to 10% or more, but is occasionally less and sometimes very near spot, just 2% or so above. The dealer of course makes no money on selling when his percentage is this low — the profit is derived from *buying,* which is done at a much larger discount than the percentage charged to buyers. If a dealer pays 15% under spot for bullion coins, and sells them at 2% over, he has a 17% profit. Though this may seem meager, larger volume and quick turnover makes it more than worthwhile.

For example:

50 ounces of silver bullion coins (not counting alloy), bought when spot is $15 per troy ounce, at 15% discount = $638

same sold when spot is $15, at 2% surcharge = $765 = $127 profit.

The value of silver bullion coins is never figured on the basis of their overall weight, but the weight of the silver contained. By referring to our charts in the coin section, you will easily be able to determine, by multiplication, the net weight in silver of any amount or denomination of silver coins you may have or wish to buy. Keep in mind that U.S. coin silver is .900 fine. This is the fineness of all our silver coins struck from 1838 to 1964, with the exception of wartime nickels. The silver content is not, however, precisely 90% of the coin's weight, because silver does not weigh the same as the copper alloy. A close approximate calculation can be made in this fashion but for precise figures you will need to use our chart.

SELLING SILVER BULLION. Silver bullion is sold in the same way you bought it. If the investment is short-term (thanks to a sudden rise in silver value), you may very likely be reselling to the dealer from whom you purchased. Don't hesitate to do this, if you find him to be honest and reliable. It isn't necessary to shop around for a different buyer, simply because the dealer from whom you bought knows how much you paid. What you paid means nothing. The price you will receive in selling depends strictly on the spot value that day, the fineness of your silver, its weight, and the percentage of discount taken by the dealer. If the transaction yields a price of, say, $300, you will get $300 whether you paid $30 or $250 for the silver, or received it as a gift.

When dealers buy .999 bars or ingots they normally work with a bigger discount than the premium charged in selling. They may sell $1,000 worth of bars at 3% over spot, but in buying $1,000 worth they may subtract 8-10% from the price or even more. This, of course, must be figured in, when you calculate the profit or loss on your investment. These are your basic working figures, to which must be introduced such items as the inflation rate to discover if your investment has made an *actual* profit — that is, whether the money it will yield today *will buy more* than the original investment cost would have purchased when the investment was made.

When selling *scrap* silver, be especially careful of choosing your buyer. Sell to a well established dealer or broker with a shop or office rather than an itinerant located in a hotel or motel, or operating out of a van. Do not sell to dealers at flea markets, shows and conventions. Sell to someone who's been at his address for a substantial length of time. These individuals are less prone to cheat because they can easily be found.

It is, of course, normal and traditional, whenever anything is presented for sale, for the prospective buyer to seek out its shortcomings and obtain the price most favorable to him. There is nothing illegal in this. But when selling scrap or melt items by weight, where condition is not important, bargaining should not be necessary if the dealer is ethical. He will have an advertised price per ounce, and he will pay this price based upon the weight of your material.

Unfortunately this is not always the case.

There are many scrap buyers, mostly in the "fly by night" category, who are expert at inventing reasons why they cannot pay the full advertised sum. By shaving just a few dollars off each transaction they can gain considerable extra profits. And sometimes the shaving is not a few dollars but much more, depending on the item and the buyer's estimate of its owner's gullibility.

Probably the most prevalent infraction is short weighting, or informing sellers that their material weighs less than it actually does. This can be accomplished by keeping scales out of public sight (which is illegal in itself, even if the scales are accurate), or fixing them to give low readings. The weight is not usually grossly misrepresented, for fear of detection; but even the difference of a few ounces can mean a big difference in price.

VALUES OF U.S. SILVER COINS

There are an estimated 28 million coin collectors in the U.S. (more than 10% of the population), the majority of whom collect U.S. coins. There is obviously a very big demand for silver coins by collectors, and by the dealers who supply them. However, their interest is mostly in uncirculated specimens or coins with scarce dates or mintmarks, or which for some other reason have special appeal. The vast majority of U.S. silver coins both old and recent going back into the later 1800's — are of more value for their silver content. These are known as "bullion coins," or sometimes "melt coins."

The Mint stopped striking silver coins in 1964, when the switch was made to "cladding," or coins with copper interiors covered in nickel. Prior to that time, our dimes, quarters, half dollars and dollars (which had not been struck since 1935) were made of 90% silver and 10% copper. In 1963 the price of bullion silver had risen to the point where the Mint was just breaking even on manufacturing silver coins. Thus it was decided to remove their silver content, but to retain the same denominations, sizes and designs.

Not long after clad coins reached circulation, the older silver issues became worth more than face value. However, the difference at first was very slight — just a few cents on a 50¢ piece for example. By the mid 1970's it became profitable, even with the dealer's commission, to sell silver coins for melting. The peak was reached in January, 1980, when U.S. silver coins climbed to 35-40 times face value — in other words, \$3.50 to \$4 for a dime, \$8.75 to \$10 for a quarter, \$17.50 to \$20 for a half dollar, and \$35 to \$40 for silver dollars. They slid back soon afterward but are still salable for a considerable profit over the face value.

The following formula will enable you to determine the bullion value of any U.S. silver coin prior to 1964, whatever the spot price of silver is on any given day. Melt value should only apply to coins that are below fine condition and/or are damaged or badly worn. Simply multiply spot that day by the net weight in silver of each coin. This will give the melt value in dollars and cents. You will need the following chart of net weights to assist you with your calculations.

Silver Coin Denomination (dates 1964 and earlier)	Amount of .999+ Silver it Contains (in fractions of an ounce)
10¢	.07234
25¢	.18084
50¢	.36169
\$1	.77344
Wartime 5¢ (1942-1945 only)	.05626

There are other U.S. silver coin denominations, but the above are the only ones that fall into the category of "bullion coins." The rest have collector value and are not sold for melting.

EXAMPLE OF CALCULATION:

A. Silver \$1. If spot was \$15: \$15 × .77344 = \$11.60
B. Silver 50¢ If spot was 31: 31 × .36169 = 11.21
C. Silver 24¢ If spot was 22: 22 × .18084 = 3.98
D. Silver 10¢ If spot was 28: 28 × .07234 = 2.03

It must be kept in mind that *some* specimens of these coins are worth more than melt value, depending on date, mintmark and condition. We have provided the following guide to determining condition of each silver coin, which should aid you in distinguishing between specimens that fall in the "melt" category and those which might be salable as collectors' items at a higher price.

SILVER 10¢, LIBERTY HEAD or "BARBER"

MINT STATE MS-60 (uncirculated). A strictly Uncirculated coin with no trace of wear, but with blemishes more obvious than MS-65. May lack full mint luster, and surface may be dull, spotted, or heavily toned. Checkpoints for signs of abrasion: high points of cheek, and hair below LIBERTY. Ribbon bow and tips of leaves.

OBVERSE **REVERSE**

EXTREMELY FINE. EF-40. *OBVERSE:* Light wear shows on leaves, cheek, cap and hair above forehead. LIBERTY is sharp and band edges are clear. *REVERSE:* High points of wreath and bow are worn, but all details are clearly defined. Traces of mint luster may still show.

FINE. F-12. *OBVERSE:* Some details show in hair, cap and facial features. All letters in LIBERTY are weak but visible. Upper row of leaves is outlined, but bottom row is worn smooth. *REVERSE:* Some details in the lower leaf clusters are plainly visible. Bow is outlined but flat. Letters in legend are worn but clear.

SILVER 10¢, MERCURY

MINT STATE. MS-60 (Uncirculated). A strictly Uncirculated coin with no trace of wear, but with blemishes more obvious than MS-65. May lack full mint luster, and surface may be dull, spotted or heavily toned. Checkpoints for signs of abrasion: high points of hair and in front of ear. Diagonal bands of fasces.

OBVERSE **REVERSE**

EXTREMELY FINE. EF-40. *OBVERSE:* Wear shows on high points of feathers, hair and at neck line. *REVERSE:* High points of fasces bands are worn, but all details are clearly defined and partially separated. Traces of mint luster may still show.

FINE. F-12. *OBVERSE:* Some details show in hair. All feathers are weak but partially visible. Hair braid is nearly worn away. *REVERSE:* Vertical lines are all visible, but lack sharpness. Diagonal bands show on fasces but one is worn smooth at midpoint.

SILVER 10¢, ROOSEVELT (up to 1964 only)

MINT STATE. MS-60 (Uncirculated). A strictly Uncirculated coin with no trace of wear, but with blemishes more obvious than MS-65. Has full mint luster, but surface may be dull, spotted or toned. Checkpoints for signs of abrasion: high points of cheek and hair above ear. Tops of leaves and details in flame.

OBVERSE

REVERSE

EXTREMELY FINE. EF-40. *OBVERSE:* Wear show on high points of hair and at cheek line. Ear shows slight wear on the upper tip.*REVERSE:* High points of flame, torch and leaves are worn, but all details are clearly defined and partially seperated. Traces of mint luster may still show.

FINE. F-12. *OBVERSE:* Half the details show in hair. All of the face is weak but boldly visible. Half of inner edge of ear is worn away. *REVERSE:* Vertical lines are all visible, but lack horizontal bands are worn smooth. Leaves show some detail. Flame is nearly smooth.

SILVER 25¢, LIBERTY or "BARBER"

MINT STATE. MS-60 (Uncirculated). A strictly Uncirculated coin with no trace of wear, but with blemishes more obvious than MS-65. May lack full mint luster, and surface may be dull, spotted or heavily toned. Checkpoints for signs of abrasion: high points of cheek and hair below LIBERTY. Eagle's head and tips of tail and wings.

OBVERSE

REVERSE

EXTREMELY FINE. EF-40. *OBVERSE:* Light wear shows on leaves, cheek, cap and hair above forehead. LIBERTY sharp and band edges are clear. *REVERSE:* High points of head, neck wings and tail are lightly worn, but all details are clearly defined.Leaves show trace of wear at edges. Traces of mint luster may still show.

FINE. F-12. *OBVERSE:* Some details show in hair, cap and facial features. All letters in LIBERTY are weak but visible. Upper row of leaves is outlined, but bottom row is worn nearly smooth. Rim is full and bold. *REVERSE:* half of the feathers are plainly visible. Wear spots show in center of neck, motto and arrow. Horizontal shield lines are merged; vertical lines are seperated. Letters in legend are worn but clear.

SILVER 25¢, LIBERTY STANDING

MINT STATE. MS-60 (Uncirculated). A strictly Uncirculated coin with no trace of wear, but with blemishes more obvious than MS-65. May lack full mint luster, and surface may be dull, spotted or heavily toned. One or two small spots may be weakly struck. Head details may be incomplete.Checkpoints for signs of wear: mail covering breast, knee, high points of gown and shield; high points of eagle's breast and wings. Coins of this design frequently show weakly struck spots and usually lack full head details.

OBVERSE

REVERSE

EXTREMELY FINE. EF-40. *OBVERSE:* Wear shows on breast, and right leg above and below knee. Most of the gown lines are visible. Shield details are bold. Breast is well rounded but has small flat spot. *REVERSE:* High points of eagle are lightly worn. Central part of right wing is well worn. Traces of mint luster may still show.

FINE. F-12. *OBVERSE:* Gown details worn but show clearly across body. Left leg is lightly worn. Right leg nearly flat and toe is worn. Breast worn but some mail is visible. Date may show some weaknes at top.Rim is full. Outer edge of shield is complete. *REVERSE:* Breast is worn almost smooth. Half of the wing feathers are visible although well worn spots. The rim is full.

SILVER 25¢, WASHINGTON (up to 1964 only)

MINT STATE. MS-60 (Uncirculated). A strictly Uncirculated coin with no trace of wear, but with blemishes more obvious than MS-65. May lack full mint luster, and surface may be dull, spotted or heavily toned. Checkpoints for signs of abrasion: high points of cheek and hair in front and back of ear. Tops of legs and details in breast feathers.

EXTREMELY FINE. EF-40. *OBVERSE:* Wear shows on high points of hair around and at hairline up to crown. *REVERSE:* High points of breast, legs and claws are lightly worn, but all details are clearly defined and partially seperated. Part of mint luster is still present.

OBVERSE **REVERSE**

FINE. F-12. *OBVERSE:* Details show only at back of hair. Motto is weak but clearly visible. Part of cheek edge is worn away. *REVERSE:* Feathers in breast and legs are worn smooth. Leaves show some detail. Parts of wings are nearly smooth.

SILVER 50¢, LIBERTY or "BARBER"

MINT STATE. MS-60 (Uncirculated). A strictly Uncirculated coin with no trace of wear, but with blemishes more obvious than MS-65. May lack full mint luster, and surface may be dull, spotted or heavily toned. Checkpoints for signs of abrasion: high points of cheek and hair below LIBERTY, Eagle's head and tips of tail and wings.

OBVERSE **REVERSE**

EXTREMELY FINE. EF-40. *OBVERSE:* Light wear shows on leaves, cheek, cap and hair above forehead. LIBERTY is sharp and band edges are clear. *REVERSE:* High points of head, neck, wings and tail are lightly worn, but all details are clearly defined. Leaves show trace of wear at edges. Traces of mint luster may still show.

FINE. F-12. *OBVERSE:* Some details show in hair, cap and facial features. All letters are weak but visible. Upper row of leaves is outlined, but bottom row is worn nearly smooth. Rim is full and bold. *REVERSE:* Half the feathers are plainly visible. Wear spots show in center of neck, motto and arrows. Horozontal shield lines are merged; Vertical lines are separated. Letters in legend are worn but clear.

SILVER 50¢, LIBERTY WALKING

MINT STATE. MS-60 (Uncirculated). A strictly Uncirculated coin with no trace of wear, but with blemishes more obvious than MS-65. May lack full mint luster, and surface may be dull, spotted or heavily toned. A few small spots may be weakly struck. Checkpoints for signs of abrasion: hair above temple, right arm, left breast; high points of eagle's head, breast, legs and wings. Coins of this design frequently show weakly struck spots, and usually lack full head and hand details.

OBVERSE

REVERSE

EXTREMELY FINE. EF-40. *OBVERSE:* Wear shows on head, breast, arms and left leg. Nearly all gown lines are visible. Sandal details are complete. Breast and knee are nearly flat. *REVERSE:* High points of eagle are lightly worn. Half the breast and leg feathers are visible. Central part of feathers below neck is well worn. Traces of mint luster may still show.

FINE. F-12. *OBVERSE:* Gown stripes worn but show clearly, except for coins before 1921 where only half are visible. Center of body worn but some of the gown is visible. Outer edge of rim is complete. *REVERSE:* Breast is worn smooth. Half the wing feathers are visible although well worn in spots. Top layers of feathers are visible in left wing. Rim is full.

SILVER 50¢, FRANKLIN

MINT STATE. MS-60 (Uncirculated). A strictly Uncirculated coin with no trace of wear, but with blemishes more obvious than MS-65. May lack full mint luster, and surface may be dull, spotted or heavily toned. Checkpoints for signs of abrasion: high points of cheeks and hair left of ear. Straps around beam, lines and lettering on bell.

OBVERSE

REVERSE

EXTREMELY FINE. EF-40. *OBVERSE:* Wear shows on high points of cheek and hair behind ear and at shoulder. *REVERSE:* High points of beam straps, and lines along bottom of bell are lightly worn, but details are clearly defined and partially seperated. Lettering on bell is worn away at center.Part of the mint luster is still present.

FINE. F-12. *OBVERSE:* Hair details show only at back and side of head. Designer's initials weak but clearly visible. Part of cheek is worn flat. *REVERSE:* Most of lines at bottom of bell are worn smoothe. Parts of straps on beam are nearly smooth. Rim is full.

SILVER 50¢, KENNEDY (1964 only)

MINT STATE. MS-60 (Uncirculated). A strictly Uncirculated coin with no trace of wear, but with blemishes more obvious than MS-65. Has mint luster, but surface may be dull, spotted or heavily toned. Checkpoints for signs of abrasion: high points of cheek and jawbone, center of neck, hair below part. Bumdle of arrows, center tail feather, right wingtip.

OBVERSE

REVERSE

EXTREMELY FINE. EF-40. *OBVERSE:* Slight wear shows on cheek, along jawbone and on high points of hair below part. Hair lines are sharp and detailed. *REVERSE:* High points of arrows and right wingtip are lightly worn. Central tail feathers are worn but clearly defined and fully separated. Three-quarters of the mint luster is present.

FINE. F-12. Kennedy half dollars in this grade of condition have no value above melt value.

SILVER $1, MORGAN

MINT STATE. MS-60 (Uncirculated). A strictly Uncirculated coin with no trace of wear, but with blemishes more obvious than MS-65. May have a few small rim mars and weakly struck spots. Has full mint luster but may lack briliance, and surface may be spotted of heavily toned. For these coins, bag abrasions and scuff marks are considered different from circulation wear. Full mint luster and lack of any wear necessary to distinguish MS-60 from AU-55 (About Uncirculated). Checkpoints for sign of wear: Hair above eyes and ear, edges of cotton leaves and blossoms, high upper fold of cap. High points of eagle's breast and tops of legs. Weakly struck spots are common and should not be confused with actual wear.

EXTREMELY FINE. EF-40. *OBVERSE:* Wear shows on hair, above date, forehead and ear. Lines in hair well detailed. Flat spots visible on edges of cotton leaves. Cheek lightly worn. *REVERSE:* Almost all feathers gone from

OBVERSE **REVERSE**

breast. Tops of legs, wingtips and feathers on head show wear. Talons are flat. Partial mint luster is visible.

FINE. F-12. *OBVERSE:* Hairline along face is clearly defined. Lower two cotton leaves smooth but distinct from cap. Some wheat grains merging. Cotton blossoms flat but the two lines in each show clearly. *REVERSE:* One-Quarter of eagle's right wing and edge of left wing are smooth. Head, neck and breast are flat and merging. Tail feathers slightly worn. Top leaves in wreath show heavy wear.

SILVER $1, PEACE

MINT STATE. MS-60 (Uncirculated). A strictly Uncirculated coin with no trace of wear, but with more age marks and other abrasions than MS-65. May have a few rim marks and may be weakly struck. Has full mint luster but may lack brilliance and surface may be spotted or heavily toned. For these coins, bag abrasions and scuff marks are considered different from circulation wear. Full mint luster and lack of any wear are necessary to distinguish MS-60 from AU-55 (Almost Uncirculated). High points for signs of wear: high points of cheek and hair. High points of feathers on right wing and leg. Weakly struck spots are common and should not be confused with actual wear.

OBVERSE **REVERSE**

EXTREMELY FINE. EF-40. *OBVERSE:* Slight flattening visible on high points of hair; most hair strands clearly separated. Entire face and lower edge of neck lightly worn. REVERSE: Wear shows on head behind eye and top of neck. Some flat spots visible on central wing and leg feathers. Partial mint luster is visible.

FINE. F-12. *OBVERSE:* With the exception of those dated 1921 and 1928, Peace dollars in this grade of condition have no value above melt value.

Now you have an idea of the grade. The following values are for properly graded coins. As dealers usually only buy common date Fine or better grade coins at higher than "melt value" prices, prices for these grades of condition are given. The reason is that common date silver coins are seldom collected in grades lower than fine. The A.B.P. at the top of the first column means Average Buying Price. This is the price most dealers will pay for that particular coin in Fine condition. The other columns represent the retail value, or in other words the price that the average dealer charges for these coins in his shop. Keep in mind that buying prices vary just as much as selling prices. When the selling price is up the buying price should be up as well.

The following prices are for *common-date* silver coins. Better dates are worth more. For values on these as well as more statistical information we recommended **"THE OFFICIAL BLACKBOOK OF U.S. COINS,"** the annual publication relied on by buyers and sellers of coins. It is available for only $2.50 plus $1 postage and handling from The House of Collectibles, Inc., Orlando Central Park, 1900 Premier Row, Orlando, Florida 32809.

The following prices are based on a "spot" price of $15. and were current as of February, 1981. As spot price changes regularly you should check the up-to-the-minute figure (normally in the financial section of your daily newspaper).

	A.B.P. in Fine F-12	**Fine F-12**	**Extra Fine EF-40**	**Uncirculated MS-60**
Silver 10¢, Liberty (Barber)	2.40	3.00	25.00	225.00
Silver 10¢, Mercury	1.25	1.40	1.75	7.00
Silver 10¢, Roosevelt	1.10	1.20	1.50	2.00
Silver 25¢, Liberty (Barber)	6.40	8.00	50.00	325.00
Silver 25¢, Liberty Standing	5.60	7.00	30.00	150.00
Silver 25¢, Washington	2.75	3.25	4.50	5.50
Silver 50¢, Liberty (Barber)	9.60	12.00	125.00	800.00
Silver 50¢, Liberty Walking	6.40	8.00	10.00	100.00
Silver 50¢, Franklin	5.50	6.25	8.00	14.00
Silver 50¢, Kennedy (1964 only)	5.50	6.25	8.00	10.00
Silver $1, Morgan	14.00	16.00	18.00	38.00
Silver $1, Peace	14.00	16.00	18.00	38.00

U.S. SILVER COMMEMORATIVE MEDALS AND COINS

A great deal of commemorative medals are struck in silver. The practice of issuing such medals, which normally honor famous persons or events, dates back hundreds of years. In modern times they have become very abundant, as not only the government but private and semi-private organizations sponsor them. Generally there is a dual issue in both bronze (or copper, or brass) along with the silver, with perhaps 1,000 of the former and only 100 or less of the latter placed on sale. The difference in quantities manufactured relates to the sharp difference in price between basemetal and silver.

What sort of opportunities do silver commerative medals present to the investor? Should they be placed in the same category as coins?

First of all, the different groups of medals should be understood:

1. Government issues. These are medals or coins sponsored by the government, struck either by the Mint or under government contract by private organizations. There are numerous kinds. An example of government-struck commemoratives are the "So-Called Dollars," or commemorative coins (actually half dollars) widely sold during the 1920's and 1930's. These came out with almost the regularity of commemorative postage stamps and honored everything from statehood centennials to the opening of a new bridge. Government-contract medals struck by commercial firms include the well-known series of Presidential Inugural Medals, one of which is struck every four years.

2. Commercial issues. In other words, medals struck by private medalers or mints, for the sole purpose of selling them at a profit to the public. The best known and most numerous of these are the Franklin Mint issues, but there are also a number of other commercial mints in the U.S. that put out medals.

3. Semi-private or quasi-official issues. This enormous group encompasses all medals issued by states, counties, cities, universities, historical societies, fraternal organizations, and every kind of non-profit alliance. That, in fact, is the criteria for placing a medal into group #2, that it was sponsored by a non-profit issuer.

Every American medal falls into one of those three categories.

As with any object made of silver, silver commemorative medals have a melt value. In some instances this is considerably higher than the melt value of silver coins, because many medals are larger in size and heavier than any government coins. The Franklin Mint has issued medals weighing four times as much as a U.S. silver dollar.

Whether they therefore represent a good buy for investment purposes is not as easily answered as this seems to suggest, however.

The matter of collector value has to be considered, for one thing. All government medals invariably have a collector value that removes them from the bullion category. Many of our commemorative half dollars, while containing $10 worth of silver or less (depending on spot), sell as numismatic items for $100 or more. A very large percentage of Category #2 medals are in that class, too. Because of their scarcity or special nature — such as appeal to topical or regional collectors — they command prices several times that of their bullion content, and must be discounted as bullion investments. They could concievably be worthwhile investments, but mainly as collectors' items, and their future price-performance and return on your cost would depend on whatever trends occur in the collector market. Objects of this nature are prone to fads and to the fickleness of hobbyists. Their values are not strongly influenced by upward or downward movement in the daily spot value of silver.

Private mint issues, on the other hand, are frequently traded as bullion and often end up in the smelter's pot. During the height of silver-buying activity in early 1980, numerous ads appeared in the press to buy commemorative silver medals for melting. When such items are bought for melting, the price paid is exactly the same (proportionately) as that of bullion coins. The medal is weighed and paid for on the basis of weight plus fineness . . . just as if it were any other kind of silver object. No consideration is taken of the design, scarcity, or original cost. These mean nothing because all the purchaser is buying is the silver it contains. If silver has risen sharply in value since the medal was issued, its bullion content could be worth more than the medal's issue price (which, naturally, was based on silver content *plus* manufacturing cost and various miscellaneous costs). Then you can realize a profit on selling silver commemorative medals.

But if you think they might be a good bullion investment, don't proceed without a few words of caution.

The people who made money on commemorative medals in late 1979 and early 1980 did so because they had been holding their medals for several years at least. They might have bought a medal when issued in (say) 1974 when silver was $4 a troy ounce, obtaining a one-ounce medal for $10 or $15 at the most. Then, with silver at $40-$50 per ounce, these items could be sold for worthwhile profits — *even though* they had been bought for more than twice the price of their bullion content.

Unless you bought silver commemorative medals before 1979, and are still holding them, the odds on making money from them are not especially favorable. The newly issued private medals have very substantial retail prices, reflecting the expense to which these firms must go in acquiring silver and the increased manufacturing and advertising cost vs. five or ten years ago. Silver would need to *more than double* from the spot price at time of issue for the buyers of these medals to gain a profit selling them to scrap dealers or melters. Remember that the scrap dealer deducts *his* margin of profit before he pays you.

Of course, secondhand specimens of older medals (issued when silver was cheaper) are available on the market. These could be dabbled in for bullion investment but they aren't as attractive for this purpose as silver coins. The reason is that the premium charged for them is generally a bit higher, over the daily spot price, than is charged for silver dollars in average condition or other U.S. bullion coins. The collector market is probably responsible for this. There are people attempting to build full sets of the Franklin mint and other private mint issues, who are not interested in investment, and will give a premium over the bullion value. This situation does not exist in the same way with coins, since coin collectors go for specimens in the best grades of condition and leave circulated pieces (unless rare) to bullion speculators. There are no circulated specimens of medals; all are in more or less the same condition. Therefore, if you want to buy for bullion investment, you must pay the same price as someone who buys for collector appeal.

THE SILVER MARKET IN DEPTH

The silver market is a vast worldwide network of refiners, jewelry makers, industries, investors, coin dealers and collectors, and others. Each utilizes silver for his own purposes. The radio manufacturer uses it for printed circuits in transistor radios, because of its conductivity. The jewelry maker fashions it into adornments that are passed along for retail sale. Demand for silver is enormous — greater than at any previous time in history. The quantity of raw silver mined each year is no more today than it was ten years ago, about 300 million ounces annually. Yet demand in 1981 is at least double that of 1971. Obviously the only way that this additional demand can be met is by melting down things that were made of silver in the past — coins, tableware, decorations and miscellaneous items.

Tons upon tons of "old silver" was bought by scrap dealers in 1980 and resold to refineries. Never in the history of the silver market had so much melting been done as in 1980 — and the 1981 totals may well be even higher. Nevertheless, silver is still not coming on the market fast enough to keep in line with the demand. Therefore, its price has risen to about ten times what it was a decade ago.

As a substance of intrinsic value, like gold, silver has attracted a great many investors. Though silver has certainly been dabbled in by investors over the years, going back centuries, the first significant wave of investor buying occurred in the early to mid 1970's. This was not only generated by the gradually rising prices of silver bullion (in those days a $2 climb in a whole year, for one troy ounce, was considered very impressive), but step-ups in industrial use and projected figures on mining yields, which clearly showed that demand for silver would inevitably hike the price higher and higher. At first, investors concentrated mostly on bars or ingots of .999 fine. Later, they began buying silver bullion coins (common-date coins made of silver, in circulated condition), and various other forms of silver. With each increase in investor activity, the daily "spot" price was driven upward. This natually encouraged still more persons to invest in silver, and for those already holding it to add to their holdings. During the late 1970's, as the price climbed from $5 to $10 to $20, it became evident that silver had the ability — as an investment — to increase in value at a faster pace than the national inflation rate.

But despite the decline of 1980, and fear-mongering warnings by so-called experts that the bottom was soon to fall out, it happened to be a very good year for silver and silver investors. The market was *strong.* Industrial demand grew. Investors multiplied, not only in the U.S. but around the world. And the spot price of silver was more than twice as high, at the end of 1980, than it was at the beginning of 1979. Anyone who bought in *mid* 1979 could have sold in December of that year, or January 1980, for very enviable profits. The only individuals who "got burned" on silver were those who bought at the peak of spot in December, 1979 and January, 1980. If they sold soon thereafter, amid the chaos and confusion of rapidly tumbling prices, they lost money — possibly a very great deal of it. If they had enough courage to *hold,* they still have the chance of making a profit. There is no guarantee that silver will ever get up around the $50 per troy ounce mark again, but there is also no valid reason to believe that it couldn't or wouldn't. Nothing has changed.

HOW THE SILVER MARKET OPERATES. Like other commodities, silver is freely traded in the financial centers of the world and "spot" prices are established for it as the result of this trading. The spot price is for one troy ounce of .999 fine silver. This is important to keep in mind. It is not for one ounce of *any other grade,* because lower grades — even the highly-respected Britannia used for top-quality flatware — are alloyed with basemetal to a greater or lesser degree. If, for example, the spot price is $20 per troy ounce and you have a full ounce of .925 sterling silver, you don't have $20 worth of silver. A deduction must be made for the proportion of alloy. We have provided formulas elsewhere in this book for calculating the values of alloyed silver, based on any spot price.

There isn't just one spot price but several of them, recorded by the various commodity exchanges of the world. The American spot price is achieved on the New York exchange, which operates Monday through Friday from 9 a.m. to 4 p.m. This price is used by many bullion brokers, scrap buyers and others in buying and selling. It may be referred to as "New York spot" or "New York close." When "New York close" is used, this can be taken to mean the price at close of trading (4 p.m., or slightly later if trading is heavy) on the *previous* day, or the *last business day* if a weekend or holiday has just occurred.

The closing price may be very different than the price at which the day's trading opened, or even quite different than the price just an hour before close. The figure changes almost constantly, though usually by small amounts, all throughout the trading day. This is an indication of the volume of buying and selling, just as with stocks and other investments that are traded on a public exchange. When the volume of buying exceeds the volume of selling, the price goes up. If there is extremely heavy buying the price will go up sharply, as brokers search frantically to find willing sellers to meet the demand. By the same token, when selling is very heavy, it is not possible for brokers to turn over (that is, resell) huge quantities as rapidly as they come in, and still maintain the same price. Thus, the price goes down; and if enough buyers do not appear, the price will go down further, until a leveling-off point is attained between buyers and sellers. When you have a great deal more of one than the other, the price will not hold steady.

Since the *London spot* is accepted as the standard for Europe and most foreign countries, U.S. brokers and dealers often refer to it, rather than New York spot. To avoid misunderstanding and confusion, the more responsible dealers do not switch back and forth between the New York and London spot but choose one or the other for their purposes and stay with it. By switching arbitrarily, it would be possible for the dealer to use whichever price was more favorable at the moment. The New York and London spot prices on bullion (silver as well as gold) are not the same. When New York closes as $23.76, London may be $23.41 or $23.98. This is because the volume is different, and the people doing the buying and selling are, largely, different also. But the two prices never get *very* far apart. You will not find silver selling for $25 in London and $20 in New York on any given day. Based just on buying and selling, this could conceivably happen; but it doesn't, because the two markets keep an eye on each other. So do the buyers and sellers. If the price starts getting appreciably higher in New York, people who would have sold on the London market switch their order to New York; and vice-versa. This drives the New York price down. If it appears that the market is being controlled, by the very close similarity in prices around the world, it *is* — but not by government. The control is placed upon it by its customers, including you if you invest in silver. It's the exact same kind of control that prevails in your neighborhood markets. When a product isn't selling, the price is reduced. When it's selling briskly, the price tends to go up. When one shop offers better terms than a competitor, it gets the business.

But, of course, the price of silver depends upon much more than simply what happens in New York and London, in a pair of commodity exchanges, between 9:00 and 4:00 five days a week. The spot price is, in a way, a reflection of what has occurred in the silver market *in the world at large,* because this (not just the daily spot) also has a tremendous influence on investors and industrial buyers. And this is not a 9-to-4 matter, but continuous, 24 hour a day, international in scope.

Some of the things that have an ultimate influence on silver prices are as follows. All of these make themselves felt in the "spot" price, because they determine to some extent whether buyers will be optimistic or pessimistic, cautions or cavalier (or, to use the Wall Street term, bearish or bullish). How quickly they have an effect is never easy to predict; it is often a matter of how rapidly investors learn of these developments, and the various details surrounding each particular case. Nor can it be flatly stated that bad news about silver, or something that could be bad for silver, always hurts investors. This just isn't so. Sometimes it can have the exact opposite result. The spot price can be driven down somewhat for a while, which allows silver to be purchased at a bargain rate. Then, sooner or later, good news comes to supplant the bad news (or perhaps the bad news is discovered to have been just a rumor anyway), the spot price rebounds, and those who bought during the slump are handsomely rewarded.

1. Gold prices. Of everything that happens or could happen in the world — economically, politically, or in any other way — the price of gold has the most direct influence on the price of silver. So far as fractional advances and declines are concerned, silver does not always rise when gold rises, nor always when gold falls. In checking the day to day spot, you will notice that some days one is up while the other is down. But these are the days of slow trading. Whenever a sizable movement occurs in the price of gold, a corresponding move is sure to follow in silver, usually immediately. Since gold is more heavily invested in than silver in terms of total cash value, it may be said that gold pulls silver along with it, up or down. When silver achieved its record price of $50 per troy ounce in January, 1980, gold was — at the same time — also at its record level. When gold began declining from that peak, silver declined with it.

This is not a modern phenomenon but has been happening throughout history, long before spot prices or any of the other present-day accourtrements of bullion trading. To show how closely the price of these two metals has been aligned throughout the ages, it was 13½-to-1 in ancient Greece (gold was worth 13½ times as much as silver), and 15-to-1 in 1792 when our Mint was established, a change of only 10% in nearly 2,000 years. Very little further change occurred until the past 10-15 years, when gold and silver began to be freely traded on the world market — not backed by currency as they had traditionally been. You will probably recall the "Silver Certificates," or notes which could be turned in for silver dollars. They were known as demand notes: the government guaranteed to pay their stated value in bullion on demand. Today, currency notes are not redeemable for anything, except what can be bought for them in the marketplace.

2. Bad economic news, such as inflation increasing, interest rates going up, gross national product going down, etc. But often these have a positive rather than negative effect on the silver market. They tend to discourage purchase of the more traditional forms of investment, and some of this money is diverted into silver.

3. U.S. balance of payments falling further in the red. This is always *good* for the silver market. It encourages foreign holders of dollars to dispose of them, and invariably some percentage of this wealth is exchanged for silver bullion.

4. War or threat of war. Usually good for bullion investment.

5. Discovery of new silver mines. Initial reaction is generally negative from investors, as this means more silver coming on the world market and the natural assumption that prices will either fall or not rise as rapidly as they might have otherwise. But such speculation is unfounded. It would be impossible to discover enough new silver mines, and to work them at minimal operation cost, to seriously effect the price of silver. Compared to the annual world production figures (more than 300 million ounces), new mines account for very little silver.

THE CRASH OF 1980

The story of silver from the late 1979 to early 1980 was one of a remarkable climb, far surpassing anything that the most optimistic analysts thought possible, followed by a resounding crash heard round the world.

In two months, the spot price of silver rose more than $30. Then, in a frantic two-week period of near-hysterical selling, it dropped $30.

There were those who predicted silver would hit $100 an ounce while it was climbing; it got half that far. There were others who felt it would totally bottom out when it was falling. It didn't.

And the silver market, though a little shaken, pulled through those two weeks of "spilled bullion" alive and fairly well. Since January, 1980, the market has firmed up admirably. No, silver isn't as high today as it was at its peak. But it's shown confidence-building strength, and a lot of investors who trembled at the mention of silver a year ago are now back in the market.

Sad to say, investors were largely to blame for upsetting the silver market. Not the ordinary cool-headed investors, but big-money operators who jumped in to get on the bandwagon. They poured millions into the market and drove prices up to vastly inflated levels, from which they had to fall. The sensible investor sees the dangers of this kind of action. He saw it in late 1979, but he was powerless to do anything about it. He was trampled by an army of financial goliaths.

At one point in December, 1979, the spot price of silver was jumping ahead by as much as *$5 per day.* Increases were so swift, and so hefty, that owners were able to sell, *at handsome profits,* silver they had just purchased a month earlier. Then, when wholesale profit-taking set in, prices fell back to saner levels.

Circumstances that caused the "rush" of late 1979 still prevail and in fact have grown more pronounced: there is *more* world inflation, *more* industrial demand for silver, *fewer* articles left to be melted to obtain bullion, and just as much investor lack of confidence in stocks and other traditional investments. But the silver market is looking particulary good these days, and nobody ought to be discouraged from silver investment because of the events of late 1979 and early 1980. Since then, well over a year ago, there have been no panics or runs on bullion. Silver has re-established its solidity as an investment by showing gradual but significant advances in price. It may well be on the threshhold of more substantial increases. If they occur in a more orderly fashion this time, without the influence of overnight profiteers and media madness, they may not be followed by a sharp readjustment.

Silver simply went up *too fast* in price in the second half of 1979, to levels that even ordinary buying and selling could not have supported over a long stretch of time. Had there been no profit-takers at all, the daily spot price would have still fallen (but slower, of course), until a level was reached that reflected the *true silver market.* We have, at present, such a level. We did not have it in December, 1979 or early January, 1980, because the people who normally control silver prices — industrial users, intelligent investors and the like — lost their grip on it, or rather had it wrenched away from them by big wheeler-dealers who gambled for quick profits.

When silver was around $50 per troy ounce in January, 1980, that kind of price could only have been maintained if scores of new investors kept getting into the market, on a daily basis, without anyone selling substantial amounts. The simple *leveling-off of investment buying,* regardless of whether any selling was occurring, would have been enough to drop prices. Silver suddenly became a hungry elephant that needed hundreds of pounds of food every day to keep his strength. Without the necessary food — investment dollars — his strength waned.

Some investors profited handsomely in the bullion spill. Others lost seriously. Everybody, even the new investor just starting out today, learned something.

SILVER BULLS — THE HUNT BROTHERS

In this day and age, with 300 million ounces of silver mined annually, with countless international investors pouring money into the silver market, it wouldn't be possible for a single family to have much influence on the rise and fall of silver prices, would it?

Of course not, except for three very intrepid, free-wheeling, big-spending brothers, the Hunts of Dallas, Texas.

Lamar, Bunker and Herbert Hunt, sons of the legendary Harold L. Hunt, one of the richest men of the 20th century, are known throughout the business world for owning bits and pieces of numerous corporate pies. Since 1979 they've made a series of headlines with their Croesus-like buying of silver. Not just silver bullion, but silver mines, royal rights on silver mines, silver refineries, silver trading companies, and other silver-related investments, to the point where nearly every scrap of silver passing through the American market has been touched by the hand of a Hunt somewhere along its route.

Nothing quite like it has ever been seen in the history of American business. What Ford was to the auto and Edison to the phonograph, the Hunts resolved to become to silver. The fact that they got a 5,000 year late start deterred them not at all. It just meant they had some catching up to do.

The whole thing started long before the headlines of 1979. Messrs. Lamar, Bunker and Herbert, but especially Bunker, were heavily into silver when it was not the chic thing to spend money on. The 300-pound Bunker's first major splash into the silver pool took place in 1973. Earlier that year, a $30,000,000 per year source of tax free income was snatched from him when Libya decided to nationalize oil wells owned by Bunker in that Arab country. Without the loss of oil income, Bunker and his brothers might — just might — not have ventured into silver.

They looked around for something that had the investment potential of oil but couldn't succumb to the game-playing of foreign dictators. Gold was out for the moment; U.S. citizens weren't allowed to own it. Silver, even though it was not exactly setting the world on fire in 1973, seemed the logical choice. Its price had been inching upward, year by year — not always keeping pace with inflation, but those turtle crawls showed promise of developeing into rabbit leaps. Industrial demand was increasing, and mining yield gave no indication of increasing along with it. Silver had been drained from U.S. coins for nearly ten years without killing the market. And if foreign investors (who were allowed to own gold) were going to dive headlong into gold, driving its price skyward, could silver be far behind?

It couldn't, so far as Bunker Hunt was concerned. He succeeded in convincing Herbert to join him in a 20-million-ounce dabble in the silver market, in December, 1973.

When word got out about that transaction, the silver market stood literally on its ear. The Hunts did not have a reputation for buying out of whimsy. There was little doubt that more orders would follow, and that if the Hunts were going really bullish on bullion it would encourage scores of other big-money operators to follow suit.

It was no coincidence that silver's market price started really firming up around that time. Other industries had likewise gotten healthy after doses of Hunt dollars.

The Hunts placed further orders and in early 1974 had contracts on 55 million ounces of silver, worth more than a quarter of a billion dollars. Thanks to the Hunts, silver peaked at a $6.70 spot price per troy ounce on February 24, 1974, the highest it had ever been. The bandwagon was starting to roll. It was estimated that in the Spring of 1974 the Hunt family owned more silver than any private individuals on earth — and more than most world governments. They weren't buying futures, either; they were taking delivery and paying cash, a total of about $160,000,000 in very cool U.S. funds. (The reason this figure wasn't higher was because the initial purchase of 20 million ounces was made at a spot price of under $3 per ounce).

Was silver a good investment? Were the Hunts overdoing things a bit? Their actions seemed more than exonerated, even to those who warned that the silver bug's bite could be fatal. Within two brief months, they had a paper profit on the initial 20 million ounces of about $60,000,000.

If those kinds of figures could be duplicated a few times, the Hunts stood to control most of the wealth in the Western World.

Storage costs on that quantity of silver bullion weren't cheap. The Hunts paid three million dollars per year to have it sequetered in Swiss bank vaults. Part of the reason for storing it in Switzerland was to escape a 4½ % franchise tax imposed in Texas. Also, Bunker believed Swiss banks were more impervious to assault than those at home.

It was said that if the Hunts managed to buy another 150 million ounces, making 200 or so in all, they would have effectively cornered the silver market. Estimates were that only 200 million ounces were available, worldwide, for delivery on future purchases.

But they made no immediate efforts to go after that other 150 million ounces.

In November, 1974, Harold L. Hunt, founder of the family dynasty and father of the Silver Bulls, died at age 85. A lengthy and much-publicized legal battle ensued to divide up the estate. Meanwhile the price of silver, deprived of further Hunt nourishment, slid to $4 per troy ounce. Just a few cents either way in the spot price meant a difference of millions of dollars for the Hunt holdings.

The Hunts, a little dismayed that silver wasn't moving the way it should, borrowed against their silver stockpile to get into other lines of investment. For the next several years they plotted various financial moves, using silver as the catalyst. One of the more ambitious of these was convincing Great Western, the sugar refiners, to go heavily into silver futures. But so far as big headlines in the silver market were concerned, the Hunts had still yet to make their biggest.

In 1977 the brothers became more convinced than ever that silver lay on the threshhold of a whopping price increase. They began their now-famous efforts to buy up as many silver mines as possible, in the U.S. and Canada, again using lines of credit secured from their Swiss bullion holdings. As the silver market had not experienced any serious setbacks in more than seven years, banks were more than willing to finance just about any proposal the Hunts laid before them. When it became evident that the brothers had made pacts with a number of very rich and very influential Arab oil magnates, and that the possibility existed of oil-for-silver trading, the credit coffers opened wide.

In the summer of 1979, the Hunts in partnership with Arab moguls established an international conglomerate: International Metals Investment Co. Ltd., with headquarters in tax-advantageous Bermuda. With Arab oil fortunes being poured into precious metal, there seemed nowhere for the price of silver to go but directly through the ceiling. And that was precisely what happened. International Metals Investment Co. Ltd. bought 90 million ounces of silver, the biggest single purchase on record. Silver was $10 per ounce, which worked out to $900,000,000. The cost was to be split between the Arab partners and the Hunts, each to put in $450,000,000. The Hunts didn't have $450,000,000, but banks gladly backed them. The First National Bank of Chicago laid out $233,000,000, Citibank of New York put up $17,500,000, and the New York branch of a Swiss bank made up the rest. Just what kind of interest the Hunts were to pay on those loans had never been made public.

In December, 1979, things looked like heaven on earth for the Hunts — for a while. They owned approximately 100 million ounces of silver and the price per ounce was near $35 — more than ten times higher than it was when they started their silver orgy six years earlier. In January, 1980, the spot price got close to $50 per ounce, meaning the Hunts were comfortably seated on about five billion dollars worth of bullion.

Then the tables began turning. Within three months, the splendid silver chariot had turned to a sour pumpkin. It all started when the Commodities division of the F.T.C. decided that the Hunts were in too deep; that they were courting disaster not only for themselves but the world market by buying on such colossal credit. It ordered that individual buyers would henceforth be limited to 10 million ounces of futures' contracts.

Then, in late January, 1980, somebody pulled the plug on silver prices.

Profit-takers came into the market and silver tumbled and shattered like the most fragile of china dolls. By March the readjustment brought spot prices down to the $15.-$18. range.

It was a double blow to the Hunts. They staunchly refused to part with an ounce. But the banks, to whom all those millions were owed, got edgy. On March 25, 1980, the investment brokers Bache & Co. of New York informed the Hunts that a $135,000,000 "margin call" had been made on them. In other words, they had to come up with that amount in cash. When they couldn't, the economic world was stunned.

Almost immediately a wholesale selloff of other Hunt holdings began, in order to pay the margin. Losses were catastrophic. In just two months, value of the Hunt holdings slid about three and a half billion dollars. Some observers put the figure closer to four billion. It was a minor point because the precise quantity of silver they owned was not disclosed.

Sadly, there was no choice but to sell and take a black-and-blue pasting. Even the stock market, which had little to do with silver, reacted when news of the brothers' plight broke. The Dow Jones averages nosedived.

The Hunts succeeded in securing a $1,100,000,000 debt refinancing loan, the money coming from a pool of U.S. banks, but only by agreeing to mortgage nearly everything they owned: property, cattle, parking lots, a bowling alley, and a long list of other items. The Wall Street Journal went so far as to report that Lamar's Rolex watch went in on the deal. Furthermore, the banks involved vowed not to approve any further commodity or stock buying by the brothers until 1990, when the loan is due to be fully repaid.

A crushing blow, maybe. But it didn't discourage Lamar, Bunker and Herbert from remaining bullish on silver. Within a few months silver was up again — not to pre-crash levels, but it was showing strength. And the Hunts, showing they were far from drydocked despite being put on the shelf by banks, were buying again. A pair of Canadian mining companies announced that the brothers bought major interests in their organizations. Terra Mining and Exploration Ltd. of Edmonton, Alberta, sold a 50% royalty interest to one of the many Hunt-run corporations (Procan Exploration Co. of Calgary) for 35 million Canadian dollars. The Hunts also spent $55,000,000 for large shares of mining and royalty interests in Cadillac Explorations of Calgary — a total of nearly 100 million dollars sunk into Canadian silver mining.

Though the average public shakes its head at stories of the Hunts' exploits, investment analysts can only reach one conclusion. If the Hunts, with their armies of advisors and sources of inside information, with their easy ability to invest fortunes in *anything, anywhere in the world,* choose to be bullish on silver, it's a pretty encouraging sign for silver investors everywhere.

Next time you hesitate before buying a roll of silver coins or a .999 bar, think about the Hunts.

ALL ABOUT SILVER INVESTMENT

Silver has become increasingly attractive for investment. Despite its availability for many years, silver began to interest large numbers of investors only in the 1970's. It could therefore be considered a relatively new area of investment. Prior to that time it appeared to offer few advantages to potential investors. It was available in very abundant quantities, with roughly 300 million ounces mined annually. It had not shown significant price increases, nor much indication that increases could be expected. During the seventies it rose like a phoenix from the ashes, leaving many persons scolding themselves for not buying it when prices were truly low.

It is unlikely under present conditions that the kind of profits realized by those who bought in the mid '70's, and sold in 1979 or early 1980, could be duplicated by anyone buying silver for investment today. In late 1976 silver was selling at a price of $4.30 per troy ounce. Therefore, 100 ounces could be had for $430 plus commission (dealer or brokeage fee). In late 1979/early 1980, the price was up to $45 per ounce, meaning those 100 ounces bought three years earlier could be sold for $4,500 (less commissions). The profit was close to 1,000% by holding for just three years. *Gold* was not even this profitable, for those who bought in late 1976.

For the same thing to occur today, with silver hovering around $20 spot, the price would need to rise to over $200 by 1984 or 1985. This does not appear a strong likelihood. However, the prospects are certainly attractive for making worthwhile gains on silver bullion in the present market, even if not as high as 1,000% in three or four years.

SILVER'S SKYROCKET. For decades it was believed that the world was amptly supplied with silver. But, just as happened with petroleum, the "never ending supply" did not prove sufficient to meet demand without prices sharply increasing. For many years the price of silver actually fell on the world market, because of increased output at the mines and introduction of cost-saving refining methods. In 1874, silver was traded at $1.27 per ounce on the New York exchange. It dropped under $1 in 1886 and by 1930 was down to a mere 38¢ per ounce. It fell further, to 34¢ in 1940, and even the heavy World War II use of silver did not succeed in hiking prices very much. The value in 1943, in the heart of the war, was just 44¢. This meant that silver dollars, which were struck up to 1935, contained less than half their face value in bullion, since the silver dollar contains just under one full ounce of .999 silver.

Silver looked like anything but a favorable investment, in those days.

Anyone who had Silver Certificates back then — U.S. currency notes, which could be exchanged for their face value in silver dollars — hesitated to change them in. They felt they had more going for them with a $1 paper note than a $1 face value coin, which contained only 40¢ or so of intrinsic value. Practically no Silver Certificates were turned in, and silver dollars all but disappeared from circulation in the 1940's.

Then, gradually, things began happening.

They happened so slowly and quietly at first that investors, who are usually alert enough to pick up any signals, did not wake up until very late. Even while silver was making price advances, during the 1950's and early 1960's, investors as a whole paid no attention. Their reasoning seemed sound enough, at the time. Silver was going up, but too slowly to arouse excitement. The increase from 1949 to 1950 was 71¢ to 74¢. By 1953 it was up to 85¢. In 1956 it was 90¢. Investors and investment counselors looked at it this way: based on its performance, and world conditions in the bullion market, there was every reason to believe silver would continue advancing in price. But with a 3¢ or 5¢ annual increase per troy ounce, the advance was not as impressive as that of many other kinds of investments, including common stocks. Percentage-wise, silver was gaining only about 6-8% yearly during the 1950's, just a shade ahead of the inflation rate. Banks were paying around 3½% annual interest on savings accounts in those days.

Since there was no commission fee for depositing money in a savings account, and none for withdrawing it, banking cash seemed just as good as putting it into silver.

Investors were looking for something with a potential of at least 10% per year, and silver just wasn't it. (Today, of course, with the rate of inflation so much higher, an investment than returns 10% annually is not attractive.)

In 1961 the spot price of silver edged over $1 per ounce for the first time since 1920. Maybe that should have made people sit up and take notice but it didn't. They looked at the percentages, and the percentages were not encouraging. The annual rate of increase was still low; in fact it was less than 1% from 1960 to 1961, and not many investors were anxious to put money into something that rose 1% in a year.

What they failed to realize was that silver bullion, as it inched up in price, was nearing the so-called *seignorage breaking point.* Seignorage is the difference between the Mint's cost in manufacturing coins and the total face value of those coins. If the Mint can strike $100 worth of coins for a total of $90 in materials and labor, it has a seignorage of $10. For years the seignorage on silver coins was running high — much better than on copper and nickel. But as the half dollar (the largest denomination silver coin struck in the early 1960's) contained slightly less than ½ ounce of silver, it could yield a seignorage only if half an ounce was purchasable for around 45¢, to allow for production cost. The Mint of course had abundant supplies of silver on hand, and the fact that silver jumped temporarily to $1 did not cause immediate problems. The general feeling was that it would readjust and go down somewhat, allowing our coins to continue at .900 silver composition.

Instead it went up further. In 1963 the price was $1.27 per ounce, which meant that our silver coins — all the way down on the dime — contained more bullion value than face value. It was impossible for the Mint to go on buying silver, to replenish its stockpiles, and maintain the same face values or compositions of its coins. Even if it could somehow succeed in doing this, the effort would be pointless; silver coins would simply go out of circulation, into the coffers of hoarders or refiners' furnaces.

In 1964 President Johnson signed a bill authorizing the removal of silver from our 10¢ and 25¢ pieces, to be replaced by a core of copper covered in nickel. Silver content of the half dollar was reduced but not eliminated until 1971. This gave them a silver appearance and retained the face values as well as sizes, though the weights changed somewhat. In terms of intrinsic value they fell drastically, and suddenly the Mint was earning the biggest seignorage in its history.

This single circumstance — a shot heard literally around the world — was the biggest "push" for silver up the investment ladder. But, oddly enough, many people interpreted it just the opposite at the time. The pages of investment publications were filled with stories that silver, thanks to the U.S. government, had been effectively destroyed on the world market.

They reasoned as follows. With this country switching to clad coins, other major nations would soon do likewise (some already had introduced substitutes for their silver coins). This would eliminate one of the major sources of silver consumption, and the price would have to go down.

True enough, other countries did discontinue silver coinage — though not all, and not all at once.

In 1968 the per-ounce of silver touched $2 for the first time in U.S. history.

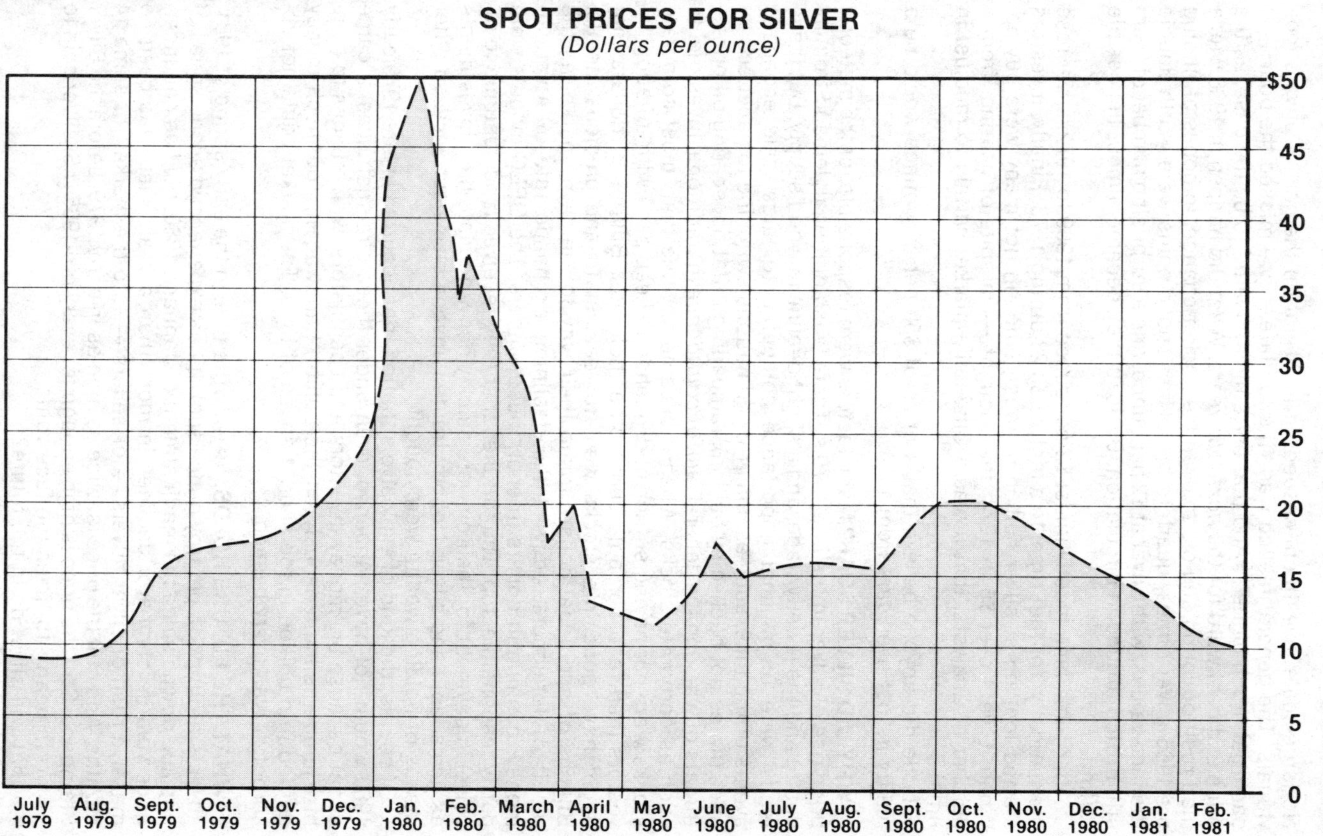
SPOT PRICES FOR SILVER
(Dollars per ounce)
$50
45
40
35
30
25
20
15
10
5
0
July 1979
Aug. 1979
Sept. 1979
Oct. 1979
Nov. 1979
Dec. 1979
Jan. 1980
Feb. 1980
March 1980
April 1980
May 1980
June 1980
July 1980
Aug. 1980
Sept. 1980
Oct. 1980
Nov. 1980
Dec. 1980
Jan. 1981
Feb. 1981

No large-scale investment ensued, at least not on the part of private individuals. The general feeling was "it's too late — we missed the boat — it can't get much higher." And that certainly appeared to be the case, as the price slid backward for the *next four years.* What did happen in 1968 was a mad rush of young and old to examine pocket change, in hopes of finding pre-1965 silver dimes, quarters or halves. Those coins were worth double the face values, with silver at $2 per ounce, and a surprising number of them still drifted around in circulation. By 1970 they became almost impossible to find.

After remaining mostly under $2 per ounce from 1969 to 1972, silver rose dramatically (for that time) to a high of $3.28 during 1973. Finally, investors started looking at silver bullion seriously, though not many were buying. When it went over $6 in 1974, they bought — in spite of hearing, from a number of analysts, that it was a Cinderella market certain to readjust in time.

Little did anyone believe that a price of $50 per troy ounce would be a reality in just five years from 1974.

WHY DID SILVER SOAR? Many factors were responsible for the meteoric price rise of silver in the late 1970's. There was additional demand from industry and the jewelry trade, and a slight decline in world supply. But these really were of minimal importance compared to large-scale economic events of the time, such as: major world nations switching to paper economies (notes not backed by bullion), rampaging inflation, soaring oil prices, threats of war, and the general *lack of confidence* in traditional investments such as corporate stocks. When it became obvious that most corporate stocks were not paying sufficient dividends to keep pace with inflation, investors (here and abroad) sought other holdings. Billions of dollars that might have gone into stocks went to real estate and precious metals. Billions of additional dollars found their way to the silver market as the result of foreigners, edgy at the declining exchange rate of American money, cashing in dollars in enormous numbers. The OPEC moguls were partly responsible, too. The fortunes that they received (and continue to receive) in payment for their oil were quickly converted into hard investments as gems, gold and silver. Nobody trusted anyone else's currency, so other means of holding wealth were sought.

Of course, the kind of explosive situation that occurred in late 1979/early 1980 would not have happened, even under these circumstances. It came about because big-money investors and speculators, with millions to gamble, jumped simultaneously on the bullion bandwagon. Too much money poured into bullion in too short a space of time. The market could not absorb it; it was overwhelmed.

WHAT THE FUTURE HOLDS. As we write this, in the early spring of 1981, silver is around $15 per troy ounce spot. It has experienced a long series of ups and downs since the readjustment of January, 1980, but has not undergone volatile climbs or declines in more than a year. There has been no massive rush of silver buyers — or sellers — into the market for some 14 months. And still the price is twice as high as in early 1979, before the Silver Stampede. Still the price is high enough for every pre-1965 U.S. silver coin to be worth nearly 15 times the face value.

What will silver do in the future?

It is, of course, impossible to make long-range predictions with any degree of confidence, but we now have a big "plus" over the investors of 1975 and 1976 — and even a bit later. Silver has now been an actively bought and sold investment commodity for nearly five years, and that provides us with a fair record to base future outlook upon. It is no longer in the class of a "sleeper" or a "possibility." Great fortunes have been made on silver by private investors, and the whole world now recognizes it as the very viable investment that it is.

The bullion market is very directly effected by world events. It reacts not only to economic news but news in general, because nearly everything of major importance that occurs in the world could eventually — if not immediately — influence prices of precious metals. It reacts to the raising and lowering of prime lending rates, wars and fear of war, oil prices, inflation, deflation, weakening and strengthing of currencies, import and export restrictions, balance of payments figures, political elections, and a great deal else.

As things stand today, world conditions are such that it would seem unlikely for silver to lose appeal as an investment.

Will the kind of $5-a-day skyrocket in silver prices, seen in late 1979, happen within the near future? The best guess is *no.* Will silver again get into the $45 and $50 per troy ounce range? All indications point to *Yes,* but this time the growth will probably be spaced over a longer period of time. If that happens, it will allow values to *stabilize as they rise,* discourage bandwagon buying by quick-buck profiteers, and eliminate the kind of dangers that investors faced in January, 1980. The very fact that silver is still being *heavily purchased* by investors more than a year after the 1980 crash is indication of world confidence in it. I personally firmly believe, based on our study of the market and various conditions affecting it, that silver will achieve levels of $45-50 within the not-too-distant future, and that a $100 per ounce spot price is a distinct possibility by mid 1982.

For silver to become a mediocre or questionable investment, a chain of events would be necessary that are so remore as to border on the impossible. Arab oil would need to get cheaper, or be so amptly supplemented by other supplies of oil that fuel costs drop dramatically. The United States and other major industrial nations would have to show a balance of payments surplus rather than a deficit. Currencies would need to stablilize in their relative values toward each other, so that holders of large blocks of foreign currencies here and abroad would trust them enough to keep holding them. Inflation would have to be reduced in the U.S. and western Europe. Nations would have to return to a policy of exchanging their banknotes for bullion on demand. All of this would need to happen, or show encouraging signs of happening, for investors to turn away from bullion. The odds on even some of this occurring within the next 10-20 years seem very, very remote. The likelihood is that conditions now prevailing will get worse, as this has been the trend for a number of years and seems beyond the ability of any single government to correct. If Arab oil gets more expensive, if world inflation touches 20% annually, if currencies become more erratic in their values, if balance of payments deficits grow larger and larger — bullion is certain to become more valuable than it is today. It will become more valuable under these circumstances even without the wild buying of speculators.

SILVER INVESTMENT IN THE REAGAN PRESIDENCY. Prior to the election of Ronald Reagan it was generally felt by most financial analysts that a Reagan Administration would be unfavorable for bullion investment, as opposed to another four years of the Carter Administration. Their logic was as follows:

President Reagan has often expressed a desire to return America to a bullion standard, probably gold, which would mean currency notes backed by gold and possibly those of low denomination backed by silver. Theoretically it could mean a return to gold and silver coins. The motive for such action is to control or possibly eliminate inflation, as the value of money would then be in direct proportion to the value of precious metals, rather than worthless paper whose value is set by inflation only. It would also presumably generate greater trust in U.S. currency abroad; foreigners would exchange their money for ours, knowing that it could be cashed in for bullion when and if desired, and the dollar might then become the strongest currency in the world (as it once was).

Whether or not this plan is feasible, and whether it would have serious effects on the silver investor if put into operation, deserve some comment.

To return to the system once employed, in which a $20 bill could not be exchanged for a $20 gold coin or a $1 note for a Silver dollar, is probably not workable under present conditions and is not likely to receive serious consideration. The values of bullion are not fixed any longer, and any attempt by government (ours or another) to fix them would not likely be successful. Instead it would probably be necessary to exchange notes for a certain amount of bullion, by weight, rather than a certain value. Whether this would cause economic chaos is questionable. This likelihood of Congress approving such a proposal, if one was ever made, seems doubtful. It would be risky, to say the least.

As for a return to silver and/or gold coins, that would appear even more remote under present circumstances. The silver coinage system is use up to 1964 could certainly not be resurrected, with the same values and compositions, as the face values would no longer be in line with metallic content. The 90% silver dime would now require a face value of anywhere from $15 to $20, or possibly higher. Silver *in small quantities* could be introduced to coins and retain the present values, but it would be an extremely minute amount (the fineness would need to be less than .100, against more than .900 of alloy). An even if that were done, the daily changes in silver values would make it impossible to maintain the face value of silver-content coins in line with market value. As soon as the coins got to be worht more for bullion than their face value, wholesale melting would occur and we'd have a collossal coin shortage, worse than in 1964. The solution (but one that might invite more problems than it solves) would be to strike coins without face values, containing so much silver per coin, which could be traded according to the daily spot price. Mexico did this with its "onza" in 1948, a silver coin containing exactly one ounce of .999 fine silver. It had no face value. Would this work in the U.S.? The odds are overwhelming against the success of such a project. Coins without face values would be an invitation to hucksters and con artists to cheat the more gulible members of the public. Debates would occur every time money was exchanged — and can you imagine waiting on line at a cashier's window, while a dozen people ahead of you debate the value of their coins?

Effects of the Reagan Presidency on the silver market are apt to be much less extreme than this.

Let's look at some of the more plausible possibilities.

1. The Republicans generally have success in bringing down the inflation rate (Ford got it to 6%). What would reduced inflation do to the silver market? On the surface it might seem a negative influence, as it could mean that other investments, now paying 15% or less return annually, could look more attractive. Actually it should prove a *bonus*. The newer investors now getting into the market cannot be expected to view silver the way it was appraised in the late 1970's, with potential for enormous yearly increases, but rather as a bluechip with staying power. If inflation comes down to around 8% or 7%, silver need only show an appreciation in the range of 15-20% annually to be attractive for a much greater number of people.

2. President Reagan may put an end to gold and/or silver ownership by U.S. citizens as a means of controlling inflation. This seems hardly likely. It was tried in the past (so far as gold is concerned) and failed miserably. The results today would be even worse. If U.S. citizens were prohibited from owning gold and/or silver in this country, there is little doubt but that they'd find a way to possess it abroad, through secret accounts and the like. This would mean countless billions of dollars flowing out of the country, as well as the need for a costly monitoring system on Washington's part to keep check on things.

3. A stiff transfer tax might be imposed on all bullion transactions. This would appear unlikely except in the case of extreme emergency, such as a 1930's style Depression.

CALCULATING YOUR PROFIT ON SILVER INVESTMENT. Profit calculation is not quite so simple a matter as comparing your cost against the current price. A number of other factors must be taken into account, for intelligent investment as well as profitable sale. It is wise to become familiar with these calculations before doing any hard investing, as you will likely become a sharper investor by doing so.

You must not think strictly in terms of spot price. First of all, there is commission to be considered, both in buying and selling, and depreciation (not of the silver, but of the money used to buy it). For an investment to be successful, it must show a greater profit after commissions and depreciation than could reasonably be expected to be realized from other forms of investment. Of course there is risk factor, too. Certain investments have the potential to show substantial profit but entail greater risk. Art and antiques (or certain classes of them) may be included in this category. A Picasso bought today for $200,000 could perhaps be salable in three years for $500,000. Increases of this sort have happened with Picasso paintings. But by the same token, it could sell for *less than* the $200,000 you paid. There is much more of a gamble with art, because the value of art depends to a large extent on current tastes and fads. Then, too, even tastes are right at which time of sale, there may be other circumstances against you. Anything which has *no intrinsic value* — including money — has to be regarded as a more dangerous investment than bullion, though the profit potential could be very great.

Your cost in investing in silver is the spot price on the day of purchase plus the dealer's or broker's commission. These commissions vary depending on what kind of silver you buy and the amount of purchase; they may also vary according to where you buy. But for sake of simplification, we'll say the commission on a purchase is 8%.

Therefore, if you buy 100 ounces when the spot price is $20, you've spend $2,000 for silver plus $160 commission = total cost $2,160.

Also for sake of simplification we'll say that the handling charge when you sell is 12% (this, too, varies quite a bit). If you sold immediately, you would get $20 per ounce or $2,000 with $240 deducted = $1,760. In other words you would be buying and selling the silver for the same price, but you'd lose $400 because of the commissions.

O.K., let's carry that a little further.

But first a word about commissions and handling charges. There are inevitable whenever you buy or sell silver. There is no way of escaping them. If it were not for handling charges, the people sold an ounce of silver for $20 when the spot price was $20, and charged no commission, he would be losing money (on cost of operating). Obviously, dealers are in business not just to meet their expenses but to show a profit. The commission charge varies depending on the kind of silver involved. When you sell .999 ingots or bars the amount deducted from what you receive is rather small, compared to selling bullion items such as pre-1965 U.S. coins or other silver meltables. This is because the dealer nearly always passes along bars and ingots to other investors, just as they come. With melt articles he's selling chiefly to refineries, which buy from him at a discount from spot. Therefore he has to discount further to allow for the refinery's profit as well as his own.

If you do not compute this handling or commission charge into the cost of your investment, along with the percentage paid when selling, you will not be able to gauge the investment's progress.

We'll say that you bought 100 ounces at $20 per troy ounces spot and paid, as stated in the example above, $2,160. This is the total of your investment, $2,160, not $2,000. All accessory costs of an investment must be included with it; that $160 is tied up just as much as the $2,000 principal that went for the actual bullion.

To sell at a profit buying at $20 per ounce, even if you solf immediately, the price would need to climb to $25.

This is why silver should not be viewed as a short-term investment. You could, of course, enter the market on the threshold of a fast substantial price jump, and in that event it would certainly be possible to sell at a profit within a short space of time. But generally speaking you should depend on holding bullion for several years and possibly longer. Remember that a bullion investment does not pay dividends. It realizes a profit only when sold; you cannot hold it and make money from it at the same time. It is therefore essential that your timing be right, so far as buying and selling are concerned, especially selling. It may be extremely tempting to sell when the spot price has advanced $4 or $5 over the figure at which you bought, but this is not likely to be profitable *at all* unless you are operating with very small commission charges.

Paper profit and actual profit are two different things and are influenced by a number of factors, the most important of which is the *buying power of money.* If there was no such animal as inflation, even a very modest annual gain would be satisfactory. As things stand, you're losing money (not actual money but its buying power) if your investment does not move ahead faster than the rate of inflation, and if the investment fails to yield a greater profit when sold — with cost deducted — than the rate of inflation.

Very few investments that offer any degree of security fill that bill. Many pay a higher rate of return than a simple savings account or bank certificate, but when figured against the rate of inflation they acutally show a loss. When inflation is 10% annually, the average investment was to gain a minimum of 20% per year to be ahead of inflation. In seven of the past ten years, silver has increased in price by double the inflation rate or better. Its average increase has been considerably better than 20% annually, while inflation during the past ten years ran around 10%.

Let's take the above example and translate it into cost vs. inflation terms. Of course we'll have to rely on very arbitrary figures, but his will at least demonstrate how to do the arithmetic.

Say that inflation is 10% per year over the next five years. After the first year, the buying power of that $2,200 you invested is down to $1,980. After the second year it falls to $1,782. The it hits $1,604. And so on. This means, in effect, that even if you sold the same 100 ounces of bullion after three years and got the price you originally paid — $2,200 — you would really only be getting $1,604. You would have $2,200 but it would buy only what $1,604 bought three years earlier. You would have a paper profit but not an actual profit.

This is a vital to keep in mind, in order to avoid selling too soon. The only way a billion investor can realize a fast profit is if the market shoots up very quickly. It would need to rise at least 30% in a single year to make this possible. Obviously, it sometimes rises much more than 30%. The 1979 increase (January to December) was in the vicinity of 400%.

AM I SAFE BUYING SILVER? If you mean, by "safe," will anyone come to your rescue in the event of falling prices, the answer is: no. As with nearly all other commercial investments, silver is not guaranteed by the government or by an insurance agency. No one can say that you take no risk. But if you buy wisely, watch the market, and are not in too great a hurry to sell, the risk in silver investment is less *compared to the potential returns* than with at least 90% of corporate stocks.

HOW TO BUY. Your investment in silver should be measured against your overall financial resources, as well as your debits and goals for the next 5 to 10 years. Among the factors to be considered are: how much cash are you approximately going to need in the coming years, to maintain or improve you present lifestyle, and what are the possible sources for this cash. Are they a sure thing or "iffy"? Will you be retiring? Do you have retirement-fund plans set up? When will you home be fully paid off? What will its market value be in 5 or 10 years? What about your other holdings? To determine the sensible amount of money to invest in silver bullion, you really need to make a balance sheet on your assets and liabilities. This will determine what percentage of your holdings are liquid and available for investment.

So far as the small investor is concerned, he should be careful not to plunge too deeply. Remember that cash put into bullion is tied up until the bullion is sold. If you buy too heavily, leaving yourself a dangerously small cash reserve, you will be defeating your own purpose. Very often in these instances the individual needs to raise money in a hurry for some unexpected purpose, and is compelled to sell a portion of his investment. Naturally in a "forced sale" you lose money, sometimes a great deal of it. Don't invest more cash then you can safely "forget about" for the next five years or longer. By all means, don't get caught up in bandwagon investment rushes. In late 1979, many people, reacting to media coverage of the bullion stampede, sold their homes, cars, emptied their bank accounts, and poured every penny they could lay hands upon into gold and silver. This isn't investing. It's gambling, with the odds stacked very much against you. Keep a level head, no matter what the public at large is doing, and your chances of coming out a winner are very favorable.

There is no need to do all your investment buying in a single purchase. It usually makes more sense to go slow at first, taking perhaps 1/3rd or less of your available investment capital and putting it into bullion. Further purchases can be made when they seem appropriate. Depending on your personal circumstances, you may decide that some of that investment capital is better put to other uses.

There is no "best time" to buy silver. The obvious answer would be: when prices are lowest, but it is impossible to determine on any given day, even if prices appear very favorable, whether they will be higher or lower tomorrow or next week. Seasoned investors do not wait for the market to go down. There is much to be said for buying during periods of confidence when the spot price has shown steady if not remarkable advances over a long stretch of time. Steady advances over a period of months are frequently followed by sharper short-term increases, since investor confidence is built and more are willing to buy. By the same token, not too many holders will *sell* when advances are small and steady, so there is not much danger of small increases being followed by substantial declines. Historically, big declines follow big advances — in bullion as in all other investments.

ARE SOME KINDS OF SILVER MORE FAVORABLE FOR INVESTMENT THAN OTHERS? The answer to this one has to be an evasive "yes" and "no." Silver bars and ingots would seem to be the most advantageous method of investing in silver, since the finenes is marked and these items are bought by dealers and brokers at a minimal discount from the spot value. The difference, however, in buyer's commission from bars and ingots to bullion coins is not very substantial, however, and coins can often be *bought cheaper* then bars since the refinery's manufacturing cost and profit are not added on. The cost of manufacturing coins was absorbed long ago by the Mint and is not passed on to investors. You may think that coin silver isn't as good bullion-wise as bars and ingots. The fineness of bars is .999 while coins are .900. However this really makes no difference, because when you buy bullion coins you pay only for the silver content. The price is figured on the weight of silver they contain, not taking the alloy into account. Therefore, one ounce of silver is the same as one ounce of bar silver (so long as the person making the sale is reputable.)

Bars, ingots and coins are probably the most attractive forms of silver bullion investment. Of course there are numerous other ways to buy silver as well. Any article made of silver or containing some silver in its composition can be purchased as a bullion investment, and occasionally bargains are to be encountered with silver scrap. If you know how to buy, it is possible to comb through antiques and secondhand shops and find silver-content items selling below the daily spot price (in terms of the quantity of .999 silver they contain). There are tens of thousands of such objects awaiting purchase at flea markets, garage sales, etc., all over the country. Many of these are offered for sale by persons unaware that the items contain silver, or the quantity or fineness of content; or they may simply not be informed about the current value of silver and are pricing ther merchandise based on some outdated guide or what they paid ten or 15 years ago. Tableware is among the most often encountered of this type of material. In the 1950's and 1960's antiques dealers were discounting table services, as modern public taste did not run to Victorian and Edwardian patterns. Even though they raised their prices in the 1970's, knowing that silver was getting more valuable, many of them failed to *continue increasing* when silver went to $10 to $15 to $20 and onward.

So you can possibly, by scrounging, make quite a few good buys in this manner. But unless you have a great deal of time, personal knowledge of silver and antiques, and some luck, this is not the best way to build an investment portfolio. For one thing, much of what appears to be good silver or heavy silver in the secondhand shop really isn't. You will come across many weighted items, such as candelabra with cement poured into the bases, and quiet a few Engligh antiques made of "Bath metal" — which looks to the untrained eye like silver but actually contains only about 1/3rd of 1% silver. This metal, used extensively for medals in the late 1700's and early 1800's, was also employed in making various trinkets and novelties that show up without end on the secondhand market.

Unless you can be your own expert, which is very difficult for a beginner, investing by "scrounging" is probably best bypassed.

Silver with a fineness rating of less than .800 should not, as a rule, be considered for investment. Even if you could purchase an article containing ½ silver and ½ basemetal for the value of its silver alone, it would not be very attractive for investment because there might be a problem selling it. Remember that bullion brokers, scrap dealers and the like have a definite preference for *marked* articles and it is unusual for silver with a grade lower than .800 to be marked. Even if you have personally carried out tests on an object (such as discussed elsewhere) to determine its exact silver content, the dealer will sometimes only buy unmarked silver at a discount from he value you have determined it to be. He doesn't want to perform all those tests an pays a lower price just to protect himself.

The best silver for investment is that in which the object is either marked or can be readily graded without need for testing, such as coins (nobody can attempt to tell you that Morgan or Peace dollar contains less than .900 fineness). *It is also essential that the item can be easily weighed.* Even if something is marked .925 (sterling), this does little good if it happens to be welded or otherwise attached to non-silver components and cannot be weighed without dismantling. Manufacturers of dinner forks, knifes and spoons in the 1800's and 1900's were serious offenders in this regard. Obvious they did not anticipate that their creations, which they sold proudly as decorative objects of art, would eventually end up in the smelter's pot. When a knife or fork has a bone or wooden handle, or when the handle is silver but the blade is stainless steel, this presents problems in weighing. In such situations most scrap dealers will either refuse to buy or will discount the price sufficiently to totally protect themselves in case the quantity of silver comes up short. They have no choice but to do this, since the refineries take the same approach when buying from them. Refineries would rather not purchase this type of material at all, since it's a nuisance for them for cut apart or otherwise dismantle it. They do so simply because it would be difficult to meet their volume needs without buying miscellaneous scrap.

Coins are an attractive bullion investment. You need not know anything about coin collecting or numismatics to buy bullion coins for investment. They aren't sold by date or mintmark or any of the considerations important to collectors, but strictly on the basis of face value vs. spot value. Bullion coins comprise all common date or circulated .900 fine silver U.S. coins, ranging in date from the late 1800's to 1964 (the last year that silver .900 fine silver coins were struck). Denominations are 10¢, 25¢, 50¢ and $1. It makes no difference for investment purposes whether you buy dimes or silver dollars. You get more silver with the higher denomination coins but the price you'll pay, ounce for ounce, is precisely the same no matter what denominations are involved. If you buy $1,000 worth of bullion dimes from a dealer, you will get the same amount of silver as if you buy $1,000 worth of silver dollars. There is no advantage in one kind of coin over another, either in buying or selling. We are using $1,000 as an example because the much-advertised "bags" of bullion coins contain $1,000 in *face value.* Their selling price is, of course, much more than $1,000, since the spot price of silver is considerably more than when these coins were struck.

When the time comes to sell, bags of U.S. silver coins can be disposed of with a minimum of fuss. The commission on them is generally about 15% of spot, but this varies so much that it would be wiser for you to check commission charges in your area than to depend on any figure we could name.

FROM DUST TO DUST. Without the scrap market — maybe an unbecoming word, but it'll do until a better comes along — investment in silver would be impossible. The simple fact is that demand for silver, by industry, far exceeds the totals yielded by the world's silver mines. The only way this demand can be met is via recycling: removing silver from old or unwanted articles and preparing it for reuse. This is done by refineries. Each year, refineries in the U.S. (where more scrap silver is recycled than anywhere else in the world) take in tons of scrap silver in every conceivable form, process it to remove the alloy material when necessary, and make it into .999 bars. This is a continuing, never-ending process. Dealers in scrap silver are among the refineries' sources of supply. Whatever the scrap merchant buys from the public is, usually turned over to the refineries. The price paid by the refineries to the scrap dealer depends on the current spot price, unless the supplier has a contract arrangement whereby he supplies a certain quantity of silver at an agreed-upon price. Therefore the price he pays when buying from the public is also controlled by the daily spot.

Coins are technically scrap silver, though it may be hard to think of them in such terms. When bought by a dealer they are customarily sent away for melting. Millions of dollars in face value of old silver coins are melted every year.

JEWELRY. Jewelry is not an attractive means of bullion investment. Jewelry is chiefly .925 fine and when purchased there is often a surcharge added for workmanship.

WHEN TO SELL. Just as there is no ideal time to buy, there is no perfect time to sell. If you have kept a record of your investment purchases plus commissions, as well as a record of spot prices and the inflation rate, you know exactly *when* you can sell for a profit. Whether or not you *should* sell, when the opportunity for a profit presents itself, is another matter. This will depend on your circumstances as well as the silver market at that moment. If there appears to be a strong and dependable upward swing under way, it would not be advisable to sell all your holdings at the first sign of a profit opportunity. Very likely the profit will increase in the coming weeks and months, and you would be better to dispose of a small portion of your holdings or none at all in the meantime.

Once the spot price has advanced to a level where you have a paper profit, taking commissions and inflation into account, you are in a very flexible position. And you should *take advantage of that position* without becoming too anxious for actual profits. For example, say the spot price advances to a point where you would gain 20% over costs-plus-inflation in selling (if that sound modest it isn't; 20% counting inflation is real money). You now have the opportunity to watch the spot quotations day by day, to discover if the upward trend will continue, stabilize, or possible readjust. If the upward advance has been gradual — not accomplished in a couple of weeks of frantic buying — the odds are strongly in favor that any readjustment, if it occurs, will also come gradually, with plenty of warning. Should the price fall a dollar or two, you have then the option of selling — still at a profit — or awaiting still further developments. You will not lose by taking a profit. Do not expect to beat the market, or to gain maximum advantage of silver's optimum highs and lows. Not even the most skilled investors can do this consistently, with silver or any other investment, simply because there is too much uncertainly about future developmens. If you take a profit, you've made a successful investment.

THE GOLD AND SILVER GLOSSARY

ALLOY

(a) To alloy a precious metal is to introduce a quantity of another metal into it. Gold may be alloyed with base metal or with silver.

(b) The metal used for alloying is referred to as "alloy."

ANNEAL, ANNEALING

To heat metal until it becomes soft enough to work into desired shapes, or to receive stamped designs (such as in coin striking). Degree of annealing varies depending upon the metal's use, as some uses call for greater softness than others. Gold, being naturally soft, requires less annealing that other metals.

ASSAY

The official determination, by a licensed annayer, of the bullion content in an object (usually a gold or silver bar). The assaying of metal requires testing that includes a measurement of its weight by specific gravity.

AQUA REGIA

A chemical widely used in the jewelry industry, especially for testing the fineness of gold. Agua regia is made of three parts hydrochloric acid and one part nitric acid.

BALANCE SCALE

A scale operating solely by the balance principal, rather than by springs or the use of a sliding weight. It consists of two pans suspended on hangers, connected at the top to a horizontal bar containing a pivot at the center. When empty, the pans are at precisely equal distance from the ground. For weighing, the object(s) to be weighed are placed in one pan, and counterweights of established weight in the other. The object(s) weight is determined by the weight of counterweights needed to precisely balance it.

BASE METAL

Catch-all term used to refer to all non-precious metals, such as copper, zinc, nickel, led, etc. These are the metals used in alloying gold, silver and platinum.

BRICK

A gold brick, also known as bullion bar, weighs 1,000 troy ounces, or approximately 68.5 pounds.

BRITANNIA SILVER.

A high grade of silver, consisting of 95.84% pure silver and 4.16% alloy. Its use is chiefly for tableware and decorative articles. The hallmark is a likeness to Britannia, symbol of the British Commonwealth.

CLIPPING

A once-prevalent method of criminally acquiring bullion, by trimming small portions from coin edges and then passing the coins at their face value. This occurred in the days of hammered coins, whose edges were not perfectly symmetrical.

COIN SILVER

A grade of silver whose content is .90 fine, or 90% pure silver and 10% alloy (usually copper). The term arose because the majority of U.S. silver coins have about this composition. However, many foreign silver coins vary in composition. It should not be presumed, as it sometimes mistakenly is, that coin silver is made from melted coins. It could be, but it can just as well be manufactured from other silver and alloy.

CORROSION

The discoloration or patina to which old, neglected (not regularly polished) silver can fall prey results from acids or oxides acting upon chemical properties in the metal. It can generally be removed or at least diminished, by treatment with common solvent (silver cleaner). However, in the case of collectors' items hundreds of years old, such as coins or religious objects, experts generally advise against its removal.

DEVALUATION

A currency rather than a metals term, but as devaluation directly influences bullion prices it seems worthy to include. Devaluation is an action by a government to reduce the exchange rate of its currency against currencies of other nations. The opposite of devaluation is *re*valuation — raising the exchange rate. Devaluation is generally resorted to when a nation's balance of payments (that is, amount of money flowing out of the country as opposed to coming in) is in serious deficit. The devalued currency buys less abroad and therefore discourages importation of foreign goods; at the same time, foreign buyers are encouraged to export the country's products, as they become available cheaper. Whenever the currency of a major world nation is devalued, gold rises in value. This is because holders of that currency lose faith in it and exchange it for other investments, gold being prominent among them. Today most world currencies "float" rather than trade at a fixed rate, and are not subject to official devaluation. When they lose value it is because they have failed to show strength against other currencies.

DICHROMATE

A chemical solution used for testing the composition of metal article. Dichromate is composed of potassium dichromate and nitric acid.

ELECTRUM

A natural mixture of gold and silver, from which the earliest true coins were made (those of the Lydians of Eastern Asia, in the 7th or 8th century B.C.).

FILE MARK

A recessed mark left upon an object as the result of filing, to test its metallic content. File marks are occasionally found on gold coins, tested for the possibility of being counterfeit. They also appear on items that proved to be of low bullion or non-bullion content, as the majority of tested objects found to be of solid gold or silver are sent for melting.

FINENESS

The degree of purity in an object of precious metal, usually expressed by hundredths in decimal form (such as .995, which means 99½ parts pure and ½ part of alloy). It may also be written in terms of a percentage; in the case of the example given, the percentage equivalent would be 99½%. The highest degree of obtainable fineness in gold or silver is expressed as .999 +, rather than 1.000, because of the impossibility of guaranteeing that all minor traces of incidental metallic substances have been removed.

GERMAN SILVER

Low quality silver, containing a high proportion of nickel alloy.

GOLDBEATERS'S SKIN

24K gold hammered or rolled into extremely thin sheets, used for various kinds of artistic decoration (such as leather tooling). Dates to the time when laborers who hammered gold were called "goldbeaters." One of the remarkable properties of gold is that it can be flattened to extraordinary thinness without becoming overly fragile.

GOLD FILLED

Gold filled articles are similar to plated: they have an exterior of gold and a core of base metal, usually copper. The difference is in the method of application. Plated objects are shaped and then bullion-coated by electroplating, in which the soft gold takes the object's form. Gold filled merchandise is made from sheets of metal to which the outer covering of gold has been applied before the object is shaped.

GOOD DELIVERY

The name applied to gold bars weighing 400 ounces, bought and sold among banks and other financial institutions and often among nations. The purity of good delivery bars is .995, meaning they contain 99½% or 24K gold, the remaining ½% being base metal not removed in refining. These bars can be and sometimes are melted for commercial use but generally held intact as investment or trading pieces. Private individuals are permitted to own them, and in fact are encouraged to do so if their available cpaital for gold investment is sufficiently high. A smaller premium or brokerage fee is charged on good delivery bars, dollar for dollar, than when buying smaller quantities of gold.

G.P.

When found on an article that appears made of gold, these letters indicate that the gold is merely surface plating (G.P. = gold plated).

HALLMARK

A decorative marking sometimes (but not invariably) found on foreign made silver articles, indicating that the metal is of sterling quality or higher. The origin of the word hallmark dates to the later Middle Ages of England, when silversmiths were members of the Guildhall.

KARAT

The method by which fineness of gold is expressed. Pure unalloyed gold is 24 karat. As alloy metal is added (usually copper, for strength or to reduce the price), the karat value declines: 22K, 20K, 18K and so on. The lowest grade of gold to carry a karat marking is 10K, or, in Great Britain, 9K. Most gold coins are 20K or 21K. Jewelry is commonly made of 12K to 18K. The word "karat" derives from the carob bean, used as a measure of weight in the ancient world. When spelled "carat" it refers to the *weight* of a precious gem and has nothing to do with fineness.

MELT VALUE

The bullion value of any object containing precious metal. When sold for melting, the full price of an item's bullion content is not received but only a percentage of it. Some articles, such as gold or silver coins of key dates or mintmarks, have a higher retail or "intact" value than melt value and obviously should not be melted.

PANNING

The technique of recovery of gold particles from streams or river beds, practiced widely by prospectors in the rush of '49 and to a lesser extent in South Africa in the 1870's. Gravel and small rocks are scooped into a pan along with water. After shaking, the upper layers are poured away. Gold, being heavier than common rock or other minerals, will settle on the pan bottom.

PLATING

The covering of base metal articles with a layer of gold or silver, which may be of various thicknesses and grades. Presence of plating may be discovered by filing and using nitric acid, or subjecting the item to specific gravity testing.

PRECIOUS METAL

The three primary precious metals are gold, silver and platinum. All others (except derivities of these three) are known technically as "base metal." Of course, the preciousness of precious metals varies, as does the baseness of base metals.

PURITY

The proportion of precious metal in an object vs. base metal. A purity of .900 would mean a content of 90% precious metal and 10% base metal alloy, or a ratio of 9-to-1.

REEDING

The faint impressed lines, running vertically from reverse to obverse, found on the edges of many coins struck by machinery. The original purpose of these lines was to discourage clipping, or removing minute portions of metal from the edges and then passing the coin at face value.

SCRAP
Material made of or containing precious metal, which has no value beyond that of its bullion content and is suitable only for melting. Old spectacle frames containing gold are an example of typical scrap.

SOLID
When an object is referred to as solid bullion, this means it is not plated or filled but that its interior composition is identical to its exterior. No inference can be drawn, however, merely on strength of such evidence that the bullion is either heavily or lightly alloyed. "Solid gold" is not necessarily 24K.

SPECIFIC GRAVITY
A method of testing the composition of metallic objects, which measures their displacement of water in relation to their bulk. Each metal element has an established specific gravity.

SPOT PRICE
"Spot Price" is the price at which precious metal is being traded at any given time. Spot prices are always calculated on the basis of one full troy ounce and must be multiplied or divided to arrive at prices for larger or smaller quantities. The spot price is achieved in day to day trading in gold markets, just as are prices for stocks and other commodities. Generally, the London spot is used as the world barometer, after conversion from pounds to dollars.

TOLERANCE
The amount of difference permitted by law between the karat marking on a gold article and the actual fineness of gold it contains. Tolerances up to one full karat are allowable, depending on circumstances (such as whether solder has been used in manufacture.) Tolerances are permitted *only* on craft or other manufactured items, not on bars or ingots.

TOUCHSTONE
A stone, of basalt or slate, used in testing gold to determine its karat. Touchstones are used in combination with testing needles and aqua regia.

DIAMONDS

THE HISTORY OF DIAMONDS

The early history of diamonds is so poorly documented that any recitation of it becomes glutted with such words as "maybe," "possibly," "perhaps" and the like. What we know as fact is about 1% of what we would like to know, so far as diamonds in ancient Greece, Rome, the middle ages and early Oriental civilizations are concerned. It is also far less than we *should* reasonably expect to know, because our predecessors left much better information about their uses of other materials (such as gold and silver).

When researching any topic with so lengthy a history as diamonds, the source for information about the ancient world is usually the writings of classical authors and/or pictures left behind on pottery, tomb walls and the like. These tell us little about diamonds. Nowhere in the Old Testament are diamonds mentioned. We can pretty safely guess that diamonds were unknown in that part of the world where most activity of the Old Testament occurred, though this does not rule out the possibility of their being known in India or Persia. That compilers of the scriptures were unfamiliar with diamonds can be deduced by a passage in Ezekiel, in which flint is given as a synonym for hardness ("As an adamant harder than flint I have made thy forehead.")

It would be reasonable to further conclude that the Greeks became acquainted with diamonds only after their expeditions into western India, beginning in the 4th century B.C. Diamonds were unquestionably being worn in India by then, and it is quite likely that the Greeks — or the Carthagenians, to be more precise — brought home collections of these baubles. The question of whether the Egyptians had access to African diamonds is of long-standing debate. Egypt is, of course, located on the African continent, but is several thousands of miles from the chief modern sources of diamonds. Could the Egyptians have penetrated that far into the Dark Continent? Might they have established trade connections with the natives and thereby purchased diamonds brought by the local tribespeople up along the coasts? Did the black native Africans even know that an Egypt existed? (Egyptians knew of the African tribes, as quite a few of their members were recruited into servitude in Egypt as early as 3,000 B.C.) Or — a less likely but intriguing possibility — might the Egyptians have taken diamonds from northern African sources whose locations are now forgotten?

We just don't know.

There are some snatches of ancient writings pertaining to diamonds. Oft-quoted (because there is so little else to quote) is the statement in Pliny's "Natural History," compiled in the 1st century A.D.: "These stones are tested upon the anvil and will resist to such an extent as to make the iron rebound and the very anvil split asunder."

That made good copy, but it was just an example — common for that time and especially common for Pliny — of authors making statements that could not be backed up. Apparently, Pliny had heard of the hardness of diamonds. He must have misunderstood and confused surface hardness, or resistance to scratching, with the power to withstand crushing. A diamond, if placed upon an anvil and pounded as Pliny describes, will not remain in one piece very long.

It is interesting to note that the word of Pliny was for many years taken on trust, and that until the Renaissance uninformed persons continued to "test" diamonds by hammering them, with the result that they were soon in possession not of diamonds but diamond dust.

It is further stated that this old belief came into handy use by unscrupulous persons, who would offer to test diamonds by splitting them. When the diamond split, they dourly informed its owner that it was only some worthless material and discarded it into their trash box (from which the pieces were later retrieved).

THE ORIGINS OF SOUTH AFRICAN DIAMOND MINING

It is not known whether diamonds were found in South Africa in the ancient world. They could possibly have been, as the Greeks colonized a large portion of that continent and had ample opportunities to explore the southern region of it. If the Greeks did no actual diamond mining themselves, they might possibly have acquired African diamonds from natives with whom they traded. Of this we can only speculate. We know that diamonds were known and used (and prized) by the Greeks and Romans, but all of their diamonds may have come from India or elsewhere in Asia.

Certainly, no mining was being done in Africa until the age of British and other modern colonization. If it had been known to the ancients that Africa contained diamonds, this knowledge was forgotten for long ages. Even the early colonists who drove deep into Africa, to the very Cape, knew nothing about the continent's diamonds. They walked over diamond-laden deposits and drove their caravans over them without the slightest idea that untold riches lay beneath the soil.

The modern discovery of African diamonds occurred in 1866 in the so-called Orange Free State, a crown colony. A young boy was strolling along the Orange River's banks when he spotted, lying upon the surface, a rough stone weighing more than 21 carats. After cutting it weighed 10.73 and was dubbed the Eureka diamond, because this was supposedly the exclamation uttered upon its discovery. Later it became better known as the O'Reilly, this being the name of an Irish trader who bought it. Mining operations did not begin immediately. Nor did the news of this find send waves of prospectors to the area. But the next one did.

In 1869, three years later, a much bigger stone was found, weighing 83½ carats. Its discoverer was also a youth, and the location was not far from where the Eureka had turned up. This time the finder was a shepherd boy. The diamond was called the Star of South Africa; it yielded a cut stone of 47.75 carats.

A 21 carat gem might have been brushed aside; but diamonds as big as 83½ carats make news. Very shortly the Orange Free State became invaded by waves of lookers and diggers, who combed the river sides and the gulches and the gullies. It was estimated that in 1870 some 10,000 people were panning in the Orange River, trying to discover diamonds amid the silt and gravel. Their rate of success was not high.

But that was just the beginning. New gem-bearing locations were found, at Dutoitspan and Bultfontein. Then in 1871 they turned up on a farm owned by the DeBeers family. Yes, this is how the DeBeers came to be connected with diamonds. They were Dutch settlers to the region, like thousands upon thousands of others, who subsisted on farming. Suddenly they found that their land produced something far more valuable than vegetables.

When scientists were brought in and more sophisticated methods started to be used, it became apparent that the extent of diamond deposits was much greater than had been imagined. Those previously found at the surface in river mush were just stragglers, compared to what could be recovered by mining. African diamonds were found to occur in kimberlite pipes. These are natural formations of rock roughly resembling long geodes, with hard crusts and crystal-bearing interiors. The problem was not just to find the kimberlite pipes but to find the right ones, as many contained no diamonds or so few that it wasn't worthwhile mining them. Huge pipes were located in the Transvaal in 1902, another British colony. Mining operations there produced the Cullinan diamond a few years later.

DIAMOND MINING TECHNIQUES

Diamonds are rather more difficult to mine than gold. They tend to occur at greater depths beneath the earth's surface and within pipes of solid rock, which renders most conventional mining techniques useless. Moreover, diamonds are extremely expensive to mine, first because of the technical problems, secondly because the yield is small compared to labor expended. South Africa has 900 volcanic pipes, but only about 50 contain diamonds. Some localities known to contain diamonds are not even worked, as the cost of operations would be higher than the value of stones recovered — or so it's believed.

African diamond mining is now largely mechanized, except for the working of alluvial sites (near or in water). This was not always the case. In the early days of prospecting, especially when numerous freelancers and fortune hunters did the work, a variety of primitive techniques and devices were resorted to, some of which had been in use for centuries. Not being able to broach the kimberlite pipes, from which most African diamonds are now taken, early "diggers" did just that — they dug the topsoil, usually with conventional shovels or spades, hoping nature had been kind enough to deposit some gems near the surface. It was an extremely hit-and-miss operation. Panners worked the streams and lakebeds, too. Here there was somewhat greater chance of success, if one had persistence. During the 1860's and '70's, quite a high proportion of diamonds found in Africa were removed from alluvial sites. Such colorfully-named devices as the Long Tom, Cradle, and Yankee Baby were used to separate diamonds (and gold, if it were present) from waste materials. These appliances operated by hand, and long days were spent throwing gravel upon them, or into them, and hoping that something better than gravel would come out. When possible the local tribespeople were enlisted as sorters; but many prospectors hesitated to accept their aid, even if available cheaply, for fear they would divulge diamond-bearing locations.

The so-called "picking table" was a common sight at early mining locales. Here the prospector or a trusted assistant sat, manually inspecting the heaps of mineral and stone particles collected during the day, often surrounded by several tons of similar material that would eventually get to the picking table. The strain on eyesight, plus the fact that this work was generally performed out of doors in temperatures beyond 100 degrees F, made the picker's life far from envious. Later, when more sophisticated mining methods came into use, buildings went up and the task of sorting came to be carried out under roofs. Still, the lack of electrical power made artificial air cooling or circulation impossible until a much later date.

Today, the techniques used by alluvial prospectors are very similar to those of "pre-DeBeers" days. The chief difference is that most laborers are now contracted to corporations and work for salary. Arrangements are made, however, for employees to receive special rewards for recovering large stones. Some independent prospecting continues to be done, though illegal in almost all regions of the continent. Under law the state owns all land and consequently all products of the land, where claims have not been filed. The practice today among most of the African governments has been to make claims difficult to obtain, leaving land free to be worked by the government when and if it so elects. Smuggling does occur.

In the earliest days of Africa's diamond rush, when attention was being paid to alluvial and surface deposits, the extent of mining possibilities was not known or even imagined by the most optimistic parties. Discovery of the kimberlite pipes brought about a radical change in approach. When the Kimberley Big Hole was found in 1871, much argument arose over its disposition. It was concluded that claims should be allotted in seven and a half foot surface strips, which could be dug as deeply as the claim owners cared to go. The strips were of considerable length and separated by roadways, for the passage of workers and equipment. Soon the Big Hole took on the appearance of a vast maze, as more and more strips were worked and digging got further and further. Though the roadways were two strips wide (that is, 15 feet), it was discovered that, as the strips were dug deeper and deeper, the land around them was weakening and threatened to cave in upon the miners. Digging at this stage was performed manually with hand tools. It was not the purpose of the diggers to examine their yield. All recovered minerals were placed in sacks and brought up to the surface, where sorting and picking was done.

By 1875 this arrangement had been abandoned, because of its dangers and general unproductivity. Wooden scaffolding was erected around the sites, equipped with buckets and windlasses. The buckets were let down and hauled up, continually throughout the day. Gradually improvements were made, such as the introduction of metal conveyors on special belts.

In 1883 the first attempt was made at sinking a shaft into the Kimberley hole. By this time other mines had been discovered and it was apparent that the success or failure of shafting at Kimberley would play a role in the methods of working them as well. Funds were not available to sink a shaft from the outside, as is done today, so the experiment was made from the inside. This was carried out by an English contractor named Edward Jones. It proved successful and was soon followed by the sinking of additional shafts. Eventually, when Cecil Rhodes acquired ownership of the Kimberley Big Hole, outside shafting was begun, and this too went successfully. At the onset of World War I, shafting at Kimberley had gotten to a depth of 3,601 feet, well over half a mile. And it was discovered that deposits at this depth were as rich, if not richer, than those nearer the surface.

Of course, many efforts were put forward to improve the traditional method of shafting, not only to save expense but time. Three years after development of the DeBeers company in 1887, chambering was begun in the mines. Chambering is the creation of artificial tunnels running out at right angles from the vertical rock shaft. The chambers are 40 feet high and 12 feet in width, their dimensions achieved with the aid of dynamite blasting. They are customarily situated at depths of 600, 1,000 and 1,600 feet. Sometimes only one chamber is mined at a time, but it is not unusual for all chambers of a shaft to be worked simultaneously. Mineral matter is loaded by native workers into metal trucks, which are then mechanically hauled to the surface for sorting.

The average pace of which diamonds are found today in South Africa is four and a half carats in every 250 tons of rock and soil. Of this, three and a half carats is of industrial grade — not suitable for gem cutting. Since the one remaining carat will lose about half its weight in cutting, **250 tons yields just one half carat of polished diamond!** Obviously, even if diamond mining is stepped up, there is no way to appreciably increase the number or size of investment-grade diamonds taken from the earth. Consequently diamonds are, in fact, one of the best investments you can make based on supply and demand.

Further improvements have been made with "block caving," in which the mines are cut with numerous interconnecting tunnels resembling a subway system, and through which, indeed, motorized train-like vehicles ride. Block caving was first used by DeBeers in 1955 but was not an invention of this organization. It had earlier been employed in the U.S. for mining things other than diamonds.

DeBEERS — THE DIAMOND MONARCHY

DeBeers Consolidated Mines Ltd., which holds an almost dynastic monopoly over diamond mining and wholesaling, grew out of small 19th century beginnings. Its history is not only the most remarkable in the industry but one of the most legendary in modern corporate business. The diamond trade as it exists today owes most of its success — and very survival — to DeBeers. Not only does DeBeers mine the majority of diamonds coming on the world market, both industrial and gem quality, it controls and protects prices.

It has also developed many of the advanced mining and recovery techniques presently in use.

It is doubtful that the diamond industry would have developed so rapidly or reached its present levels without DeBeers. Anyone who deals in, invests in, or simply wears diamonds has a debt of thanks owed to DeBeers.

DeBeers was a Dutch farming family that had very little to do with the diamond business. In 1871 a Dutch prospector named Corneilsa was given permission to dig at the DeBeers farm, in exchange for 25% of the proceeds of all diamonds discovered. This was the era of diamond fever in South Africa and many other farms were being worked, too — some successfully and some not. Various claim-grabbers moved in and the DeBeers family was offered 6,300 British pounds for their farm, by a syndicate of miners (then equal to about $30,000).

Up to the present time, the land on which it originally stood has yielded more than two billion dollars worth of diamonds. It is now owned by DeBeers Consolidated Mines Ltd. Though the DeBeers family made a good profit — they had paid just 50 pounds for the land — they were by no means justly compensated for the riches it contained.

Next into the picture came Cecil Rhodes, a young Oxford-educated Englishman of precarious health. He had been sent to South Africa at age 17 by his physician, who considered his chances of improvement better in the hot, dry climate of that area than in clammy, foggy Britain. In 1873 Rhodes bought a claim at the DeBeers mine and seven years later established the DeBeers Mining Co. Ltd. It was his aim to buy out all claim-owners on the property, and this he succeeded in doing. But it was a slow and extremely costly operation. Other claim-owners held out or raised their prices as business became more lucrative. They, too, tried to buy out each other, and "claim wars" were common. Finally in 1887 Rhodes achieved his dream. DeBeers Mining Co. Ltd. owned all the original DeBeers land.

But it was not the only major mining organization in the region. Another of considerable importance was the Kimberley Mine, owned partly by Barney Barnato (an ex-vaudeville trouper) and partly by a French syndicate. Barnato was taken in as partner by Rhodes, in spite of objections by DeBeers stockholders. They considered Barnato a rake and a buffoon. So did Rhodes, undoubtedly, but knew that DeBeers' mastery of the mines could not otherwise be accomplished. This virtually eliminated all competition in the South African diamond industry. The company was now renamed DeBeers Consolidated Mines Ltd., as it continues to be known in the present day. Date of incorporation was March 13, 1888. Almost immediately, diamond prices — now freed from the pressures of one company trying to undersell the other — began steadily rising.

When Rhodes died in 1902 he left one of the largest personal fortunes ever recorded in the British Empire.

DeBeers not only carried on, it expanded. Its next important phase came after World War I, when demand for jewel diamonds resumed. The 1920's witnessed the highest prices for diamonds in history up to that time (far surpassed today!). In 1926 Sir Ernest Oppenheimer (1880-1957) became a director of the company. A British subject born in Germany, Oppenheimer had risen from the menial task of sorter for a London gem dealer to owner of an important South African mining conglomerate. After his appointment as a DeBeers director, he arranged for DeBeers to purchase the controlling interest in his former firm. Once again DeBeers controlled close to 100% of diamond mining activity in South Africa.

Oppenheimer was a business master who restructured the firm along totally new lines. He set up many subsidiary corporations to perform the various functions of DeBeers, mostly aimed at gaining more efficient worldwide distribution. By the time of his death in 1957, he was director of more than 40 DeBeers-related companies and board chairman of nearly 30 others. Harry Oppenheimer, Sir Ernest's son, then became chairman of DeBeers, a position he has held since then. Sir Phillip Opperheimer, a nephew of Sir Ernest, holds the important post of Managing Director of the Central (diamond) Selling Organization of London, which places all DeBeers-mined stones on the market and regulates their prices.

CELEBRATED DIAMONDS

History has demonstrated that diamonds are not only a girl's best friend. They have been equally admired by sultans, princes, nobles, sheiks, shipping magnates and royalty. And the bigger the better.

Nature occasionally produces diamonds of prodigious size. Stones so big that, even after cutting, they almost fill the palm of the hand. Naturally, such specimens have always attracted great attention, not to mention great prices. They have been given names to identify them (Hope Diamond, Orloff, Cullinan, etc.) and treated with an almost divine reverence. And their histories have been as closely chronicled, from the moment of discovery down through their various changes of ownership, as the lives of Popes and Presidents. Some have led swashbuckling lives, getting lost or stolen or disappearing from sight for ages and then turning up with a different cut. All have, at one time or other, served as household words to denote things of unattainable price. "As valuable as the Hope Diamond" is a phrase still heard today, despite the fact that this aristocrat of aristocrats has been reposing quietly in the Smithsonian for 23 years.

Are these super stones the world's most valuable objects, ounce for ounce? Technically, no. There are some chemicals worth more by weight than any diamonds. But among articles of beauty and adornment, nothing comes within miles of approaching their value.

It might be presumed that the story of famous diamonds would begin in the 1800's, when full-scale mining began in South Africa. By then, however, multitudes of prize-winning specimens had been unleashed on the world. Most of them came from India or Persia. Before the days of African mining, India held the lead in diamond selling. Many of these stones were not freshly mined and some did not come from India but places like Ceylon and Nepal. Such was the reputation of India as a diamond source that numerous westerners traveled there, in days when India was not so pleasant a place to be, to browse among its gem shops. Even as early as the 17th and 18th centuries, the larger European jewel dealers used agents in India to supply stones for them. Indian gem traders of that era were a breed unto themselves, of which no parallel exists any longer. They carried the equivalent of multi-thousands of dollars worth of gems wrapped in torn rags, tucked away in baskets and ebony boxes. Their places of business were masterpieces of disarray. Despite the large-scale transactions going on, the shops often had earth floors with some straw strewn over it. Flea-riddled dogs played around. Chickens strolled in and out. In the next shop or stall, an elbow's rub away, a merchant would be pouring rice into a sack and nearby there would be a soothsayer telling somebody's fortune. Europeans were always a little overwhelmed by all of this. They expected prices to be cheap, considering the low overhead. But they were mistaken. Indian merchants knew to the fraction of a shilling just how much their stones were worth in England. And their bargaining powers knew no equal.

The rule was for no actual retail prices to be set on anything. Gem sellers charged, or asked, what they thought they could get — doubling or tripling the real values if a customer looked rich and gullible. Anyone not expert in diamond buying was dragged through hot coals. Nearly every fair-sized diamond was claimed to be "the biggest stone in India," "the finest diamond on the market," and so forth. In many instances they were big but poorly cut, or contained serious flaws, which the merchant would argue, until the sun set and long thereafter, were not flaws at all. You needed lots of endurance to buy diamonds in India.

One of the best-known diamonds to come from India was the Mughal, variously known as the Grand Mughal or Great Mughal. An early commentator reported seeing the Grand Mughal at Delhi in 1665. He described it as having the appearance of an egg cut in half and recorded its weight as 280 carats, against a rough weight of 793 carats. Apparently it was a fairly new discovery at the time; it was said to have been found around 1650. The Grand Mughal was then in the possession of the Shah of Delhi, who proudly displayed it among the baubles of his treasury. It was not to remain there long. Another Shah, named Nadir, took it upon himself to relieve the Delhi treasury of most of its higher-grade valuables and carry them away to Persia. Its subsequent fate is not known. The Grand Mughal never appeared again. Or, it might be better to say, it never again appeared with the same cut and a 280 carat weight. Very likely it was recut, to better escape the prying eyes of those seeking its return to India. The opinion of some authorities is that the Grand Mughal was reincarnated into one of the other celebrated diamonds of the world, possibly the Orloff.

The Koh-i-nor, not quite as big, went through a no less harrowing existence but remains safe and sound today — extremely safe, as one of the British crown jewels in the Tower of London. (The term "crown jewel" is sometimes mistakenly assumed to refer to gems used in royal crowns. Some of them were, but the expression has nothing to do with this. It is applied simply to jewels *in the crown's possession — meaning state possession.)*

The Koh-i-nor's history has been traced back as far as 1304 — the earliest date, by the way, at which the whereabouts of any famous diamond has been established beyond reasonable argument. It was then in possession of an Indian potentate in the neighborhood of Delhi. Later it was handed down through several generations of the Mughal emperors. In 1850, after the colonization of India by Great Britain, it was presented by the East India Company to Queen Victoria. The queen, born of the manor royal and having a temperament typical to queens, was not overly enthralled by the glittering goliath. Impressed by its physical proportions, its manner of cut left something to the royal desire. It was not shimmering enough for her taste. So the queen decided to sacrifice a bit of its bulk and shipped off the Koh-i-nor to her diamond cutter. After he was done with it, it weighed 108.93 carats — barely half as much as before. But she was now satisfied that it was as eye-knocking as it could possibly be, and everybody was satisfied that Her Royal Majesty was satisfied. No further cutting was done and the Koh-i-nor still carries a weight of 108.93 carats, plus nearly 700 years of colorful history behind it. Technically, it may be worn by the present queen, Elizabeth II, on state occasions. But this isn't done; it would present a huge security problem.

Small compared to most other historic diamonds, the Hope has something going for it in addition to size: a rare rich blue color. It is without question the most famous diamond currently on U.S. soil. Its story begins in 1668 and takes us across several continents. In that year Tavernier, a well-known diamond agent, brought it back to France from India. It weighed 112.50 carats and was purchased by Louis XIV. At this time its popular designation was "The French Blue." Louis decided to have the shape changed and in 1673 it was recut into a heart pattern, reducing the weight to 67⅛ carats. For many years it was hailed as the finest diamond in France, if not all of Europe, and served as an object of adoration not only for Louis XIV but his successors, Louis XV and Louis XVI. At the outbreak of France's revolution in 1792 the stronghouse in which it was stored suffered the same fate as the Bastile: it was broken into, and the French Blue disappeared.

Who had it?

Nobody knew, or those who knew weren't talking. The revolutionaries were known to be in need of money and general opinion was that the French Blue, along with anything else of value on which they succeeded in laying hands, was probably smuggled out of the country for sale. Officially, it was never heard from again. But unofficially, there is little doubt that the gem now displayed in Washington, D.C., is the slightly transmogrified French Blue.

In 1830, more than three decades after the French revolution had faded into memory, a diamond weighing 44½ carats appeared for sale in London. It was bought by Henry Hope and thereafter identified as the Hope Diamond. The experts are convinced that this was the French Blue, after a bit of additional recutting and reshaping — which had either been done shortly after its theft or, possibly, at a considerably later date. Even as late as 1830, long after Louis XVI was in no position to make a claim for its recovery (he had been guillotined), it would not have been prudent for a London dealer to offer the French Blue in exactly the same condition it had left France. The French authorities certainly would have wanted it back.

From England the Hope Diamond found its way to America, where it was purchased by Evalyn Walsh McClean of Washington, D.C., a prominent socialite, in 1911. Following her death in 1947 it was acquired by a New York diamond dealer, Harry Winston. After holding it for nine years, Winston gave it to the Smithsonian: the largest gift of a precious stone, in terms of its current value at the time of presentation, ever made to a public institution.

The Regent diamond also came from India. It was dug in 1701 and had an in-the-rough weight of 410 carats. William Pitt, an English politician, purchased it for an undisclosed sum the following year. It was still uncut. Pitt had it cut down to 140½ carats. A number of years later it was sold to Phillippe d'Orleans, regent of France (then a child, later to reign as Louis XV), and it acquired the title of Regent diamond. Like the French Blue/Hope, the Regent was also stolen during the French revolution. But it was recovered before any cutting or other mischief could be done, and deposited in the Louvre museum. It remains there today, and has the distinction of being the largest diamond on public exhibition in France. The Regent has a yellowish tint.

THE ANATOMY OF A DIAMOND

Until fairly recently no clear explanation could be given for the legendary lure of fine diamonds. It was known for at least 2,000 years that diamonds were somehow above the class of other minerals, that they were harder and more pleasing to the eye, but the reasons for their unique characteristics remained beyond the scope of scientific knowledge. Today, the atomic structure of gems is no longer a mystery. We know the makeup of diamonds and this knowledge has led to an even greater appreciation of them.

Diamonds are formed of carbon with a slight admixture of nitrogen. The proportion of nitrogen is never more than one-fourth of one percent; the composition is at least 99 3/4 carbon. If additional elements are present, which they can be, their percentage versus carbon is extremely infinitesimal. Consequently the carbon atom gives the diamond its structure and hardness. Within each diamond is a vast and complicated network of atoms and electrons, visible only under very powerful magnification. Though tiny, the atoms are all perfectly circular and connected one with another in distinct, orderly patterns. Magnification shows them to have the appearance of tinkertoy construction, as if wood balls were connected by wood rods or dowels into artistic geometrical designs.

The positioning of these atoms, in the millions and multi-millions within a given stone, dictate the direction of cleavage. A diamond will cleave only in the direction of its atomic structure; it will not cleave against the atoms, as the atoms will cling fast to each other and prevent a clean break.

DIAMOND CRYSTALS

The majority of diamonds as found "in the rough" are octahedrons. Ideally these are smooth crystals, greasy looking at the surface, and very glassy. They are not, however, always clear, nor even mostly clear. Generally, the glassy diamonds are more likely to be colored, to a greater or lesser degree. The more desirable cutting stones tend to occur in other types of crystals. Many octahedrons are not cut for jewelry but end up as industrial stones, where coloration is not important.

Though the basic shape of an octahedron is eight-sided, with six points, irregularities of shape are common. Rough stones of symmetrical proportions, in which all sides are equally formed, are much in the minority. One side may be perfect and the other side squashed or stunted. This happens because diamonds do not form under ideal conditions. If a rough is large enough, it may be worthwhile to cut away the inferior portion. Often, octahedrons have rounded rather than the more desirable pointed corners.

BANDED GROWTH. These are crystals, usually but not necessarily cubic, displaying alternating colorless and colored layers. They are often not recognized as diamonds except by skilled individuals. Though banded crystals are colorful, their quality as diamonds is low.

COATED CRYSTALS. Rough diamonds are sometimes discovered whose exterior displays a deep coloration but which prove to be less highly colored, or uncolored, internally. This is a result of natural formation and is not truly a "coating" but part of the diamond itself. The reverse can also be the case, that a rough whose external coloration is clear or nearly clear has a deeply colored interior. The former in naturally preferred for cutting.

CUSHION SHAPE. This is a flattened crystal, more or less circular at the girdle but extremely distorted at top and bottom.

DISTORTIONS. Various names are sometimes applied to miscellaneous crystal shapes. In nearly all instances these are octahedral roughs which have failed to form correctly and have sides that are rounded or sloping, are larger on the bottom than the top, or bear other characteristics of irregularity. Nearly circular or spherical crystals are encountered. These, too, are really octahedrons, very imperfectly formed. There is no such thing as a "round crystal." Crystals are formed with angles and points, and when these are not present, or so distorted as to appear not present, it is simply a mistake or trick of nature — not a different kind of diamond.

DOG TOOTH CRYSTAL. Technically known as a hexakis octahedron, the dog tooth crystal has the appearance of a canine incisor tooth. The surface is generally rough.

HEXAHEDRON. Hexahedrons are cubic roughs, having six sides. The sides are not necessarily of equal dimensions and the stone may be misproportioned in other ways too, such as having a sloping side or sides. Normally the points or corners are somewhat rounded, but hexahedrons have been found with knife-like points. Amateur prospectors frequently bypass this type of stone, assuming it to be quartz, especially if internally cloudy. It is just as much a diamond as the best octahedron and can yield handsomely cut stones. There is, however, usually somewhat more carat loss when cutting a hexahedron.

MACLE. A common variety of twinned crystal, it can occur in stones of a number of different shapes, including triangle and star. The chief characteristic is that the "attached" crystal appears to have been turned about 180 degrees on an octahedral plane.

MULTIPLE AGGREGATES. These are collections of many crystals, generally of small individual size, fused together. The shaping tends to be very irregular.

NEGATIVE CRYSTALS. These are grooves or hollows occurring at the surface of a crystal. The cause is not positively known.

RHOMBIC DODECAHEDRON. This is a rough which began as an octahedron and developed further, giving the appearance of a crystal-within-a-crystal or, more precisely, a crystal with an additional interior wall. Technically a rhombic dodecahedron is still in process of development and if left to nature the internal crystal would disappear.

Dodecahedrons are more usually of yellowish coloration than white, sometimes a deep yellow that disqualifies them for gem purposes.

Dodecahedron and octahedron shapes also occur within the same roughs, occasionally. There is no limitation to the crystal forms that can be combined within a diamond, but some are considerably rarer than others. This does not mean they will yield a valuable cut gem; they may not even be suitable for gem cutting, depending on the individual specimen.

TWINS. When two or more crystals are attached to each other, this is called twinning. The crystals are not wholly or perfectly formed; consequently, separation does not yield good stones. But twinned crystals may still be useful for gem cutting, if large enough to withstand a great loss of carat weight. There are various types of twinned crystal, each with its own properties and characteristics.

GUIDE TO CRYSTAL SHAPE TERMINOLOGY

The following terms are used in reference to uncut diamond crystals:

Hexahedron - 6 faces (cube shape)
Octahedron - 8 faces
Rhombic dodecahedron - 12 faces
Tetrakis hexahedron - 24 faces
Icositetrahedron - 24 faces
Triakis octahedron - 24 faces
Hexakis octahedron - 48 faces

DIAMOND HARDNESS

Relative hardness of minerals (precious and otherwise) is expressed by the so-called Mohs Scale. Mohs, a noted mineralogist, worked out a listing of 10 mineral elements ranging from very soft to the absolute hardest, the principle being that each has the ability to produce a scratch on the minerals ranked beneath it but will not scratch those graded above it. It must be kept in mind that the Mohs Scale measures *only* vulnerability to surface scratching. The hardness ratings have no relation to resistance to crushing, if the minerals are struck blows with a hammer. It can be safely stated that every mineral will crush, and fairly easily, if subjected to extreme pressure. For many years this fact was little known, and the auther ticity of diamonds was frequently tested by subjecting them to blows. Naturally, many genuine stones were destroyed in this fashion.

The Mohs Scale is as follows:

1. Talc	**6. Feldspar**
2. Gypsum	**7. Quartz**
3. Calcite	**8. Topaz**
4. Fluorspar	**9. Corundum**
5. Apatite	**10. Diamond**

Quartz, rated #7, will scratch feldspar (#6) but will not scratch topaz (#8). Talc (#1) can be scratched by all the other minerals — as well as by the human fingernail. Diamond scratches all the other minerals and is not scratched by any of them.

Technically the Mohs Scale is deceiving because the relative hardnesses of the minerals vary a great deal. In other words, the degree of difference in hardness from feldspar to apatite is not the same as between corundum and topaz. But is has become so universally accepted that the suggestion of revising the Mohs Scale is looked upon as tampering with sacred scriptures.

Will one diamond scratch another? Yes, positively. Diamond dust or powder is applied to the metal saws used in cutting diamonds. And quite a few gem owners have discovered, much to their grief, that diamonds stored in the same container and allowed to contact each other have acquired scratches. Two diamonds should never be permitted to touch. Scratches caused in this fashion may be too minor for detection by the unaided eye but are certain to be noticed when the time comes for selling.

It is naturally because of the diamond's hardness that it finds such extensive use in industry. About 80% of all mined "roughs" go to industrial use, where, of course, the color or configuration play no important role.

THE GEMOLOGICAL INSTITUTE OF AMERICA

This organization, with offices in New York, Los Angeles and Santa Monica offers courses in gemology and provides graduates with accreditation as gemologists. Perhaps more importantly to the private buyer and seller of diamonds, it provides an expertising service both to the public and to dealers (the fee charged to dealers is somewhat lower). Diamonds submitted for its opinion are subjected to a variety of laboratory procedures and are issued a diamond grading report, known commonly in the trade as a "G.I.A. Certificate," stating whether or not the stone is a true diamond, its weight, color grading and clarity grading as well as all measurements. The G.I.A. certificate has come to be regarded as the "Standard of the Industry," as stones accompanied by it can be traded in confidence without suspicions or the differences of viewpoint that frequently occur over matters of grading. Many gem dealers automatically submit every stone they acquire to the G.I.A., if it does not already possess a certificate, as the presence of one adds greatly to its sales appeal. It acts as a kind of pedigree and is universally relied upon, representing as it does the findings of an impartial body that stands to gain nothing by sale or ownership of the material.

Investors are advised to restrict their buying as much as possible to G.I.A. certified stones. It will be found that the majority of stones offered by brokers are furnished with a G.I.A. certificate. This is not the case, however, when buying from jewelry shops or other sources. When reading auction catalogues, it should not be presumed that any of the lots are accompanied by G.I.A. certificates unless this is specifically stated. Many jewels sold at auction have come out of old estates and were never subjected to G.I.A. testing.

DIAMOND GRADING TERMINOLOGY

The grading terminology of diamonds as developed by the Gemological Institute of America (G.I.A.) employs letters and letter/number combinations to refer to clarity and color. This terminology, though frequently a cause of debate, is almost universally used by diamond traders, sometimes with local additions or amendments. No system can please everyone; the G.I.A. has at least removed much of the confusion from describing and grading diamonds.

COLOR RATINGS. The letters used in the G.I.A.'s system of reference to diamond colors bears no relation to the initial letters of the colors. It is a descending scale, just like the clarity scale except a bit lengthier. It begins with D, which refers to the best color (completely colorless) quality of a brilliant blue-white diamond (the most desirable color for investment diamonds). There is no A, B or C in the scale. The letters toward the beginning of the alphabet represent the more desirable colors; toward the end the less desirable.

D, E, F — These are all crystal clear or completely colorless diamonds. They represent the most attractive investments, assuming their other qualities are comparable.

G — Nearly colorless, fine white.
H — Nearly colorless, white
I — Nearly colorless, commercial white
J — Nearly colorless, top silver cape
K — Slightly tinted, ranging from top silver cape (better) to silver cape (not quite so desirable)
L — Slightly tinted, silver cape
M — Slightly tinted, light cape
N — Slightly tinted, light cape, but not as high a grade as M
O — Pale Yellow, cape
P — Pale Yellow, cape, lower grade
Q — Pale Yellow, cape, third lowest grade of this classification
R — Light Yellow (stronger yellow than above), cape
S — Light Yellow, dark cape
T — Light Yellow, dark cape, more heavily colored
U — Yellow, dark cape
V — Yellow, dark cape, strong coloration, very little light refraction, not a gem — quality stone.
X, Y, Z — Very heavily colored
Z + — Extremely heavily colored and are considered "Fancy Colored." These are very rare and considered the most valuable of diamonds, more so than say a "D" flawless.

TERMINOLOGY RELATING TO CLARITY. The most complicated terminology refers to gem clarity. This is a series of grades ranging from Flawless — expressed as FL — down to badly defective or "I-3." The point to be kept in mind, so far as clarity grading is concerned, is that the quality of a diamond is measured in relation to perfect examples of that shape or cut. Because not everyone has equally keen vision, what appears flawless to one individual could very easily look otherwise to a sharper sighted person. Therefore, the grading criteria are based upon examinations made not only with the unaided eye (which is unreliable) but the use of various equipment, such as the jeweler's or diamond appraiser's 10X loupe. (NOTE: 10X magnification is the maximum limit for inspecting and grading diamonds throughout the world).

FLAWLESS. (FL) Stones in this grade do not reveal imperfections of any kind when magnified with 10X magnification.

INTERNALLY FLAWLESS. (IF) Slight surface imperfections but internally the stone is as perfect as an FL (above).

VVS1. Has very tiny inclusions which can be distinguished with extreme difficulty using 10X magnification.

VVS2. Like VVS1, but inclusions are not quite so difficult to see under 10X magnification.

VS1. Minor inclusions slightly more pronounced than VVS2, but still difficult to see with 10X magnification.

VS2. Minor inclusions more noticeable than in a VS1, fairly easy to see with 10X magnification.

SI1. Inclusions can be seen without difficulty under 10X magnification.

SI2. 10X magnification readily reveals inclusions, which may possibly be noticeable with the naked eye looking through the pavilion.

I-1. Inclusions very apparent with 10X magnification and can be seen with the naked eye.

I-2. Inclusions noticeable without magnification.

I-3. More pronounced inclusions, visible with naked eye.

Such are the classifications. Getting two parties to agree on their application to any particular stone is another matter. Any grading system is left open to personal interpretation and can be abused, willfully or otherwise. What one appraiser calls a I-1 will be a I-2 or an SI-2 to another, and there are instances of stones termed VS by one party being declared I-1 or I-2 by someone else. Since price is very closely allied to a stone's grading, this is a matter of no small importance. It is naturally commonplace for a prospective buyer to grade stones one category lower than he believes them to be. This provides him not only with the usual 10% or 15% profit on a transaction but the leverage of obtaining an additional 10% or 15% if the stone sells in a higher grade. Also, this is done because usually when a purchase is made, examination is done only with a 10X loupe in less than desirable conditions, and the buyer needs that latitude for his protection. This practice is so widespread that it is no longer looked upon as unscrupulous. It is simply one of the "facts of life" of diamond trading and occurs in transactions between dealers, too, not only when dealers buy from the public. There is not much effective defense against undergrading, except to present a G.I.A. certificate, but even this is likely to be challenged by a buyer intent on making an advantageous purchase. "They always overgrade," is the common rejoinder when papers are offered.

What can you say?

Nothing, really, because if the buyer has determined to himself that he will not pay the full market value (less a reasonable percentage for his profit), it makes little difference whether he chooses to offer inferior condition as an excuse, or the state of the market, or the fact that his back aches. If he will not pay a satisfactory price, the reason is unimportant. You must simply go elsewhere.

Of course, it *is* possible for a diamond to be overgraded, and this really is not a rare circumstance when the grading has been performed by profit-making appraisers. Professionally appraised diamonds are overgraded much more frequently than undergraded. Why? Because the appraiser stands to gain, if he charges by percentage of the appraised value. Placing a stone into the next higher category could increase its value by hundreds or even thousands of dollars, of which he receives from 1% to 5% as his fee. In borderline cases, the appraiser will automatically place the diamond in the higher of the two categories. Unfortunately, this is often done in cases that are not borderline as well.

You should not expect a prospective buyer to agree with opinions given by professional appraisers, even if they happen to be colleagues of his. The stone will be "taken down a peg or two," which probably will bring it more in line with its true level of quality.

When buying investment diamonds accompanied by G.I.A. certification, or appraised by an independent authority in whom you can place faith, those of FL or flawless rating are naturally to be preferred. They are not the only specimens suitable for investment, however, as the values of the slightly lesser grades advance about as steadily as do values of FL. Any grade down to VS (very slight imperfection) is acceptable as an investment purchase, *but* as you begin to sacrifice quality of clarity this should be compensated for by demanding excellence of color.

DIAMOND GRADING

Correct grading of a diamond is essential in establishing its value, either as a commercial property or investment piece. Many factors are involved in grading, but the chief ones are:

Carat Weight | **Clarity**
Color | **Cut**

These are known collectively as the "Four C's." An accurate determination of the Four C's of a diamond will establish its value. The key word here is *accurate.* Misinterpretation of any of the four characteristics will result in an incorrect value.

Some experience in handling diamonds is necessary before reliable estimations of value can be made. Grading diamonds is a science, at which the beginner cannot expect to become expert overnight. It is recommended that, after studying this chapter and becoming familiar with the basic points of grading, the potential buyer spend some time visiting diamond dealers and examining gems at first hand, with the aid of equipment used by the dealer. This can be thought of as "going to school." It provides an education that books — even a library of them — can only supplement. As you examine diamonds, compare them against the dealer's description (either verbal or, preferably, the description in his inventory list). Look for the characteristics mentioned. Notice how one stone differs from another, and why the more costly specimens are highly valued. Sometimes you will encounter stones that are not accurately described. The more experience you have, the better you can recognize these specimens and avoid their purchase. The intelligent diamond investor has sufficient knowledge to serve as his own appraiser.

CLARITY. Clarity is perhaps a misleading term; purity would be more descriptive, as the clarity of a diamond is just that: the degree to which it is pure and unadulterated internally and externally. The purer the diamond, the greater its value, compared to other stones of the same color, cut and weight. Absolute purity is an elusive quality in diamonds. Therefore, the occasional specimen that reveals no major blemishes or imperfections of any kind, even under 10X magnification, is extremely desirable and rates as a good investment piece.

The purity of a diamond can be spoilt by nature or man, or both. Diamonds are crystals, just as are quartz (with which most of us are more familiar). Despite the expression "crystal clear," very few crystals, of whatever mineral, are entirely clear. They may appear so, to casual observation, but careful examination under magnification will generally reveal a variety of flaws of one kind or another.

Internal flaws are the fault of nature and have been carried by the diamond for millions of years. To understand the cause of internal or natural flaws, it is necessary to examine the formative process of minerals. Most minerals in the earth today were created between 100 and 400 million years ago; some are even older. Diamonds were formed through 80 to 150 million years of enormous pressure plus intense heat — one and a half tons per square inch and a temperature of 5,000 degrees F. In the case of crystal minerals, the admixture of just a minute trace of some other mineral or element, which, of course, occurred frequently as these substances were jumbled about indiscriminately, resulted in the crystal not being strictly pure. Just like a fly in amber, these traces of foreign minerals became entrapped within the crystal, to remain there forever. In the event of a rough diamond being sufficiently large, and bearing mineral or metallic admixture along the outer surface only, it is sometimes possible by judicious cutting to remove the flaws and achieve a stone of good clarity. In most instances, however, this cannot be done. The stone after cutting still bears some evidence of the jailed-in element. When the flaw is serious, the stone will be ranked as industrial grade rather than attempting to use it for jewelry (the next higher grade over industrial). Obviously such specimens are never considered of investment quality.

There are other kinds of internal flaws, too. During the early stages of formation, the elements comprising the soon-to-be diamond may have begun to cool and harden, when suddenly another explosion or shifting about of earth took place. No foreign substances were imparted into the stone, but it was squeezed or contorted. Hence it showed, when dry and hard, internal lines or "creases," which have the resemblance of cracks and really are cracks of a sort.

Cloudiness is another variety of internal imperfection.

External flaws are generally the fault of misuse or accident, either in cutting, mounting or handling. The stone may have a surface scratch or nick. Its grading will depend upon the seriousness of this blemish (the length and depth of a scratch, for example), and its quality in other respects. Minor imperfections do not destroy the value of an otherwise good stone, but they do understandably reduce it somewhat. Investment-grade stones have rarely suffered such accidents. They are frequently encountered in jewelry stones, often as the result of careless handling or storage (allowing two diamonds to rub together, etc.)

External flaws also encompass imperfections of shape. The perfect diamond, after cutting, is symmetrically proportioned; if imaginarily divided in half vertically or horizontally, these two halves would be exact duplications of each other. If the two halves would not perfectly match, the stone is not regarded as flawless. It may still, however, merit a fair grading if the fault is not severe and all other points are satisfactory.

COLOR. The average public believes that all diamonds are as colorless as window glass, just as it believes all jade is green and all wood is brown. Such is not the case. Diamonds may be found in a variety of colors, or rather color tints, as the degree of coloring is never so intense (as in many minerals) to destroy their transparency. Color tints have the same origins as internal flaws, though, of course, they are not flaws. Certain chemicals or substances became mixed with the basic elements at the time of formation and the diamond today bears the color of these substances. Rarity is not an important factor so far as color is concerned, as some colorings or shadings of them are quite uncommon but are nevertheless not desirable. Preferences of color were long-ago established by purchasers of jewelry and have remained fairly constant. Most highly rated are crystal clear examples with icy whiteness, which under careful inspection (sometimes a mere glance, if the stone is large enough or its shading characteristics pronounced) reveals highlights of blue. Public admiration for this coloring is perhaps misdirected. It is presumed by individuals without gemological knowledge that blue tingeing is an assurance of absolute clarity of color, the belief being that the clearer and sharper a crystal is, the more prone it will be to acquire this touch of blue coloring. Technically, that is not the case; but a gem of ideal crystal clarity, with blueness, is nevertheless extremely handsome and probably deserves the high admiration it receives. The determination of color is made by comparison using stones that have been certified by the G.I.A. and given accurate color grades. This set of stones is refered to as a "Master Set." You will read more about this in the chapter "Examining The Color of a Diamond."

The Gemological Institute of America (G.I.A.) ranks the blue-white color grades as D, E and F. Stones rated in any of these categories are, if their remaining characteristics are satisfactory, regarded as investment quality.

But these are NOT THE ONLY COLOR GRADES suitable for investment.

Also considered as suitable investments are stones falling in the next three descending categories of classification, H, I and J. (It should be noted that the G.I.A. scale, on which all interpretations of color are based, begins at the letter D; the previous three letters of the alphabet are not used.)

The ranking "G" is applied to stones whose official designation is "fine white." They are not "borderline colorless" with the faint blue tinge as are the D, E and F rankings. This would appear to place them into a lower category and technically it does, but "fine whites" are still high grade stones and are in fact preferred by some purchasers. As with most commodities, individual taste plays a role. If everyone were to favor the same characteristics, and avoid diamonds not exhibiting these characteristics, values would be much more clearly determined. Fine whites have a long and noble heritage in jewelry, especially in Europe among the old aristocratic families.

The letter "H" is applied to ordinary white, a cut beneath fine white, while "I" refers to "commercial white," a grade of coloration commonly employed in jewelry.

The lesser classifications, all the way down to "Z", may also be used in jewelry but their values are lower. For the purposes of investment they are best avoided. The *color* of a diamond is one of the chief matters that will influence the price paid when your investment gems are disposed of. It might logically be presumed that if $5,000 is given for a blue-white and $5,000 for a yellow, both would have the same resale value. This, however, is not the case. The blue-white will invariably carry greater resale value, because a potential purchaser can liquidate such a diamond to an investor. He will not be generally able to sell a yellow to an investor; at least not to one who has some knowledge of diamonds. Thus he will more readily purchase, and give a somewhat higher price for, the former. These are matters well worth taking under consideration before buying.

Of course, whenever color is discussed, whatever the color or grade may be, the diamond's desirability and value are influenced by *distribution of color.* Stones are sometimes encountered in which the coloring is not even. These are called occluded stones. The color is crowded more in one area of the diamond than another, as if improperly "mixed." This is a case of nature not doing her job. After millions of years, her mistakes cannot be corrected. Improper color distribution can be better understood by examination of quartz crystals, which are considerably larger and show this feature more noticeably.

CUT. Cut and weight are both human-influenced, unlike color or internal purity. A mediocre diamond can be turned desirable by skilled cutting, and the reverse is likewise true (and is sadly of more common occurrence): an essentially good-quality stone may be reduced in value, or not brought up to its full value potential, by inartistic cutting. An investment diamond should, first of all, be *cut.* This seems elementary to point out, but deserves mention. Rough diamonds may be purchased for investment, and this is not uncommon. However, the private individual is urged strongly not to invest in roughs. The rate of return they bring upon sale is invariably lower than finely cut gems.

It may in fact prove difficult to find a buyer for rough stones, unless extremely attractive. The argument will be raised, by a prospective purchaser, that cutting is not only expensive but its results uncertain, and that he would rather buy diamonds already cut. As an investor you ought to do likewise, even though it means paying more. Rough diamonds are not the bargain they seem, unless you can obtain them well under wholesale.

Cut must be considered from two points of view: the shape, which will be obvious at sight, and the excellence with which each individual cut was executed. This is not so obvious and will be determined only through inspection under magnification, by a person sufficiently familiar with the craft of diamond cutting. The term "proportioning" is sometimes applied. We mentioned above, in discussing surface imperfections, that these may be sometimes revealed by thinking of a diamond in terms of two equal horizontal or vertical halves. If the diamond is perfect, its halves would be mirror images of each other. The same is true of proportioning. The stone must be cut so exactly that each facet and cleavage line on one side agrees perfectly with its counterpart on the opposite side. Also, the cutting must have produced a well-proportioned stone. It is quite easy for diamonds to be cut "out of proportion," when handled by unskilled artisans. This is sometimes done deliberately to save carat weight or satisfy local tastes. Perfect proportioning requires that the cut be ideal for that particular stone, allowing light to enter at the correct angles, to be reflected and to exit upward toward the observer. This is how a diamond achieves its "sparkle," a misused word but one which conveys the basic message. When ill-proportioned, the light may enter properly but is incorrectly refracted upon reaching the sides or base, and is expelled along the lower portion of the diamond. When this occurs, the brilliance of even an exceptionally fine stone is diminished, as it cannot attain the gentle play of light and nuance of tone imparted by that play of light, which is so essential to a good diamond. The term "beauty is in the beholder's eye" applies to few things so aptly as to diamonds. The ability of a diamond to enchant, to dazzle, to beguile its beholder is responsible for a very large measure of its cash value. The diamond incapable of doing this, no matter the color or clarity or size, is regarded as impotent, and should not be considered as an investment.

Of course, unsatisfactory proportioning can sometimes be corrected by recutting. You will perhaps occasionally be told, by zealous salesmen, that a certain misproportioned stone is being offered at an irresistible bargain price, and can by recutting be increased by double or triple the value. Be wary. There is no guarantee that the recutting will go successfully. It is also quite likely that the stone will be considerably reduced in weight, and even if the recutting is satisfactory the loss of weight might result in its cash value working out no higher, or only slightly higher, than originally. The claim that such a stone is offered at a bargain figure should be treated with caution. The price is likely to be a bargain only in comparison to the full retail value of the same stone if well cut. It is probably the average sum at which a miscut specimen of that size, color and purity normally sells, and therefore is not a bargain at all.

Some expertise is necessary to judge proportioning. Bad cuts will generally look acceptable to a beginner, who invariably has the habit of taking a loupe and probing around the cleavage, searching for rough or misaligned cuts. The cuts may be very respectable in that regard — nice and even and smooth — but the proportioning can still be wrong, if the cuts were not made where they ought to have been. This is not to suggest that cleavage be ignored, nor any other consideration.

The chief errors of proportioning are cutting too deep, and not cutting deep enough. When a diamond is cut too deep, light will exit through the sides. When cut too shallow, it will exit through the bottom. Both these situations are undesirable. Proportioning must be mathematically exact to achieve proper refraction of light.

No matter what shape of cut is used, the various surfaces on a diamond are classified into five basic divisions.

TABLE. This is the uppermost surface, which will be flat and uncut (and hopefully unmarked in any way).

CROWN. The sloping sides, extending down from the table to the girdle.

GIRDLE. The widest or mid-portion of a diamond. Though called the midsection, its location is not necessarily at the center of gravity.

PAVILION. The inward-sloping sides, leading down from the girdle.

CULET. The point of the base.

When considering a diamond from an investment point of view, stones with a depth percentage in the region of 58% to about 64% are most desir-

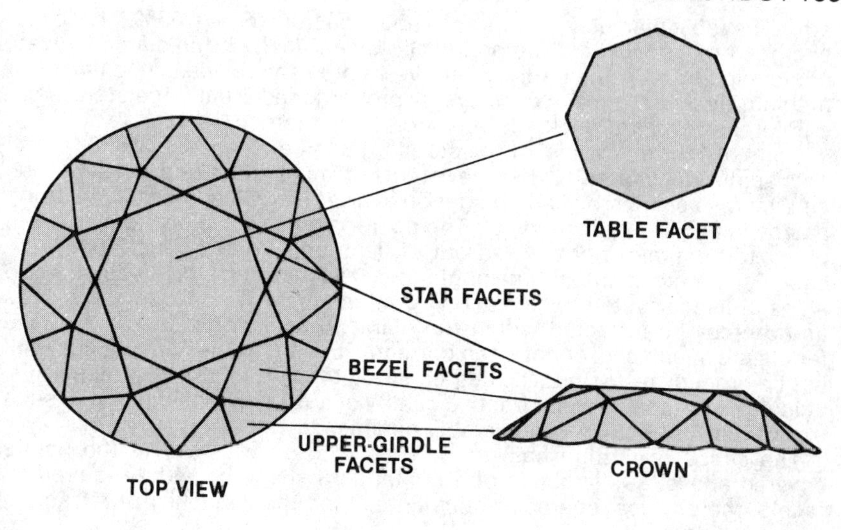
TABLE FACET
STAR FACETS
BEZEL FACETS
UPPER-GIRDLE FACETS
CROWN
TOP VIEW

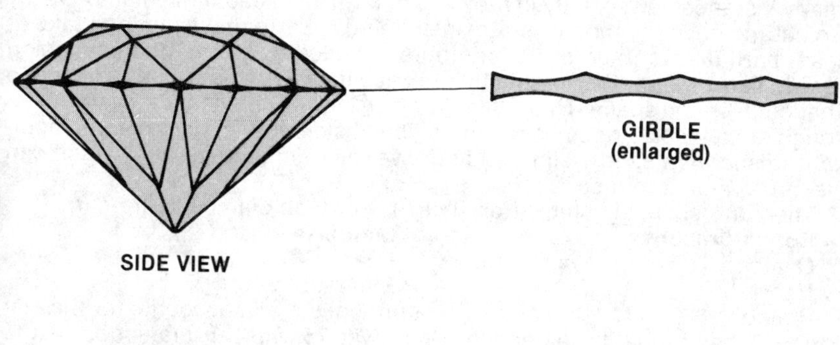
GIRDLE (enlarged)
SIDE VIEW

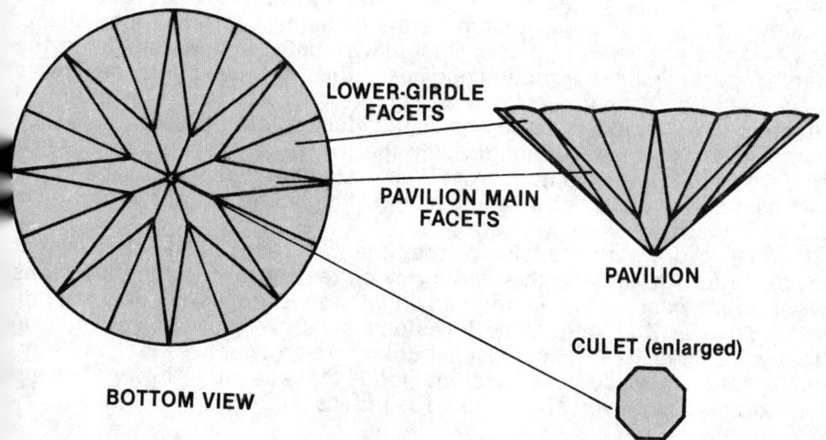
LOWER-GIRDLE FACETS
PAVILION MAIN FACETS
PAVILION
CULET (enlarged)
BOTTOM VIEW

able. The table diameter percentage should be from 55% to 65%. These percentage ratings will be given on the G.I.A. certificate, if the diamond is accompanied by one. The girdle or middle section should ideally be thin or of medium thickness, in any case evenly proportioned around the stone's circumference and not thicker in one area than another.

Correctly cut diamonds, of the standard popular shapes, have 58 facets. This applies no matter if the stone is large or small; the facets will simply be smaller on a small stone and bigger on a large, but will number 58 if cutting has been accurately carried out. The positioning of these facets may seem either to be aimless or devised out of decorative motive. Such is not the case. Their placement and the angle of cleavage is performed according to an established system, which allows light to enter at certain critical angles and thereby be refracted within the diamond to best advantage. If these facets are misplaced, or not sized correctly, or if the angles are off, light will not be properly refracted. The degree of tolerance is slight. Very slight miscalculations can ruin the refractive quality of a diamond, or impair it to such extent that its value is considerably diminished.

The *shape* of cutting has really nothing to do with any of the points covered above, as diamonds of any standard shape have the required 58 facets, the physical characteristics noted, and the capability of refracting light if properly cut.

The choice of shape into which a rough stone will be cut is influenced in many instances, especially in the case of large or exceptional diamonds, by its natural shape in the raw state. In shaping, an attempt is made to take at least partial advantage of the contours provided by nature, thereby losing less in carat weight than would be the case if choosing a shape opposed to the rough or raw shape. This will not be done, however, in instances where a rough stone has a "good" side and a "bad" side, it then being more important to sacrifice carat weight and remove the offending portion, which can be put to industrial use.

There are six basic shapes or styles into which diamonds are cut:

Round Brilliant
Oval
Heart
Marquise
Pear
Emerald

Round is the so-called classic or traditional cut and accounts for the majority of better-quality diamonds. Well over 75% of all diamonds in the market, for use in jewelry and of investment quality, carry the round shape. It is perhaps not very original or imaginative but it results usually in the greatest possible light refraction and hence the most pure brilliance. This is because basic shape does play a role in refractive ability of a diamond. In the other five shapes, as listed above, the stone's width does not perfectly match its vertical measurement. Only the round cut measures the same from North to South as it does from West to East across its top. Therefore, light as it enters through the facets meets at more precise junctions, and is thrown out a bit more powerfully.

If you have drawn the conclusion that finely cut round diamonds are most advisable for investment, this is entirely correct. Any of the other shapes might, in the case of top-quality individual stones, be just as desirable investment-wise. But overall, the investor makes his best choice when he stays with round. He will not risk encountering a prospective purchaser who claims not to "have customers for diamonds of that shape," because round diamonds are as universal in demand as red roses. Of course, the other considerations of quality are not to be sacrificed or even interfered with merely for sake of obtaining a round cut. A round cut diamond which has flaws, is not of the best color, or otherwise is below the best quality grades, is certainly less desirable than one of the other shapes that measures up favorably to the other points.

CARAT OR WEIGHT. The size of a diamond is never expressed by linear measurement but rather by its weight, expressed in the form of *carats.*

The uninformed buyer of diamonds is generally more impressed by a statement of carat than any other consideration. Thanks to this, numerous badly colored, impure and miscut stones are successfully sold at prices higher than they ought to command. This should perhaps not be overly surprising; we live in an age when "big" is taken to mean "best," though rising gas prices and the switch to compact autos may signal a reversal of this philosophy. Big diamonds are not necessarily best. A large-carat stone of good purity, attractive color and successful cut will certainly be worth more — often a great deal more — than a small of the same quality. But where the quality is different, carat alone is not sufficient to save the value and imperfect large-carat gems are definitely not to be regarded as investment pieces. The prospective buyer to whom your diamonds are offered for sale will not be impressed by the carat size so much as by the quality. He will think in terms of resale and he knows from experience that most buyers of investment diamonds are more concerned with quality than size.

One carat equals a fifth of a gram or 1/42 of an ounce. As many diamonds weigh less than one full carat, it will be necessary to carry out mathematical divisions of these figures to arrive at an equivalent. To achieve more precise communication of weight, "points" are sometimes employed instead of carats. A point equals 1/100 of a carat. Therefore, a 25-point diamond is the equivalent of ¼ carat, 50-point would be half a carat and so forth. In the days before diamond prices got so high, nobody bothered about splitting infinitives so finely. No attention was given to the possibility of a diamond described as 1 1/8 carats being slightly more or less in weight. Today, when every point means dollars, you are being most unfair to yourself if you do not purchase from a dealer who can provide point weights for his merchandise. These should be available even for large diamonds (432 points would translate, for example, into four carats and 32 points, or roughly 4 1/3 carats).

With stories of diamonds such as the Cullinan being well-known, weighing over 1,000 carats in the rough, it is naturally presumed by most persons that diamonds when discovered are at least the size of small pebbles. This is not so. The vast majority of diamonds taken from mining and sifting operations are less than one carat in weight in the rough, and therefore end up even smaller after cutting (though, of course, most are not made into jewelry: they go toward industrial use, where such considerations as light refraction are not significant).

Loss of carat weight is inevitable in cutting. For a rough diamond to be properly cut, with introduction of all 58 facets and correct shaping (no matter which of the six popular shapes is chosen), at least *half of* the original weight must be sacrificed. There is no alternative. In the case of extremely large rough stones, which are of equal clarity and color throughout, it is sometimes decided to cut them into two or more gems, as two smaller or moderately sized diamonds are likely to be more easily salable than one super-stone. This was done with the Cullinan, which became two individual diamonds as well as nearly 100 "brilliants," fashioned from the odd chips removed in faceting.

Investors frequently think in terms of buying the largest carat diamond consistent with quality that their budget will permit. This is not the best approach. It is true that the larger diamonds are scarcer and worth more, carat for carat, than those of lesser size. But it is likewise true that the market on large specimens is not so steady. Overly large diamonds can prove a problem in disposal. If a dealer or broker has no waiting client to accept a five or 10 carat stone, he may not wish to make the investment himself, fearing that it might move slowly and result in too much capital being tied up. Of course, if you have the right buyer, a large gem is very profitable to sell. On the other hand most dealers will take unlimited quantities of good-quality diamonds weighing three carats or less (one carat should generally be the lowest for investment), because there is an almost constant demand for stones of this size. They can be turned over easily and quickly at a predictable rate of profit. Therefore, if you have the choice as an investor of buying five one-carat stones or one weighing five carats, it would be much more sensible to choose the former, even though the latter may be more tempting. This advice does not apply if you have substantial sums of money to invest and/or are certain to be in a position where rapid sale is not required.

GRADING MOUNTED DIAMONDS

Mounted diamonds cannot be graded as accurately as loose stones. The best that can be hoped for is an approximation of grading. This is why mounted stones which the owner declines to have dismounted are bought by dealers at a discount from the price that would be given for an unmounted specimen in similar condition. The discount allows for the risk that, when and if unmounted, the diamond might prove less desirable than it appeared in its setting.

Mounted stones present grading problems both in terms of clarity and color. The clarity cannot be read as reliably as on an unmounted gem because certain areas are obscured by the mounting. A dark included crystal may exist directly behind one of the setting prongs. If this seems a slim possibility, it should be realized that gem mounters take pains to cosmeticize their stones as much as is practical; it is obviously more to the stone's advantage (and theirs) to hide flaws that can be hidden. Looking through from the opposite side does not tell the full story, even if examination is carried out with 10X magnification under strong light.

Color grading is a problem with mounted stones because the color of the mounting is reflected into the diamond. If this is yellow gold, it will inevitably tinge the stone yellow. There is less color reflection when the mounting is platinum or white gold. Still, the color cannot be inspected as well as if unmounted. A mounted diamond in a setting by colored stones is even more troublesome to grade. When the surrounding stones are blue, this tends to artificially improve the diamond's color, as their reflection imparts a suggestion of "blue-whiteness."

GRADING DIAMONDS FOR CUT

An important step in grading cut diamonds is carefully examining the quality of cut. This includes overall proportioning as well as the cutting of each individual facet and the girdle. Grading for cut is difficult for the inexperienced person, as the ability to distinguish between qualities of cutting is mainly acquired by handling and inspection of many diamonds.

It should first of all be realized that vast difference will be encountered in qualities of cut, regardless of the diamond's size, shape (Round Brilliant, pear, etc.), or source. Furthermore, many stones that appear very impressive when first seen prove on closer inspection to be mediocre or bad cuts. It is not simply a matter of the cutter failing to do his work satisfactorily. Some diamonds are intentionally misproportioned for the sake of saving carat weight, as the average jewelry buyer understands carat weight much better than the fine details of cutting.

Obviously, investors should try to restrict their purchasing to stones with high quality cutting. Remember that you might be selling — when the time comes — to individuals who know about diamonds, and any deficiencies in cut are certain to be used in beating down the price.

THE MAKE. This is the trade term for the diamond's proportioning, generally referred to either as a "good make" or "bad make"; the word "perfect" is seldom used. Essentially the stone should have been cut so that it reflects light to its maximum potential, which is somewhat greater with a Round Brilliant than the other shapes (and is influenced, too, by color). The table and facets can be looked upon in the sense of transmitters of light. They admit light into the diamond, from which it is bounced outward after traveling through the interior on an established path. If these transmitters are not angled just right, or if some are too large or small, not quite as much light will enter. Or it will enter in the wrong direction, and not travel on the path it ought to.

Differences between a good and bad make — or a good and almost-good — may be so slight as to be indistinguishable with the naked eye, or even with magnification. Actual measuring is often resorted to, in the case of stones large enough to submit to measuring.

The diameter at the girdle is measured, using a Leveridge guage (these are available at most jewelry supply houses). The diamond's other proportions

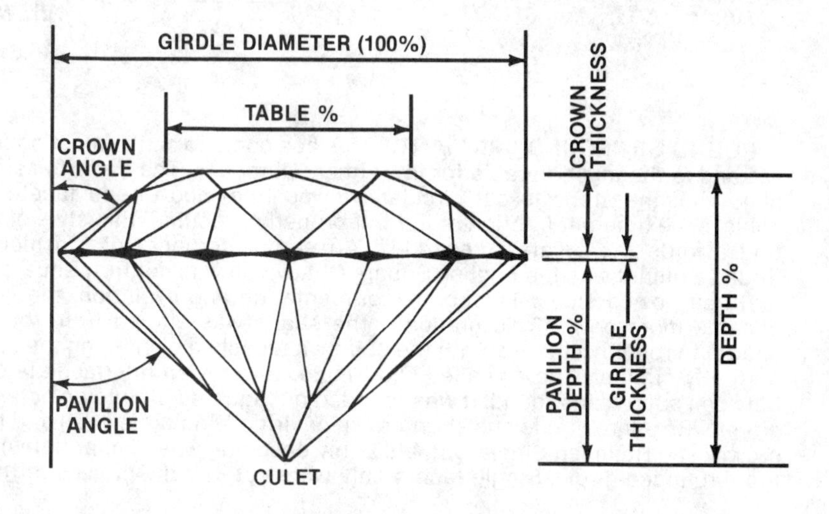

are then matched against this reading, including table diameter, crown height, and pavilion depth. According to the much-respected Tolkowsky scale — he developed the American Brilliant Cut — the table diameter should be 53% of girdle diameter. Crown thickness should be 16.2% of girdle diameter. The pavilion should have a thickness of 43.1% of the girdle diameter. Depth from table to culet should be 59.3% of girdle diameter. The crown angles should be 34.5° and the pavilion angle should be 40.75°. The crown and pavilion facets must also be cut at precise angles. Some variation is possible, but only if planned in advance, using a different set of percentages that will yield predictable results; not when variation is the result of bad mathematics or poor cutting.

When the table is larger than it should be, crown thickness is reduced. Consequently the crown facets will be too small. This is more common than cuts with too-small tables.

European buyers are somewhat less critical of stones with wide-cut tables than are American.

ALL ABOUT DIAMOND SHAPES

There are six traditional or popular shapes into which diamonds are cut — Round, Marquise, Pear, Emerald, Heart and Oval. Many variations in shaping and/or faceting of these shapes are possible and will be encountered on the market. You will also find diamonds of other shapes — usually referred to as fancy or miscellaneous shapes. Diamonds with shapes other than these six are normally but not invariably European cuts and many are old. For example, the Mazarin cut, named after Cardinal Mazarin (17th century), is a French version of today's Round Brilliant. It is almost but not perfectly circular. By and large the older cuts are not as desirable and unless the stone is of exceptional quality are not recommended for investment.

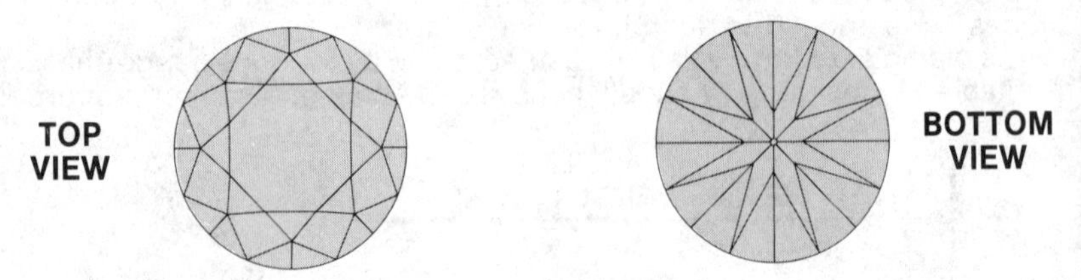

ROUND OR "ROUND BRILLIANT." This has come to be the most popular cut and is the most suitable for investment purposes. The name is self-explanatory: the stone is cut circular (viewed from above) and faceted to achieve maximum refraction of light. If properly executed, this style of cutting affords the greatest "sparkle." An early forerunner of the modern Round Brilliant was the English Square Cut, which was not truly square but featured bowed sides. Through experimentation and evolution, the sides became more bowed and gradually the shape was altered from roughly square to roughly circular, until the point was reached of shaping the stone perfectly circular. The so-called Old Single Cut was an intermediate step between square and round. It was rounded but squared off into an octagon, either with a large table and short crown or virtually no table at all and high crown. The Rounded Single Cut, also now obsolete, was similar but with a more rounded girdle. Single facets only were cut into the crowns of these stones. They were attractive but the single faceting did not make full use of a diamond's ability to refract light. These cuts were admired in their time because buyers were not exposed to anything better. None are being produced any longer. They are truly "antiques" and have some curiosity appeal, but the investor will not care to purchase them.

One of the more familiar intermediaries between old diamond shapes and the Round Brilliant is the Old Mine Cut. This term originated from the practice of some mining companies in early days to employ cutters and place already shaped stones on the market, presumably at more attractive prices than independent cutters would charge. Quite a few Old Mine Cuts are still turning up, in possession of persons who have owned their diamonds for two or more generations. Old Mine Cuts are square with bowed sides. The faceting can take several forms. These are considered unattractive and are not desirable. They are usually purchased, when purchased at all, at liberal discounts. An Old Mine Cut weighing several carats, which could be recut into Round Brilliant without reducing its weight below one carat, will have some appeal. But such stones should not be acquired by investors.

Other early versions of the Round Brilliant were: English Star Cut, Perruzzi Cut, Brazilian, Lisbon, and Early Modern Brilliant. The names are romantic and the stones often have long impressive provenances or histories of ownership, but they are not for investment.

The modern Round Brilliant has several characteristics worthy of notice. Its table is octagonal or eight-sided and is always a perfect octagon, regardless of stone size. Ringed around this table is a crown composed of alternating kite facets, star facets and upper girdle facets, each of its own standard contour but always with straight edges (except along the girdle which, of course, is rounded). The girdle itself, or the circumference of the stone at its widest part, has a wavy cut. Investors should seek out specimens in which the girdle is not too thick, as this is regarded as an indication of inferior shaping. The culet or point at the base is cut octagonally as a miniature duplication of the table.

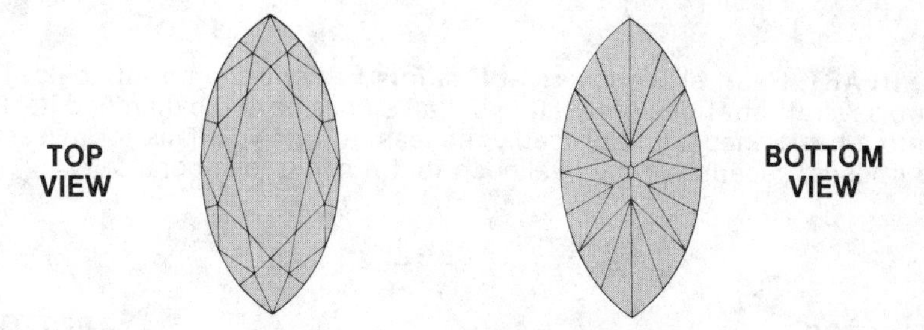

MARQUISE. The Marquise is a variation of the brilliant cut, in which the stone is shaped ovally and comes to a point at either end. It may be cut into the classic Marquise, featuring a long table squared at either end and bowing out slightly into a semi-triangle at the sides, or the less-common Navette Marquise, which has a star pattern. The Navette is not very popular in the U.S. and is not suggested for investment.

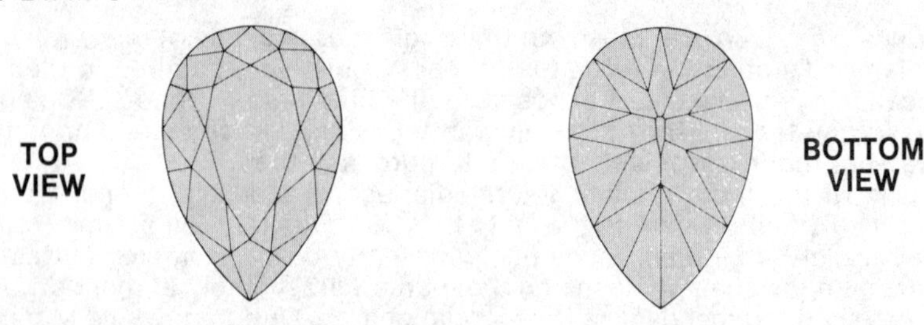

PEAR. The Pear cut is also sometimes referred to as Teardrop. It is actually egg-shaped, coming to a point at the small end. The table is roughly rectangular, intersected with both straight and curving cuts.

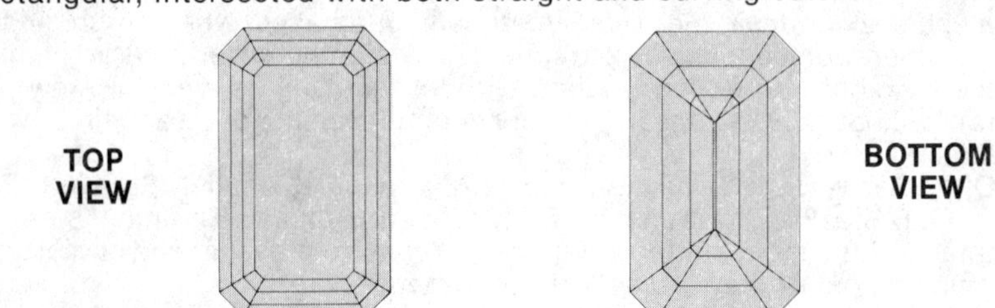

EMERALD. This is what the name suggests, a shape following that into which emeralds are normally cut. It is rectangular with the corners removed and features a very large rectangular table, also with the corners removed.

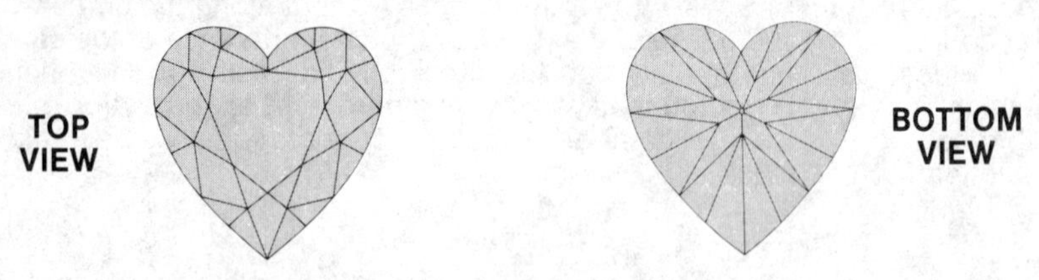

HEART. Heart shapes were at first rated among the novelty cuts. There are several variations of faceting but all stones have the diamond itself cut into a heart shape. It is probably the least attractive shape for investment purposes, because of the likelihood that it might lose popularity.

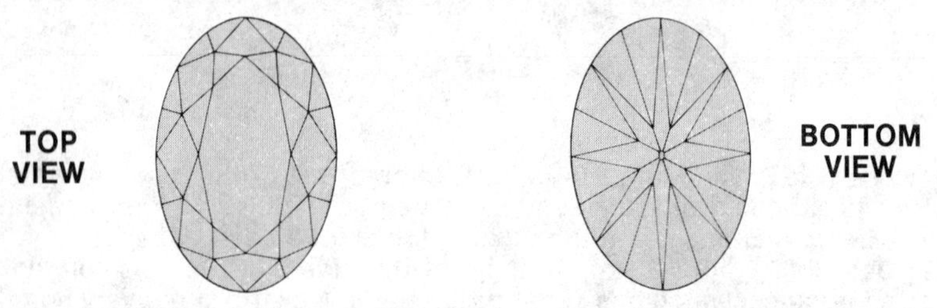

OVAL. The Oval shape is just what the name implies. The table is of modest size and all cuts are curved.

THE OLD MINE CUT

The "old mine cut" is generally found in jewelry made before 1900. This is most commonly a round shape, very crudely cut. Proportions are very inaccurate. They are not advisable for investments unless mounted in an exceptionally rare piece of jewelry, in which event the item has more antique value than value as a diamond.

The term "old mine cut" originated from the belief that in the 1800's diamonds were cut at the mines before wholesaling. This was seldom the case. These poor cuts were simply the result of inferior workmanship and reflect the lower standards of the jewelry buying public at that time.

Old mine cuts can be recut by an experienced gem cutter. In the U.S. this is almost always done in New York. You should probably check several good jewelry trade journals available at your public library for help in locating a qualified cutter. In recutting, 30-50% of carat weight will be lost, on the average. Recutting can either be done for best clarity or for size — that is, retaining the highest possible carat weight. Your cutter should adivse you of the options and give his opinion on which approach will yield the highest value stone.

HOW DIAMONDS ARE CUT

The operations of modern diamond factories, through which millions of dollars worth of stones pass every few months, are not greatly different than those of their predecessors in Renaissance Europe. Tools, though basically similar, have been modernized, and volume of output is considerably greater. But the daily routine is more or less as it was 400-500 years ago.

Cutting of diamonds is, of course, the most significant phase through which they pass from discovery at the mines to ownership by the eventual private buyer. In the act of cutting and shaping, their value is increased several times beyond that of the "rough" price. The operation demands not only skill but adequate planning and judgment, for a cut that might suit one diamond is not necessarily best for another. Decisions of this kind are not made by the cutters but by a "designer," who carefully surveys all arriving roughs. The goal is to achieve the maximum possible value from each rough. As there is no standard formula for doing this, each rough stone must be considered individually just as if it were a hospital patient.

The shape must be taken into account. Is the rough shaped well enough so that it could yield a single cut diamond with minimum loss of carat? Or does its shape seem more suited to division into two gemstones, which will mean greater loss of weight? When possible, roughs are cut into single stones, because a single stone weighing two carats is worth more than two stones of one carat each. In the case of very large roughs, it is sometimes possible to cut a series of small stones from the shards left behind.

The rough's shape also influences the cut shape. A basically spherical rough will lend itself well to a round cut. If elongated, it is a better candidate for an oval, emerald or some other shape.

The chief diamond cutting terms are:

BRUTING. Removing portion of a stone by use of friction (with another stone).

CLEAVING. Breaking away a portion of surface along a plane or cleavage.

GRINDING. Leveling off a surface (of the table, for example) with a high-speed wheel coated in diamond dust.

POLISHING. The final step, also accomplished by use of a wheel laden with diamond dust.

SAWING. Division of a diamond by use of a diamond saw.

Cutting also has other objectives. Most roughs contain flaws and the style of cut can eliminate some or all of them. Some may be simply cleaved or bruted away. Others, while remaining, can have their severity diminished by cutting the stone so that flaws such as inclusions of foreign mineral particles are at the *top*, where they will be less noticeable. It might be presumed that inclusions would be better positioned at the bottom; but as light refracts from inside the base, inclusions there interfere with the stone's sparkle.

The ideal shape for a diamond may not be readily apparent from inspection of its exterior, even when this is carried out under magnification. Exterior inclusions or cloudiness may be so extreme that clear viewing of the interior is hampered. In these instances it is common for some preliminary cutting to be done along the outside, removing areas containing flaws or which, because of odd shaping, would need to be removed anyway. These preliminary openings are referred to as "windows." After several have been cut, the stone is re-examined. When the decision is made as to shape, the stone is marked with ink to indicate where the table or upper flat surface is to be cut. Additional markings may also be made by way of instruction to the cutter. This practice varies from country to country and often from factory to factory.

BRUTING. Bruting is likewise done on a machine (of the lathe variety) but calls into play more human labor than sawing, as the diamond (or rather the stick holding it) is at all times worked upon by the bruter or cutter. It is fastened to a holder known as a "dop," which spins round at 800-1,000 r.p.m. or about 15 revolutions every second. While rotating at this intense speed, the diamond is contacted by a cutting diamond mounted on the bruter's stick. His skill in maneuvering the stick, and removing it from contact at the proper moments, will determine whether the stone is correctly bruted. As the subject diamond is so tiny an object, the high success ratio is ample testimony to the dedication of cutters.

THE CUTTER. Some diamond cutters work independently, as did the majority of their profession in olden times. But independent operators are now the exception; most are employed by the factories and paid an hourly wage. Nevertheless, they still rank as artisans, and those of greatest skill are highly respected within the trade. They must serve apprenticeship before being employed. Thereafter, their tasks are confined mostly to the simpler cuts or work upon stones of modest value, until their talents are fully proved. The cutters are men of intense personal pride. There is much competition and even rivalry between them, in the large diamond cutting centers such as Amsterdam and Tel-Aviv. The trade is financially rewarding for those of acknowledged skill. The whole diamond industry depends upon them — a fact they never fail to recognize. They must not merely be technicians adept at handling machinery and tools, but require a thorough knowledge and understanding of diamonds: their structure, qualities, and reactions under given circumstances. Much of this can only be gained through long experience. Nearly every cutter has spoiled diamonds at some point in his career. Spoilage is accepted as an inevitable price that must occasionally be paid. It is reflected in the cost of diamonds whose cutting goes well.

There is a constant play of opposing forces in diamond cutting, somewhat akin to that of the mythological gods who played tug-of-war for heaven and earth. On one hand, to cut a rough in symmetrical perfection is the ideal. Production of a diamond is this class certifies the cutter's expertise and wins admiration of informed buyers. But there is something else to be considered. By widening out the girdle a bit (the band around the stone's circumference), somewhat greater weight can be retained, and in all likelihood the stone will be accepted as High Grade by the majority of potential purchasers. Do you make a perfect cut, or go for added weight? This decision is faced constantly.

In the case of roughs which would not appear capable of yielding cuts of IF or even VVS grade, the latter route will normally be chosen. But if the cutter is working with an IF or FL rough, its value if transformed into a perfect cut will almost certainly overshadow the slight loss of carat weight.

The word "make" is used, in reference to cutting results vs. the ideal proportions for a cut of that nature. If a diamond agrees with the usual qualifications of proportioning, it is called a good make — possibly a fine make or even (though the trade is not too fond of superlatives) an excellent make. If not it will be saddled with some derogatory designation, such as a "poor make" or "bad make." These terms are freely used by the merchants and factory personnel but rarely are passed along to the public. Actually, a "bad make" is seldom so bad as one might imagine. It is nine times in 10 only fractionally out of line, to a degree noticeable only by a trained observer.

In cutting operations, all work is done in relation to the grain. Cutters saw the grain and polish against the grain. Unless the "rule of grain" is strictly observed, desired results will not be achieved. The grain may be seen under magnification, or with unaided vision in larger stones. A good conception of diamond grain may be obtained from observation of quartz crystals, whose graining is similar and whose larger size displays it more readily.

Cleaving is done, too, in relation to grain. The cutter cleaves in an octahedral direction. When the crystal is an octahedron, cleaving is parallel to any of the facets. This is a delicate step in the procedure and, obviously, any mishap brings ruin. The stone must initially be glued to the tip of a cleaving stick, a wooden dowel rod about eight inches in length. A special composition paste is used, which holds the diamond firmly even after it receives the cleavage blow. A second diamond is similarly glued to another rod. This is the "cleaver," the first being the "subject." The cleaver diamond is a special cutting diamond with a cleavage edge. Actual cleaving is not performed with this second diamond. It is used merely to mark the desired line of cleavage on the "subject," in the form of a deep scratch. This done, the rod holding the subject diamond is laid into a special box which holds it securely in the manner of a vise, while a sharp knife blade is positioned above it guillotine-like. This is done strictly by hand and requires calm nerves and some measure of confidence. The blade is rapped smartly across the top, which drives it downward into the guide-scratch. If properly carried out, the stone will divide along the cleavage plane. It will not shatter or divide unevenly. The instrument used to drive home the knife blade is normally a short iron rod.

Cleaving is also performed on some diamonds destined for industrial use. Here, however, the degree of accuracy is not of such great importance.

GRINDING FACETS. Facets are ground into the diamond with equipment similar to that employed in bruting. This, too, is an operation calling for precision. A stone which has successfully passed through the earlier stages of its treatment could still be spoilt, or at any rate its sales value seriously reduced, by bad grinding.

A skilled cutter known as the "cross cutter" is responsible for applying the first 18 facets. These include the table, the culet, the four corners, the four upper bezels, and four corners and four pavilions at the lower portion. This is standard regardless of the stone or shape, as all shapings must carry these cuts. The table is always ground before the other cuts or grindings are made. This provides the central direction for the remainder of the operation. The first facet is then ground. As the other facets must match it, the correct grinding of this initial facet is extremely important. Normally, the position of the first facet is at one of the top corners. A gauge is used to judge the size. However, the gauge alone, in the hands of an unskilled operator, cannot produce satisfactory results. Nor can any phase of diamond cutting ("cutting" used here in the sense of all phases of manufacture from rough to finished stone) be performed without skilled human aid. The machinery itself, no matter how sophisticated, is merely an accessory to the talents of its operators. When grinding in the facets has been completed, the stone is then polished, on the rotating wheel of the scaife or scaive. This apparatus, used in grinding as well, has somewhat the appearance of a huge phonograph turntable. Its chief component is a central wheel, fixed horizontally on a table, which spins around at high speed. There are various grades of abrasive surface on the scaife, as one gets nearer or further from the center, which can be compared in a sense to rough and fine sandpaper.

The stone is then sent along to the so-called "brillianteer," or "brillianteerer," whose task is the cutting of the final facets. Though the gem is by now well along in its travels, having received its shape and its large facets, it can still be spoilt by accidents or faulty judgment. These small facets are of extreme significance in the admission of light and determine, by their correct positioning and proportioning, if light will enter the stone at proper angles and thereby be refracted and expelled to the fullest capability. Diamonds have extraordinary refractive abilities, if cut in the right way. An improperly faceted gem will not sparkle to nearly its full potential and its sales value — despite color, shaping and carat weight — will be seriously reduced.

This done, all work is not yet completed. The diamond is now physically in the form it will display to a retail purchaser (unless, of course, its destiny is to be mounted into jewelry). But it still requires checking, to determine if some minor repairs or additional grinding are necessary along any part of its surface. Inspection is carried out with the aid of magnification. Occasionally, depending upon the traditions of an individual factory and the nature of the diamond, it may be washed in acid prior to final polishing, for removal of any grease or other surface matter that was acquired in the preceding operations.

The stone is then polished, usually with an automatic machine, the use of which is of modern origin. This process is more painstaking than might be presumed and adds considerably to production expense, but is a necessary adjunct to turning out diamonds of the best quality.

SAWING. The process of sawing calls machinery into play. In early ages the "machinery" was powered by water wheels, or treadmills driven by horses, dogs or humans. These provided a minimal number of r.p.m.'s (revolutions per minute) compared to modern devices run by electricity. Sawing is done to fashion the cleaved stone into the approximate shape it is desired to achieve, as well as remove flaws. The sawing blade is made of bronze of a special composition, to which diamond powder or dust is applied. Application of this dust is necessary because the bronze alone would not be capable of cutting. The dust is prepared by mixing with olive oil. The subject diamond is affixed in a holder, secured to the sawing machine. There are various techniques for attaching the diamond to the holder. This holder is rotatable to any position, so that the diamond may be sawn in whatever direction is necessary or required without the trouble of remounting. Though the sawing machinery is highly developed, its supervision and operation by skilled personnel is essential to successful results.

DIAMOND RECUTS

A recut diamond is one which has twice, or more frequently (though this is rare), gone through the cutting process. As a certain amount of carat weight is lost in recutting, there must be some strong motivation to have this done rather than simply wishing to change one shape into another. Usually, recutting is done for one of the following reasons:

1. (the most common) To transform an obsolete cut into something more currently fashionable.
2. To correct errors in the first cutting.
3. To conceal the identity of stolen gems.

So far as the first two are concerned — we will not give any advice concerning the third — careful thought must be given and frequently some mathematics entered into before the decision for recutting is made. The obvious question is, in the case of recutting stones of obsolete or unpopular shapes, will the loss of carat weight be compensated for by the increase in sales appeal? This depends upon the stone's size and present shape. A stone weighing two carats or more is pretty certain to yield a good return in recutting. In smaller stones, when a recutting would bring the weight down below a carat, there may be nothing gained or so little gained that the operation is not worthwhile. Remember that it is not merely a question of present weight less the loss of weight in recutting; *the recutting itself costs money* and this sum must be added to the loss of carat weight. It is rare for an Old Mine Cut to be transformed into a Round Brilliant without losing at least 30 to 50% of the carat weight as previously stated in the "Old Mine Cut" chapter. However, a modern well-executed Round Brilliant outsells an Old Mine Cut of the same size by anywhere from 300% to 500%. So it is usually a profitable undertaking, if the stone is large.

As far as recutting to correct errors in the old cut is concerned, this is generally a matter of improving the proportioning. It involves the loss of more carat weight than might be anticipated and is often not profitable.

BROKEN DIAMONDS

Despite their resistance to scratching or other surface damage, diamonds can be (and sometimes are) broken. In ordinary cutting they must be broken and this is accomplished not with superhuman strength but the mere tapping of a knife blade along an etched line. When diamonds break accidentally, they cannot be mended back together because, even if all portions are salvaged, they would be so noticeably flawed as to grade in the reject class. The only logical approach is to have the largest pieces recut, which will unfortunately reduce them further in size, and perhaps sell the smaller pieces (if the stone is crushed) as they are for whatever can be obtained for them. It might be possible to trade the smaller pieces for the recutting work. There is no way to fully or even substantially reclaim the value of a broken diamond.

DETERMINING THE CARAT WEIGHT

The matter of a diamond's weight is of course a prime consideration in establishing its value, or at least its potential value in relation to other diamonds.

Diamonds are weighed by carat.

In the distant past, seeds of the carob bean were employed by merchants and traders in the Middle East for weighing delicate merchandise, and the word carat is simply a derivation of "carob." Another common measure of weight, the grain, evolved from a similar practice: that of using wheat grains as counterbalances of primitive scales. A carat is a greater measure of weight than a grain because the carob bean is heavier than a grain of wheat.

But weighing diamonds is, today, a far less casual (and unfortunately less simple) endeavor than tossing beans on a scale.

It is a matter of precision, for which a variety of devices, some of them costing large sums of money, have been developed. Nevertheless, many dealers prefer the use of traditional non-electric balance scales, operating in the same fashion as those of 2,000 years ago. Use of these naturally demands counterweights whose weights are precisely established.

ROUGH WEIGHT AND CUT WEIGHT. It is believed by some persons unfamiliar to the world of diamonds that only cut stones have a carat weight, that the carat is somehow imparted to them in grinding and faceting. This, of course, is not the case. Roughs have their carat weight, too — and all are weighed upon being received at the central office after the day's mining operations. Rough stones are sold by weight in the same manner as cut stones. There is, of course, a difference. Not only is the price considerably lower, it does not advance so sharply from one carat to the next for rough stones. A cut diamond of three carats will normally sell for twice as much — or even more than twice — as one of two carats. Rough stones do not. This is because the cut stone has ended its life cycle. It has arrived at the completed stage, and whatever its present size or shape or proportion it can be expected to retain these characteristics. A rough diamond is rather an intangible. There is no telling for certain how the factory into whose hands it passes might choose to cut it. It may be cut into any of various shapes, resulting in a small or substantial loss of weight. Also there is some risk of accident or of the proportioning not working out just right. Therefore the great premium attached to finished cut stones of large carat is not applied to roughs.

EXPRESSION OF WEIGHT BY CARAT. Proposals have for many years been advanced to revise the method by which weights of diamonds are given, replacing the carat with something more universally understandable to the public. These have so far all met rejection. There is no great difficulty with the carat system so long as one learns it thoroughly.

Expressed in metric terms, the carat equals one fifth of a gram. It is therefore readily apparent that even very large diamonds, excepting of course those of museum proportions, do not attain to even one full ounce in weight. No cut diamond exists with a weight of as much as five ounces.

Where carats alone are used for expression of weight, fractions of a carat are normally given by decimal. A full carat is written as 1.00, which means "one carat plus nothing extra." A stone weighing one and 1/10th carats would be recorded as 1.10. Depending upon the sensitivity of the weighing equipment, readings can get to hundreds and even thousandths of a carat. The figure 1.16 indicates a weight of one and 16/100th of a carat. When two digits appear behind the decimal, the weight is being expressed in hundredths of a carat. If there is just one digit, such as 1.1, the weight is being given in tenths. In this case the weight is one and one-tenth carats.

The following may simplify this:

1.00 = one carat
1.10 = 1 1/10
1.20 = 1 1/5
1.50 = 1 1/2
1.75 = 1 3/4ths
2.00 = two carats
2.34 = two and 34/100ths, or approximately 2 1/3rd carats
2.546 = two and 546/1,000ths. A figure such as this can be better understood by mentally knocking away the final digit, reading it as 2.54, then using the last digit to make a calculation in hundreds. Thus we would then get 2.54 carats plus 6/10ths of the hundredth part of a carat.

When the weight is lower than a full carat it will be expressed in terms of a zero followed by a decimal, with digits behind the decimal, such as:

0.72

This indicates a stone weighing 72/100th of a carat, or about 3/4ths of a carat. 0.50 would be half a carat, 0.25 one quarter of a carat. There is no limit, technically, to the minimum weight which can be expressed by carat, as you can get down to readings such as 0.08 (less than 1/10th of a carat) and the like. Luckily the investor need not trouble himself about these.

Though the system of expressing weight by carat is readily mastered by anyone of reasonable intelligence, it is not considered as plainly comprehendible as the point method. The latter is in wide use today in the American diamond industry and is gradually — but grudgingly — being adopted in Europe. It is regarded as an adjunct only to the carat system, not really as a replacement for it. The carat system cannot be entirely replaced because the mining companies and C.S.O. (Central Selling Organization) are far too dedicated to it.

The point system presupposes that the average human being can more easily understand figures in which decimals are not used. This is probably true. In the point system, 100 points is the equivalent of one full carat. 200 points stand for two carats and so forth. A stone weighing 0.81 of a carat would be indicated merely as 81 points.

Equivalents are as follows:

Carat system	Points		
0.10	10	=	1/10 of a carat
0.50	50	=	½ carat
1.00	100	=	1 carat
1.50	150	=	1½ carats

And so on. A ten carat stone would be 1,000 points.

THE ART OF WEIGHING. Far trickier than the reading of carats or points is the actual weighing of stones so that reliable figures can be arrived at.

All manner of equipment has been tried for this purpose, some of it discarded through the years. There is still no single scale in universal use or preference. However, weighing to the fraction of a carat is now a reality — which it definitely was not in the days of carob beans.

Rough stones are often weighed in groups and sold in lots of 20 or 50 or 100 carats, with no assurance given of the quantity of stones that will be contained. Lightweight cut stones may be traded in this manner, too, but for specimens of more substantial weight it is necessary to weigh each individually.

DIAMOND ESTIMATION. The most popular method of determining approximate carat weight is the diamond estimator. These are of many types, the most common of which is a plain piece of aluminum with holes of graduated sizes cut in it. Approximate carat weight is indicated by the circles below. It is thereby possible to roughly guage the carat weight for stones of these diameters.

We have illustrated a selection here, for use in the event you are not able to obtain a carat estimator. There should, however, be no trouble locating one through a jewelry supply house.

NOTE: These are approximate sizes and should be regarded as such. Before you buy or sell any diamond its carat weight should be determined by a professional using accurate equipment.

ROUND BRILLIANTS

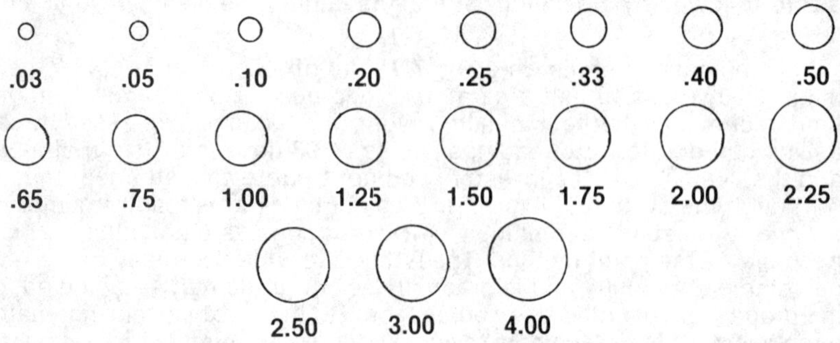

.03 **.05** **.10** **.20** **.25** **.33** **.40** **.50**

.65 **.75** **1.00** **1.25** **1.50** **1.75** **2.00** **2.25**

2.50 **3.00** **4.00**

NOTE: With ROUND BRILLIANT cuts you may also estimate by measurement. If you have a ruler or calipers that measure in millimeters, the following table can be used for round cuts.

CARAT WEIGHT	DIAMETER IN MM.	HEIGHT IN MM.
0.01	1.38	0.78
0.05	2.37	1.33
0.10	2.98	1.67
0.25	4.04	2.26
0.50	5.09	2.85
1.00	6.42	3.60
1.50	7.35	4.12
2.00	8.09	4.54
3.00	9.25	5.19
4.00	10.19	5.72
5.00	10.98	6.16

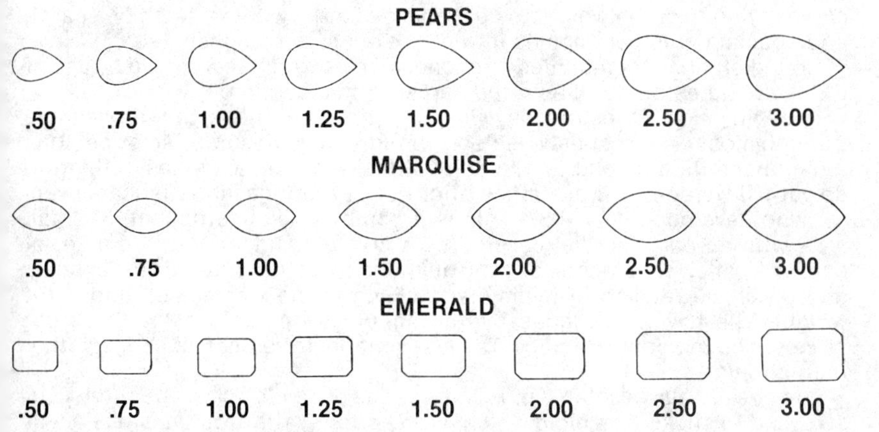

BALANCE SCALES OR PANS. This is the ages-old method of weighing, still employed to some extent today for diamonds because of the ease with which such scales are transported, their resistance to damage, their ability to be used where electrical current is unavailable, and their extremely low price in relation to the modern devices. The principle of the balance scale is that if an object is placed in one pan, and another object in the other, the pan holding the heavier object will fall while the other rises. The extent of fall-and-rise determines the difference in weight, whether it be great or tiny. No springs or anything mechanical whatever is employed in balance scales. However, to arrive at a reliable reading it is necessary to use counterbalances (to place on the pan opposite that of the item being weighed) whose weights are established beyond doubt. The balance can only give readings to relation to the counterbalance's weight; it cannot weigh anything — as do modern scales — independent of a counterbalance. Jewel traders generally rely upon using diamonds of established weight as their counterbalances.

Balance scales do not give the most accurate obtainable readings for fractional weights. They weigh a tenth of a carat very well, but their reliability on hundredths of a carat cannot be trusted.

Among the more sophisticated weighing machines on the current market is the Oertling diamond balance, used extensively in Europe and to some extent in this country. Based on the principle of the pan balance, it offers extreme sensitivity and accuracy of readings impossible with simple balances. It is supplied with counterbalance "rings," each of a stated weight, and by the use of these rings singly or in combination the weight of virtually any diamond in the world can be determined down to 0.01. Fairly advanced portable scales are also on the market, usable without electric power. They are more prone to damage if dropped or knocked than the old-fashioned balances, and their price is not low.

MOUNTED STONES. There is far greater difficulty in weighing mounted stones, a problem that has long vexed the industry. Owners of jewelry given over for appraisal will seldom agree to having the stone removed for weighing. Therefore it must be weighed while mounted, which, technically, is an impossibility. The best that can be done in such circumstance is for a *close estimate* of the weight to be made, generally within a tenth of a carat, and special equipment comes into play even to accomplish this.

Round brilliant cut mounted diamonds can be weight-estimated by use of the diamond estimator illustrated earlier in this section.

More advanced investors may wish to use the Leveridge gauge, available through most jewelry supply dealers. Though often presumed so by persons unfamiliar with diamond terminology, the Leveridge gauge has nothing to do with "leverage." It was named after A. D. Leveridge, an American inventor who developed it in 1937. This is a compass-like instrument, of small size, with an encased dial covered by a crystal. Attached to it is a set of calipers, which are placed upon the diamond to be measured. The dial spins and gives the reading in millimeters, which is then translated into carat weight. The Leveridge gauge has an accuracy degree of 98% for larger stones. The readings are of course less reliable for stones of shapes other than circular.

Gauges are also available in which a series of "mold" sizes are furnished, attached to sticks. The mold which most perfectly fits atop the stone being weighed indicates the approximate carat of the latter.

These are all uncertain operations but nothing so far has been developed to make more accurate estimations of the weights of mounted stones.

DETERMINING THE COLOR OF THE DIAMOND

Reaching correct or reliable conclusions about the color of a diamond is somewhat more challenging than grading for clarity, as a number of variables enter the picture. It is not only a matter of differences in the human eye, from one individual to another, to perceive color, but interference from color reflection of other objects. This is an extremely delicate operation. If conditions are not ideal, the results obtained are likely to be unreliable and will be challenged when the stone is subsequently examined by a person using more sophisticated techniques.

Remember here that we are speaking of cut stones. Grading cut stones for color is quite a different thing than grading roughs, whose external coloration may differ from the underlying color. As the investor or other private buyer is not likely to be in a position of grading roughs we have omitted discussion on the subject.

If your stone or stones are accompanied by a G.I.A. certificate, the color grading will be stated and there is no need for further investigation. If not, the grading is left open to determination, and you should at least become familiar with the methods of grading in order to intelligently buy and sell. This is not to suggest that a beginner can grade as accurately as an experienced person, simply by learning the correct approaches, because knowledge acquired through handling and inspecting many diamonds of different color grades aids greatly in building expertise.

It should also be pointed out that color grading is not an absolute science and that many stones, of both high and low ranking, could easily be placed into different grades by persons of equal expertise.

Sophisticated equipment is now available on the market to assist in color grading.

By far the most accurate means of diamond grading is "comparison grading," used by the G.I.A. when issuing a G.I.A. certificate. You must use what the industry refers to as a "master set of diamonds." These are stones that have been graded by the G.I.A. into specific color categories. They are then put in a row under correct lighting and the stone of undetermined color is compared to each, until the closest match is found. Example: if you have a stone that appears lighter or more colorless than a J grade but is definitely a shade darker than an H, then the obvious conclusion is that its color is an I. This is really the only *true* method of determining diamond color. Size of the master set varies with the individual's needs. The G.I.A. maintains two full master sets of stones D through Z. One is a .50 carat set and the other 1.25 carats. The former is used in grading smaller stones and the latter for larger. For precise and exact grading this is necessary. However a dealer who has only occasional need for a master set may only require a 3-to-5 stone set: let's say an F, G, H, I and J set in .50 carat size. This should suffice to give him a general idea of color for buying purposes as it will show either a colorless state, a slightly tinted state or a heavily tinted state. In most cases this is as involved as he need get to calculate his buying price. Not to mention the fact that a 23-stone master set is extremely costly to assemble. The dealer will hardly ever encounter such a broad range of colors. In buying better quality jewelry, a stone of less than L color will almost never be found mounted in a piece of jewelry.

Recently there have been developments in the manufcturing of Cubic Zirconia "master sets" or "CZ master sets." Placed on the market within the past year or so, these have proved to be most accurate. They are fairly inexpensive and can be transported without fear of losing a $30,000 or $40,000 genuine master set. The cost of a 1.00 carat 5-stone CZ set is under $1,000.

This innovation should prove to be a real landmark in the diamond business.

When grading a diamond yourself, it is first of all important that the surroundings be ideal. Reflections of color can occur from great distances, even in lighting which is not particularly strong, and will interfere with testing. The very nature of diamonds is such that they amplify nuances of color fed into them by light, and it is not possible for the human eye to distinguish between the natural color of a diamond and introduced or reflected color.

The testing room must be set up, so far as is practical, to simulate conditions under which diamonds are graded in a laboratory. This means it ought to have white walls, which have been covered in flat rather than gloss paint. There should be no highly reflective objects in the room. Light entering through a window should not pass through curtains, even if filmy and white, nor should the glass itself be tinted.

It is important that the subject diamond be tested against the proper background. Testing against haphazard or non-standard background is certain to give unreliable results. The stone must be placed on a sheet of good white non-reflective paper. Do not use colors other than white, and do not use typewriting or other similar paper as the surface is too glossy. In the absence of special diamond testing paper (which is available), ordinary white blotting papers may be substituted. The stone is not merely laid upon the paper as it sits flat on the desk. If this is done it will not be viewed at the best angle. Instead, the paper is folded lengthwise to create lines of fluting, so that when laid on the table it presents a series of ridges of perhaps ½ inch each in height. The stone is now placed in one of the valleys between these ridges and is in correct attitude for examination. Instead of being viewed from the top it will now be examined from the side, which will give a more reliable reading. Tests conducted from looking down at the top, or

DIAMOND COLOR GRADING COMPARISON TABLE

NOTE: Color grading is generally based on increased amounts of yellow tint. This color may also appear in brown tints and grey tints. Any other tint should be considered fancy colors no matter to what degree they are saturated. (Examples: blue, pink, orange etc.)

COMPARATIVE AND OLD WORLD TERMS

				G.I.A. COLOR SCALE
FINE BLUE WHITE			JAGER	D
FINEST WHITE	FINEST WHITE	COLORLESS	RIVER	E
				F
	FINE WHITE		TOP WESSELTON	G
WHITE	COMMERCIAL WHITE	VERY CLOSE TO COLORLESS	WESSELTON	H
				I
	TOP SILVER CAPE		TOP CRYSTAL	J
VERY, VERY SLIGHT YELLOW		SLIGHT YELLOW TINT	CRYSTAL	K
	SILVER CAPE		TOP CAPE	L
VERY SLIGHT YELLOW	LIGHT CAPE		CAPE	M
			LOWEST CAPE	N
SLIGHT YELLOW		LIGHT YELLOW TINT		O
				P
YELLOW			VERY LIGHT YELLOW	Q
	CAPE			R
				S
				T
		YELLOW TINT		U
				V
HEAVY YELLOW	HEAVY CAPE		LIGHT YELLOW	W
				X
		HEAVY YELLOW CAST		Y
				Z
FANCY COLOR	FANCY CAPE COLOR	CANARY YELLOW	FANCY YELLOW	Z+

table, are hampered by the much greater reflection of light from within the diamond in that position.

The lighting should be natural if possible. When diamonds are to be graded under artificial light, it is wise to avoid the standard incandescent bulb in favor of white florescent. Do not place the source of light too near the stone, and be certain that it falls centrally from overhead rather than at an angle.

Beginners are advised to make color judgments against the gradings of stones bearing G.I.A. certificates, or otherwise established to be a particular color. If you do not have access to a G.I.A. certified stone you might try a local jewelry store. The larger ones generally have certified stones on hand and might allow you to inspect one or more.

CLARITY CHARACTERISTICS

Clarity characteristics of diamonds are really *defect* characteristics. As explained elsewhere in this book, every mark on a diamond — even if very, very tiny — is a strike against its clarity. These can be of many different kinds, caused by nature or man. When they occur on a stone's surface, they can often be removed by polishing with very little loss of carat weight. Internal defects are frequently impossible to remove; even when this can be done, the diamond loses a great deal of weight.

It is *important to note* that BLEMISHES are marks or other characteristics on the *surface* of a stone. INCLUSIONS are trapped or imbedded within the diamond itself.

The more commonly encountered BLEMISHES are:

ABRASION. Chip on a facet edge, nearly always caused by two diamonds coming into contact with each other. Sometimes called Paper Marks.

EXTRA FACET. An additional facet or plane surface, beyond the number required in shaping. This generally occurs through accident in the cutting process.

NATURAL. An overlying portion of the crystal covering or skin. Found, if at all, near or at the girdle.

PIT. Small nick or cavity. Also known as CHIP.

SCRATCH MARK, WHEEL MARK. Scratches on diamonds may result from contact with other diamonds or defects in the polishing wheel.

SURFACE GRAIN LINE. Evidence (at the surface) of irregular crystal development.

The more commonly encountered INCLUSIONS are:

CLOUD. An area within a diamond that is not perfectly clear but appears opaque.

FEATHER. Break within the structure of a diamond.

FEATHERED GIRDLE. Networks of very fine feathery lines radiating outward from the girdle into the stone's interior.

INCLUDED CRYSTAL. A second crystal within the first or main crystal. It may be clear or colored. When the included crystal is colored or has the appearance of black, it is called a "dark included crystal."

INTERNAL GRAIN LINE. Internal marks of abnormal crystal development.

KNOT. Included crystal (second diamond crystal) which has broken through the surface.

LASER DRILL HOLE. Tiny hole caused by drilling with a laser beam (in an effort to launder the stone).

PERCUSSION MARK. Crumbling in the surface of a cut stone, with uneven cleavages. Also known as bruise.

PINPOINT. Tiny included crystal, having the appearance of a white dot when viewed through 10X magnification. Pinpoints sometimes occur in groups and can then easily be mistaken for cloudiness.

Obviously, the *size* of a blemish or inclusion is important in determining how seriously it detracts from desirability and value. Most of the above vary considerably in size, from very minute (visible only with 10X magnification) to glaring. Also, whether just one of these defects is present in a stone, or several of them, will influence the grade into which it falls. It should likewise be realized that blemishes or inclusions on the table area (the most visually strategic part of the diamond) are more damaging than when they occur elsewhere.

Dark inclusions, as a rule, are more damaging than those of a very light color or colorless.

The grader must become familiar with these various defects, not only in detecting but identifying them, before he can grade accurately. The following grading section of this book will provide further aid.

DETERMINING DIAMOND CLARITY

Examination of diamonds for clarity should first be undertaken with the naked eye, then with a 10X jeweler's loupe and finally with a 10X stereo microscope, if available. It is suggested that the operation be carried out in the following manner.

If possible use a bench or table that permits examination while seated. There should be maximum light and it should come from overhead, rather than from a lamp or other source placed on the work table. Natural light entering though windows may have to be supplemented by artificial lighting. Be sure that all surfaces of magnification devices are clean. Diamonds should be handled with tongs or tweezers only by the girdle.

Do not be in a hurry. Study the diamond from all angles. Move it closer and further from your eye. Take notes as you work. Compare your findings with the descriptions of various grades of clarity given below.

FL (flawless). The highest grade. It is presumed by beginners or uninformed persons that to qualify as FL a diamond must be so crystal clear that no degree of magnification reveals even the slightest blemish or imperfection. This is not true. Minor deviations from perfection sometimes do exist; it is an extremely rare stone which, magnified to 10X, exhibits no flaws whatever. There may be slight imperfections that are visible only a magnification greater than 10X, but the "legal limit" universally used throughout the world is 10X. Therefore if an imperfection or blemish is not visible at 10X, for all intents and purposes it simply does not exist.

IF (internally flawless). As with FL, the blemishes or departures from absolute perfection on an IF stone can be observed only with 10X magnification and only with extreme effort. There are perhaps more of them, but they are not in any way serious or distorting. In addition to those mentioned above, an IF stone may reveal such blemishes as minor (very minor) pitting, but this cannot occur in the table — the diamond's most vital area — or else a lower grading is certain to result. There could be infinitesimal facet abrasion but not a network of scratches. A good grading rule to keep in mind is this: any surface fault or blemish not readily eradicated by simple polishing, in other words blemishes which must be ground out or are impossible to remove without recutting, disqualify the specimen from an IF or FL ranking. This applies even if the injury is not revealed by examination with a 10X loupe.

VVS (Very Very Slight blemish or imperfection — broken down into VVS-1 and VVS-2 to permit use of more grading categories). VVS stones are blemished in some way or other. There will be somewhat more faults than with an IF stone, or the faults are slightly easier to observe with 10X magnification. Typical characteristics of VVS stones are minute spots outside the table. There can be a tiny colorless crystal, more than overshadowed by light refraction. When examined from the underside a minute "feather" could be observed. The girdle or outer circumference may reveal minor natural irregularities. These should not be the result of a bad cutting job. The facet edges could be slightly rough. In short the negative features of a VVS stone should be largely, though not entirely, remedial by simple polishing.

VS (Very Slight blemish or imperfection). This grade is also broken down into VS-1 and VS-2. Here we are still using 10X magnification, under good strong light. We are looking for any internal or external markings that are not consistent with absolute perfection. The VS stone reveals such markings to a slightly more pronounced degree than the VVS. However, they do not appear obvious as soon as we place the stone under 10X magnification. They must be searched for. At first, we are perhaps confident that the stone grades higher. But we persist in investigation, and we locate internal growth lines which exhibit pale color from the front. Once we have encountered such lines we have no alternative but to grade the stone below VVS. Upon further inspection it may be necessary to reduce the grading even more. The VS diamond may show small colorless crystals or groupings of pinpoints. There could be insignificant cracks, as well as minor scratching to the surface caused by contact with other diamonds in storage or errors of the cutter. The girdle may show indented naturals not related to cutting. All in all, there will be general abrasion and possibly a slightly larger extra facet than would be allowable on stones of higher grade. The VS stone is not, despite this lengthy catalogue of possible shortcomings, by any means an outcast. It is still an extremely worthy specimen because its faults, while many, are all of the minor variety and cannot be observed without 10X magnification.

SI (Slight Imperfection; SI-1 and SI-2 are commonly referred to in the trade as "eye-clear"). We are using a 10X jeweler's loupe and the blemishes we find are relatively easy to see with it — not as hard to find as in a VS stone. There will usually be groupings of pinpoints, but not glaring. There are likely to be colorless crystals — not just one but several. One or more of these may be of a dark color. There could be minor cracks or cleavages. Cloudy areas are apt to be notices. There may be a roughness to the culet (the tip of the stone's base) or nick in the girdle. SI stones are not generally regarded as investment pieces, regardless of color or carat. But as diamonds continue to become scarcer, even SI'S should prove to be investment worthy.

Their imperfections are too glaring — despite the fact that they can be noticed only the the 10X loupe — for these diamonds to carry a high resale potential. It might be possible to purchase them cheaply, but they will not advance in value as steadily or rapidly as higher graded stones and very likely the margin of profit on their resale will be slightly lower.

I-1 (Imperfect - first degree). We are now abandoning artificial aids to vision and are examining with the naked eye. Of course, examinations carried out in this fashion do not bear quite such reliable results, being dependent on the individual's keenness of vision. I-1 stones have flaws that can be seen, but just barely, by persons with approximately 20/20 vision at close range. There will be minor cloudiness of flouresence beneath the table. The crystal exhibits darkness. There is a colorless reflecting crystal located beneath the table. Cleavage may be observed from the front. The girdle is likely to show minor cracking radiating outward, either in one restricted region or across most of its circumference. At the surface there will be small waves or indentations on the table. Additional facets are larger than on more highly graded stones.

I-2 (Imperfect - second degree). Blemishes of the above nature, but somewhat more pronounced.

I-3 (Imperfect - third degree). The extra facets are larger, there are collections of dark colored spots beneath the table which can be seen with the unaided eye, as well as cloudiness, possibly feathering below the table. The surface shows scratches observed without magnification, and usually shows large dark included crystals. Generally speaking, this grade should never have been cut into a finished stone.

NOTE: The European market generally refers to imperfect stones as "pique" stones, with various degrees of included crystals. They will be graded as I-1 = P-1; I-2 = P-2; and I-3 = P-3.

Many stones fall into a boarderline category, between one grade and the next. They could be placed into the higher grade by one appraiser and the lower by another. This is why the VVS and VS gradings have been sectioned into VVS-1, VVS-2, VS-1 and VS-2. Even so, specimens will be encountered that seem to defy safe placement into a given category. In such instances the opinion of the G.I.A. serves to resolve argument.

DETERMINING THE VALUE OF A DIAMOND

Simply stated, the value of a diamond is determined by its quality and size, "quality" meaning not only its natural characteristics but the cutting and shaping.

Many diamonds that score high on one point are deficient in other respects. A stone of exquisite color may have blemishes visible to the naked eye and will therefore rank I-1 or lower. The clarity on the other hand may be fine enough to grade IF or FL, but the stone has a bad "make," the trade term for improper proportioning. Whenever a diamond scores poorly on one of these quality considerations, its value is less than that of a perfect stone of the same size and characteristics. Of course, some shortcomings are more detrimental to value than others. Nor should it be presumed that specimens failing to grade high in all respects are near worthless. It is mostly a matter of the individual stone's overall appeal and salability. Some stones can carry a defect better than others. Some have their defects well camouflaged by ingenious cutting.

Diamond appraisal is not an exact science. The appraiser operates from the standpoint that certain colors are more valued than others; that strong light refraction is desirable; that prospective buyers will give a premium for a well-executed cut; and so forth. The diamond must be taken account of as a whole, after careful inspection and consideration of its characteristics, and value determined (or estimated) by a weighing out of good and bad features.

The experts themselves are often in disagreement over value of a given stone. This is why prices realized at major gem auctions, such as those conducted by Sotheby/Parke-Bernet and Christie's, bear less relation to the presale estimates than prices at most other kinds of auctions.

Even the word "value" is open to interpretation. There are a number of meanings of "value," in the world of diamonds.

RETAIL VALUE. Usually taken to mean the price that the average customer pays at the average jewelry store for a diamond to be used chiefly for personal adornment.

INVESTMENT VALUE. The price that an investor could be expected to pay, with fair prospects for a profitable sale at some future date. This will be considerably beneath the retail value.

WHOLESALE VALUE. The price a wholesaler would charge a jewelry manufacturer or other purchaser for the stone.

APPRAISAL VALUE. This might be even higher than retail value, depending on the appraiser's practices. Appraisal value is often referred to as "insurance value."

CUTTING VALUE. A stone that is large enough for recutting may be purchased on the basis of "cutting value," to correct a poor or obsolete cutting job. This will be a low price as it means reduction of carat weight, along with the inevitable risks taken in cutting.

Therefore, any potential buyer, after determining a stone's quality and weight, thinks in terms of the value *to him,* based on the purposes to which it will be placed. A very attractive purchase for one class of buyers may be unprofitable for another. A wholesaler cannot pay more than a fraction of the retail value. To a jewelry manufacturer, a diamond is worth anywhere from 10% to 30% of its retail value. And, of course, the ultimate retailer must buy at a good margin, paying around 50-60% of the price at which he sells (or less, if the stone requires mounting).

It may therefore safely be stated that exact values for diamonds are impossible to fix.

Luckily, the investor need only think in terms of his own position.

First, he can summarily ignore or dismiss a great number of stones on the market, which are simply *not suitable* for his purposes. Even if offered at attractive prices he will not wish to purchase them. Any diamond weighing less than one *full* carat should generally not be considered for investment. There may be only one point in difference between a 99 and 100 point score, but the 99 is technically under one full carat and this fact is sure to be pointed out by the eventual buyer. Old or obsolete cuts should not be bought, regardless of weight or the prices at which they may be available. These, too, will prove difficult to sell. A clarity grading of less then VVS or VS places most stones in the questionable category so far as investment goes. If large, and if the color and cut are good, they might be worthwhile; but generally as an investor you will be seeking VVS or better.

Consequently the investor should be able to tell, without much difficulty, which diamonds *do not* meet his needs, thereby leaving him to concentrate upon the ones that do.

COLOR. It is debatable to what degree color counts in the value of a diamond. But when a diamond is highly graded in other respects, its color will count very much in fixing sales potential. An IF stone with round brilliant cut is certainly worth much more in D, or the highest grade of colorless/bluewhite, than in G or H or some other grade. The difference may be 50% or more. But do not make the mistake of presuming that color counts this much, or even half this much, toward the value of diamonds in general. Say we have for example two stones. One weighs 1½ carats, has a clarity rating of VVS and the color is L (slightly tinted, silver cape). Both have identical shapes and proportioning is equally good. The only difference between them is that diamond #1 ranks a couple of notches lower on the color scale. Their values will be extremely close, perhaps less than 5% apart.

If a stone has superb color, does this override defects if might otherwise exhibit?

The answer is an emphatic NO. Certainly as an investor you cannot become bewitched by color, as tempting as this may be. Many diamonds are wonderfully colored — in the D, E and F class — but are otherwise quite ordinary or have characteristics which *automatically disqualify* them as investments.

ONE CARAT STONES. When a single carat stone has a clarity grading of VS, its color should be generally no less than IF to qualify for investment, regardless of the merit of its other characteristics. If the grading is less than VS, you need give it no further consideration. By the same token, a one carat stone grading from VVS or FL whose color is less than G (nearly colorless/fine white) is not an investment piece. Marriage of good color and good clarity grading is necessary to produce an investment diamond. They need not both be of maximum superiority, but perfection of one does not cancel out the shortcomings of the other.

ONE AND A HALF CARAT STONES. A 1½ carat diamond is VS clarity grading may be suitable for investment in the F color class. That extra half carat compensates for the slight deficiency in color. Here, of course, we are speaking of a weight of 150 points; a diamond weighing 149 points is *not* 1½ carats, as the eventual purchaser will be quick to inform you. The rules of investing cannot be bent. Many attractive and really worthy stones must be passed up simply because of technicalities such as these. You cannot buy what you like, any more than can an investor in anything else.

TWO CARAT STONES. Or 200 points. The larger stones are more in demand and it would be safe to purchase for investment a 2 carat diamond whose clarity rating is VS with a color of G. With less than G you assume some risk, as the lesser colors are not as scarce or as highly desirable. A two carat stone in H is, however, a good investment when the clarity rating is VVS or better.

TWO AND A HALF CARAT STONES. Or 250 points. There is difference of opinion over whether 2½ carat diamonds in VVS merit investment purchase when the color is less than H. It is probably wiser to forego them and concentrate on the more reliable combinations of grade and color.

THREE CARATS AND MORE. When a stone weighs three carats or better — that is, more than 300 points — it is acceptable for investment in FL to VVS grading all the way down to I coloration (commercial white), though if the grading is VS it is necessary for the color to be G or something higher on the scale. Again we are "balancing," and even though we're dealing with large stones there is not a great deal of room for maneuvering. The large stone has much going for it, in weight alone. But it will still not prove profitably salable if it grades low in one respect or another: there are simply too many 3 carat stones in the marketplace that do measure higher in quality. Major sacrifices can only be made with larger specimens, and they are not as a whole recommended for investment anyway. Stay with those of 1-3 carats or possibly 4 carats if a good opportunity presents itself. Five is rather large for the average investor.

CLARITY. Refer to the section on grading terminology for a detailed explanation of the various gradings. This is a major consideration in determining value. When a stone has an imperfection visible to the naked eye, there is really nothing that can save it. It may be brilliant bluewhite, well proportioned, substantial in carat weight, but the imperfectness will chop down its commercial value by 40-70% against the value of the same stone in VS or better condition. As far as investment value is concerned, imperfect diamonds (regardless of whether I1, I2, or I3) are not to be considered under any circumstances.

Do not be misled by fancy trappings. It is quite possible that an imperfect stone was, at some time in the past, set into a piece of good jewelry, and the item as a whole may be quite handsome — especially if the stone is several carats or more. This was done frequently in the past. In days before the public became discriminating, there was a market for *large stones* at *cheap prices.* A woman who wore a 5 carat stone with an imperfection did not concern herself with the imperfection; she was happy to wear a diamond as large as Mrs. Post's or Mrs. Vanderbilt's, figuring that not many people would notice its fault. But things are different today. The market for that kind of stone has deteriorated to the point where it must be more sharply discounted than in the past. Many brokers will not buy imperfect stones at all. A jewelry dealer will, usually, but his offer is likely to be about 5% of the retail value of the same stone without an imperfection.

SI stones, or Slight Imperfection, are readily salable if their other characteristics are acceptable, but they are still not suggested for investment. They simply do not pay as good a rate or return as the higher clarity rankings. A broker may or may not care to buy them. He may have no customers for SI. Even if he does, he will discount these stones more sharply than VVS or FL/IF. Remember when you buy for investment that the purchase price is not the only important consideration. Every day there are brilliant opportunities to acquire diamonds cheaply. But in nearly all instances these are cheap diamonds, which sell at a low figure because they just aren't worthy of a higher price. Their owners wish to dispose of them to place whatever cash they will realize into better grade stones. You should do this, too, if you own diamonds with a clarity grading below VVS. It is not advisable to hold them in anticipation of an appreciation in value, as their sale will be very uncertain even if held for a considerable length of time and the market rises steeply. They will never be anything but VS or lesser and potential buyers will react to them no better in 1985 or 1990 than today.

If it could be stated that 5% or some other figure can be added to the value of a stone, for each higher grading into which it can be placed, the task of appraisal would be marvelously simplified. Unfortunately it cannot. An appraiser must simply operate from the standpoint that the stone would be worth its maximum potential in FL and work down from there.

SHAPE. All other things being equal (but when are they ever?), a circular round will lend more value to a diamond than any of the other shapes. It is not a matter of rarity but quite the opposite. The other shapes are less common but in much less demand. Circular diamonds are highly sought-after. It makes sense for the investor to concentrate his purchasing upon round stones or at least show a representative sampling of them in his portfolio, as their popularity to future buyers can be trusted a bit better. Here again we may be paying more but initial outlay must be weighed against the prospects of eventual sale.

PROPORTIONING. Also called "make." This is the degree to which the cutting job approaches perfection. There are not many absolutely perfect cutting jobs but an investor would not want to place capital into a stone that is obviously misproportioned: the girdle too wide, the crown too short, etc. Improper proportioning can interfere with light refraction. The more perfect a diamond the greater it is likely to appreciate in value, and the easier it will be to sell.

CARAT WEIGHT. For purposes of investment it is probably safer to think in terms of point weight than carat weight. One hundred points equals one carat. If one talks in carats it is natural to classify a 99 point stone as one carat. But it is less than one carat by the point system, and when you attempt to dispose of it you will be told that demand isn't as strong for specimens under 100 points. Get the point weight on every stone you contemplate purchasing, before you buy.

In figuring value by weight (assuming we are dealing with stones of the same clarity grading, color, shape and proportioning), it would be easy to assume that a 200 point stone has twice the value of a 100, and that a 300 pointer is worth 1½ times as much as a stone of 200 points. But this is not the case. The percentage of increase in cash value rises with the weight. A 300 point or three carat gem is generally worth about 25% more than the same stone of 200 points. A 5 carat or 500 pointer will be worth about 45% more than a 3 carat. Whether it can readily be sold at its full potential, at the time you wish to sell it, is another matter: but the potential is there.

The following can be used as a rough guide for tabulating percentage advances. We are assuming that we have a selection of stones which are all Round Brilliant and grade FL for clarity and D for color. *These prices are not intended to be taken as anything more than an indication of percentage advances.*

⅓ carat (0.30), 30 points	*$ 6,000 per carat*
½ carat (.50), 50 points	*16,000 per carat*
1 carat (1.00), 100 points	*54,000 per carat*
2 carats (2.00), 200 points	*60,000 per carat*
3 carats (3.00), 300 points	*75,000 per carat*

Advances for D color VVS-2 are approximately as follows:

⅓ carat	*$ 3,000 per carat*
½ carat	*7,500 per carat*
1 carat	*22,000 per carat*
2 carats	*26,000 per carat*

Figuring values of uncut stones by carat weight is considerably more difficult. A proportion of weight will be lost in cutting and this portion is never precisely known in advance.

* * *

The following chart reflects current New York diamond market prices as of February, 1981. As an investor you should be able to buy diamonds from a good New York broker at these prices plus a 10-15% commission. If you have a diamond to sell you could probably sell to a broker at these prices less 10% to 15% commission for handling. As an example, if you purchased a $1,000 market value stone from a broker your total cost plus commission would be $1,100.00 to $1,150. If you sold the next day, before it had a chance to gain in value, your net proceeds would be $850 to $900 — which reflects a sale price of $1,000 less the $100 to $150 discount for commission. Commissions of brokers vary with the geographical location. It is a good idea to shop around

Keep in mind that these figures are for round brilliant stones accompanied by current G.I.A. certificates, with good proportions. Other shapes have correspondingly less value. These are:

1. *Marquise, 45-50% less than round*
2. *Pear, 60% less than round*
3. *Oval, 65% less than round*
4. *Emerald, 45-50% less than round*

NOTE: All prices are PER CARAT.

.50 CARAT TO .99 CARAT SIZE STONES

COLOR GRADE	CLARITY GRADE FL	VVS1	VVS2	VS1	VS2	SI1	SI2
D	$15,000	9,000	7,250	5,000	3,500	3,000	2,500
E	9,000	7,250	6,000	3,800	3,000	2,500	2,100
F	7,250	6,000	4,200	3,200	2,800	2,000	1,850
G	6,250	4,250	3,700	2,850	2,400	1,900	1,750
H	4,250	3,500	3,000	2,500	2,000	1,700	1,500
I	3,200	2,800	2,600	2,000	1,700	1,500	1,350
J	2,750	2,500	2,200	1,750	1,500	1,300	1,200
K	2,450	2,150	1,800	1,400	1,300	1,200	1,100
L	1,850	1,600	1,450	1,250	1,050	850	700

1.00 CARAT TO 1.99 CARAT SIZE STONES

COLOR GRADE	CLARITY GRADE FL	VVS1	VVS2	VS1	VS2	SI1	SI2
D	$52,000	30,000	20,000	15,000	11,000	8,000	6,000
E	31,000	20,000	15,500	10,500	9,300	6,240	5,250
F	20,000	16,200	11,500	9,200	7,800	5,000	3,800
G	16,000	12,000	9,500	8,000	6,200	3,800	3,200
H	12,000	9,500	8,200	6,000	5,150	3,200	2,800
I	8,000	6,000	5,000	4,200	3,900	2,800	2,600
J	6,000	5,000	4,250	3,800	3,200	2,600	2,450
K	5,000	4,200	3,750	3,200	2,800	2,400	2,200
L	3,800	3,200	2,800	2,650	2,400	2,250	2,000

2.00 CARAT TO 2.99 CARAT SIZE STONES

COLOR GRADE	CLARITY GRADE FL	VVS1	VVS2	VS1	VS2	SI1	SI2
D	$58,000	36,000	25,000	17,000	13,500	9,500	7,500
E	36,500	25,000	18,000	14,000	10,000	8,000	6,750
F	26,000	19,000	15,000	10,500	9,000	6,800	5,800
G	19,500	15,000	12,000	9,250	8,000	5,750	5,000
H	15,000	12,000	9,500	8,050	6,250	5,200	4,400
I	9,500	8,000	6,500	5,800	5,200	4,200	3,800
J	8,000	6,200	5,800	5,250	4,200	3,800	3,400
K	6,200	5,400	4,850	4,400	3,800	3,450	3,000
L	4,800	4,250	3,800	3,550	3,200	2,900	2,700

* * *

Also, to keep tabs on the current diamond market check the **Wall Street Journal** every Monday. Several diamond brokerage houses run the current New York price quotations in the Monday edition. Using these published prices in conjunction with our chart, you will be able to roughly calculate the value of most investment size stones.

CLEANING DIAMONDS

Despite their non-porous surfaces, diamonds do require cleaning from time to time, just as does glass. The frequency of cleaning will depend upon the regularity with which your diamonds are worn or touched, as they acquire a greasy film when handled. Investment stones kept in bank vaults and seldom disturbed will need cleaning only occasionally. The operation is simple and should not be cause for alarm. It can be performed without risk by anyone, observing just a few simple rules.

The chief point to be kept in mind is that diamonds ought to be cleaned individually, as there is danger of scratching if two are allowed to come into contact with each other. If you do not have commercial jewelry cleaner at hand, which is available at most jewelry stores, you can follow the following instructions using simple ingredients. You will first of all need a small bowl; porcelain does very satisfactorily for the purpose but just about any bowl may be used. Into this is introduced a mixture consisting of one cup warm water, two tablespoons liquid dishwashing detergent, and a teaspoon of clear ammonia. Mix this around thoroughly until a frothy lather appears. If it should overflow the bowl, skim some of it away. Now drop one diamond — just one — into the bowl and allow it to remain for about 15 minutes. This soaking will sufficiently soften the grease so that it can be wiped away. The wiping operation is performed while the diamond is still submerged, by grasping it with the fingers of one hand and brushing it on all sides with an old toothbrush or some similar instrument. An artist's brush with stiff bristles can be used. The diamond is then rinsed under lukewarm water and patted with a lintless cloth. It is left out to "air" for a while before being returned to the jewel box or whatever it is normally stored.

IMPORTANT: Do not, when rinsing, hold the diamond over a sink drain as it may disappear into the plumbing.

HISTORY OF SYNTHETIC DIAMONDS

Synthetic and imitation diamonds, though often spoken of interchangeably, are not at all the same. Imitations are fake stones, which could be glass or quartz or any of a variety of other materials, cut or shaped to give the appearance of a diamond. Synthetics are actual diamonds which have been produced by man in the laboratory rather than by nature. Obviously the value of a first-rate synthetic is considerably higher than that of a mere imitation, though not so high as the value of a natural diamond of the same size and quality.

Efforts to counterfeit diamonds began in antiquity, probably as soon as diamonds began to sell for impressive prices. Though technical knowledge was lacking, early fakers probably enjoyed great success since their customers were not expert at telling real from the unreal. For centuries the properties of diamonds remained mysterious. Anyone who claimed expertise and had a flair for salesmanship could readily show why his "diamonds" were superior to others on the market. Even in the time of Pliny (1st century A.D.) so much misconception existed about diamonds that the gates were open wide for clever hucksters. In addition, we must also suppose that a good deal of imitations were honestly made and sold to persons who admired the real thing but could not afford it, just as is done today. Numerous rings, necklaces and other adornments have been found, dating from ancient Greece and Rome, set with stones cut in the usual shapes of diamonds. This activity was even more pronounced in the European Renaissance (16th/17th centuries A.D.). Of course, the cuts bear little relation to those of current popularity, as the science of faceting was not then fully understood.

Just as alchemists of the Middle Ages attempted to make synthetic gold by heating up ordinary rocks, believing that real gold was formed by nature in that fashion, they tried likewise to make diamonds. This was done without knowledge that diamonds are composed chiefly of carbon. Consequently, various experiments were carried out, using heat as their basis, on all manner of subject materials — without results. Minerals of similar character to diamonds were thrown into furnaces, including quartz, and each successive experiment seemed only to prove the mastery of nature over man.

As scientific knowledge increased, the likelihood of manufacturing synthetic diamonds appeared dimmer. But this did not totally eliminate the hope, and from time to time ambitious persons, often outfitted with bizarre or primitive equipment, made efforts. Even a few magicians and swindlers got into the act.

The most celebrated of the latter was a Frenchman named Henri Lemoine, who parlayed his skill in sleight-of-hand into a considerable sum of money. In 1905, after some slight success had been reported in the making of synthetic diamonds and the public eagerly awaited news of further advances, Lemoine approached Sir Julius Wernher, a member of the board of directors of DeBeers. Lemoine excitedly explained to Wernher that he had developed a perfect formula for artificially manufacturing diamonds. All rights in their sale could be Wernher's, he further explained, if only the former would advance enough money for Lemoine to set up a full-scale manufacturing operation. Wernher asked to witness these diamonds being made, before any further discussion. Lemoine agreed. The two went to Lemoine's London apartment, arrayed with more than enough apparatus to convince even the skeptical of his scientific turn of mind. Before Wernher's eyes he mixed ingredients in a tube, placed the tube over intense heat for a period of time, stirred it, and poured out 25 genuine diamonds. It was, of course, a magic trick — just like pulling a rabbit from a hat. The diamonds were real, but not made by Lemoine. Wernher was sufficiently impressed to sign a contract and put up a sizable amount of cash. For the next three years Wernher advanced money, and occasionally received packets of diamonds in return by mail. Finally it dawned upon him that the stones he was receiving were not worth nearly as much money as he was laying out. They were also strangely similar in appearance to those mined by DeBeers. In fact, they *were* mined by DeBeers. Lemoine was using small portions of the money to buy diamonds, from ordinary trade sources, and the rest for himself. He was eventually imprisoned for fraud.

As late as 1952 another case, very similar to the above, occurred in Germany. Again, discovery and legal action followed.

HONEST EFFORTS. Efforts at manufacturing synthetic diamonds with honest intent began to bear fruit only in the 19th century, and even then long periods of time passed between one small success and the next. This was due probably to the unwillingness of scientists or other researchers to divulge their methods, for fear of losing copyright. Consequently, almost every "diamond maker" was required to proceed on his own without benefit of accrued knowledge. In 1823 a Russian scientist named Kazarin succeeded in making carbon crystals that had the general appearance of diamonds, but were a very far cry from the synthetics later produced. There is not much information on his activities. It is said only that Mendeleer, a noted scientific researcher, inspected Kazarin's handiwork and was impressed by it.

Nothing of great note was thereafter accomplished until the fourth quarter of the 19th century, when a Scottish druggist named Hannay came upon the scene. Young Hannay — he was only 25 when he "made diamonds" — was of a deeply inquiring mind, which delighted in fooling with chemistry sets and amateur experiments. His synthetic diamonds were born out of a series of tests made to discover a solvent for potassium. One thing led to another and after some 80 experiments, Hannay had produced some tiny crystals which gave the appearance of diamonds. Not being the world's most skilled scientist, Hannay blundered right and left: sometimes his test tubes exploded while being heated, or his furnace would melt. He was also not an expert on gems and hesitated to declare these crystals diamonds. So he brought them to the British Museum, where M. N. Story-Maskelyne, keeper of minerals, placed them under careful examination and pronounced them to be diamonds. The story broke in the London Times on February 20, 1880.

Hannay was ahead of his time. Using equipment that was very archaic by modern standards, he achieved remarkable results. Though detailed records exist of exactly how Hannay went about his work, the materials and procedures he used failed to yield diamonds when employed by later generations of scientists. His secret, if there was one, died with him. He passed away in 1931 at age 76. The possibility has been advanced that Hannay might have used trickery.

Henri Moissan was the next to claim production of artificial diamonds, in the early 1890's. All suggestion of fraud has been eliminated from his efforts. He produced small crystals that were capable of scratching ruby. Whether or not they were true diamonds was a matter of debate among the experts, some believing one way and some the other. They did, however, excite great curiosity and encouraged other experimenters. As Moissan's crystals are no longer in existence, analysis of them with modern equipment is not possible. Hannay's stones do still exist (at the British Museum), and have proved under modern inspection to be authentic — but a little *too* authentic, in the view of some, to have been created artificially.

Various other efforts were made, both in Europe and the U.S., following the publicity of Hannay and Moissan's experiments. These were greeted with little positive results until after World War II. In 1953 a Swedish firm, Allmana, produced crystals of about one mm. in size. It was the intention of this organization to manufacture diamonds for jewelry use and it withheld announcement of its progress until first-quality large stones were produced. By then, however, General Electric of America, which had been working in secret on such a project for a number of years, had arrived at the capability of making synthetic diamonds. News of the G.E. synthetics was circulated in 1955. Its diamonds were extremely small but fitted the purpose, as the firm intended them for industrial use.

As it became increasingly likely that artificial diamonds for jewelry purposes were to be a reality, the DeBeers company turned much attention to developing its own synthetics. It naturally envisioned the position it would be in, if buyers turned in wholesale quantities to synthetics. Major results were announced in 1958, followed quickly by establishment of a DeBeers subsidiary, Ultra High Pressure Units Ltd., whose exclusive function was making gem synthetics. A branch was later opened in Ireland.

Gem quality diamonds were not artificially produced until 1970. Again, General Electric won the race — but it was not certain whether the victory entailed some loss. G.E. had developed the capability of manufacturing diamonds of one carat and larger, suitable for cutting, but there was a catch: cost of production was several times that of the real thing!

Work then began on reducing costs while maintaining the same quality level. While this seemed at first to present insoluble problems, much progress has been made in that direction.

DIFFERENT TYPES OF DIAMOND SUBSTITUTES

The following listing of common substitutes may prove frightening. Before concluding that diamond buying is too risky for his taste, the potential investor should realize that he will generally be dealing with certified stones (accompanied by G.I.A. papers), and that the likelihood of acquiring imitations when buying through legitimate channels is quite small.

He should, nevertheless, try to familiarize himself with substitutes, by examining actual specimens when possible.

PASTE DIAMONDS. These are the oldest varieties of imitations. They are not obviously in the nature of synthetics, or real diamonds produced by artificial means, but are true fakes. Paste diamonds have been manufactured for at least 2,000 years and the market for them is apparently stronger today than ever. Their fate is normally to be mounted into "costume" jewelry, to sell for a tiny fraction of a diamond's price. And no wonder — the material is intrinsically worthless. Paste diamonds are made from the same substance as window glass or colorless glass in general. If well shaped and cut, the appearance can be most convincing to persons unfamiliar with real diamonds. Paste diamonds will reflect light almost as well as genuine diamonds.

The scratch test is conclusive with paste gems, as their surface hardness is considerably beneath that of a diamond. Paste diamonds can be scratched by quartz.

CUBIC ZIRCONIA. A singly refractive, high dispersion synthetic. Cubic Zirconia has false "naturals" and wispy inclusions. It is a very high-grade synthetic which cuts and polishes attractively. Not distinguishable from diamonds except by trained observers.

RUTILE. Synthetic rutile is produced under a variety of trade names, the most popular being Titania. Titania diamonds are always somewhat tinted, the tint being yellow of one intensity or another. Rutile refracts light very well and a stone of this material will have greater sparkle and brilliance than a diamond. It is not overly deceiving to an experienced eye but may fool the unwary.

STRONTIUM TITANATE. The popular names for Strontium Titanate "diamonds" are Fabulite and Starilian. The substance is man-made. Though well-cut strontium titanate gives the appearance of a diamond, its surface hardness is considerably less. It can be scratched by quartz, which ranks only #7 on the Mohs hardness scale.

Y.A.G. This is the term by which the not easily pronounceable material Yttrium Aluminate is commonly known. It is a man-made substance and nearly ideal for the simulation of diamonds. To date, "Yag diamonds" have shown up in greater numbers in Europe than in America, but this state of affairs is not likely to maintain very long. One of the better properties of Y.A.G. is its surface hardness, which rates as 8½ on the Mohs scale (that is, just ½ beneath corundum). Yag diamonds are heavier for their size than the real thing, but not so heavy as those fashioned from strontium titanate.

ZIRCON. This is a colorless synthetic which has become very abundant on the market. It is quite like diamond in most respects, but not as convincing as Djevalite.

ZIRCONIUM OXIDE. This product, merchandised as "Djevalite" (the "D" is silent), is patented by a Swiss organization and can legally be manufactured only by them. It is sold in white as well as tints. The properties and characteristics are extremely similar to those of diamonds. They have been on the market only since 1977. The unaided eye is incapable of distinguishing between Djevalite and true diamonds, but several methods for their detection are described below.

HOW TO TELL REAL DIAMONDS FROM FAKES

The eternal question confronted by diamond buyers is: **Is it real?**

Is it a true diamond or something else?

Great advances in technology have given birth to very sophisticated testing apparatus, unknown 50 or even 20 years ago. But this same technology has made possible the production of artificial and imitation diamonds that could not be made with earlier methods.

Diamond substitutes are not illegal in trade because they have definite uses in industry, and in jewelry making as well — if properly labeled. Most of these are man-made materials to which various names are given, though it is still possible to encounter "diamonds" faked from one or more natural mineral substances, such as quartz and white topaz. Once these stones have passed from the hands of their original seller (who, hopefully, has sold them without deceptive intent), their identification hinges upon the expertise and care of any subsequent potential buyer.

METHODS FOR DETECTING ARTIFICIAL OR SIMULATED DIAMONDS. As each of the materials used in production of artificial diamonds has its own properties and characteristics, methods successful in detecting one will not be useful in testing all.

A number of the available tests require use of high precision (and high priced) equipment. Others can be performed without aid of any tools.

VISUAL INSPECTION. The ratio of success by visual inspection depends mostly upon the individual's experience and expertise. A newcomer will usually be able to distinguish only the more obvious diamond substitutes and imitations, while a gemologist will score much higher. Knowledgeable diamond handlers look for certain characteristics: the surface lustre, straightness and flatness of facets, high light reflectivity, and (internally) the foreshortening which is peculiar to well-cut diamonds. This foreshortening, which makes the stone appear shallower than it really is, is in the nature of an optical illusion, caused by play of light; it is nevertheless a characteristic that other minerals and most of the synthetics do not possess in quite such a degree and can be taken as good evidence of a diamond's authenticity. To examine for foreshortening, the back facet edges must be inspected while looking through the table or uppermost flat surface, under a good light.

Surface reflectivity is not perhaps so reliable an indication of authenticity, but it can at least be said that when this characteristic is *not present* the odds are good that the stone is not a diamond. Holding the stone near the eye and turning it slowly, it should catch in mirror fashion reflections of objects in the room, if the area is well lighted. The less good the lighting, the less that can be expected of a diamond's reflectability.

These procedures are not of much use in identifying rough stones. It is also much more difficult to reach conclusions on the genuineness of mounted than unmounted cut stones, as they pick up reflections from the mounting and cannot be inspected as completely.

TILT TEST. This is a common preliminary test used by all diamond merchants. Despite its simplicity it is very useful. The stone is held close to the eye, table upward, and slowly pointed away from the body. If genuine, the brilliance or sparkle observable through the table will remain even at this angle. Most imitations and fakes lose some measure of brilliance when the table is tilted away.

HEAT CONDUCTIVITY. Diamonds have a high level of thermal conductivity. That is, they acquire the temperature to which they are exposed. They become warm in a warm room and cool if the surroundings are cold. Other minerals do not possess such a high degree of thermal conductivity. Consequently, simple tests may be done, exposing stones to warmth and cold and then touching them to the lips to discover their approximate temperature. Such tests are more conclusive when other gems, known not to be diamonds, are tested at the same time.

BREATH TEST. Another simple test is the breath test, which involves nothing more than breathing upon stone. For results to be meaningful, the subject stone and one known to be a diamond should be tested simultaneously. If the coating of mist clears from both at the same time, it is indication that the subject stone is likely a diamond. If it clears noticeably sooner from the known diamond, the subject stone can be presumed to be some other material — but further testing is necessary to reach an irrefutable conclusion. Thermal conductivity is once again the cause. The diamond heats up faster and therefore evaporates the mist quicker.

STICKINESS TEST. If the subject stone can be picked up with the tip of a moistened finger, this points to its likelihood of it being a diamond. The majority of stones cannot be picked up in this way. Of course a large diamond is not suitable for the stickiness test, as its weight will cause it to fall from the finger.

WATER TEST. This test is inexact but worth performing before more complicated procedures are entered into. The diamond table must be perfectly clean. If not recently cleaned it should be and dried before attempting this test. A drop of water is placed on the table. If it begins spreading about, this is an indication that the stone is something other than a diamond. Diamond has the ability to almost "magnetize" water and hold it firmly.

HARDNESS TEST. This old traditional test is still of value; no other gems have the hardness of diamonds. The hardness test is objected to by many persons because it entails risk of injuring the stone, even if it is a real diamond. If carried out properly there is little danger of injury. No attempt should ever be made to test hardness by trying to scratch a possible diamond with another stone or object, but rather using the test stone to make a scratch upon something else. The best material is ruby or sapphire, which cannot be scratched by any mineral except a diamond. Use the diamond *girdle* — not the culet or one of the facet edges — and draw it with moderate pressure across the ruby or sapphire. If the scratch it leaves cannot be removed by rubbing with a moistened finger, the stone being tested is probably a genuine diamond. Beware of shallow surface scratches that can be easily rubbed away, as these can be created by softer minerals or synthetics.

CUTTING ACCURACY. A diamond will generally exhibit more precision of cut than synthetics or gems of lesser value.

SURFACE CHARACTERISTICS. The surface characteristics of true diamonds, while important in identification, are so subtle that a beginner is not apt to learn much from their examination. Straight lines or ridges in the polished surfaces are an indication of authenticity. If examined under 10X magnification, the surface will appear to be slightly rippled or to contain minute hills and valleys. This is called texturing and is peculiar to diamonds. The girdle or central circumference of a cut diamond should display a more waxy appearance than the stone in general, the result of cutting.

INTERNAL CHARACTERISTICS. Internal cleavage is good indication of authenticity. The only other gemstone to show internal cleavage is topaz, whose brilliance is considerably less than that of diamonds.

SPECIFIC GRAVITY. Diamonds have a specific gravity of 3.51½. The reading must be taken accurately to be of any service. Obviously it is not possible with mounted stones.

We now come to what is probably the most foolproof method in the industry. It is called a "diamond probe." Several models are available on the market. The diamond probe measures reflectivity and gives a specific reading when the tip of the probe is placed perpendicular in the center of the stone's table facet. The indicator will either read "imitation" or "true diamond." To date, this method has been the most successful in detecting even the most sophisticated fakes. Even graduate gemologists, who have extremely well-trained eyes, always use this as part of their inspection of a diamond's authenticity.

THE DIAMOND MARKET

The international diamond market is unique unto itself. Its operations and its way of life cannot be compared against any other business. It is true that diamonds, like gold, are mined chiefly in Africa. But this is the end of market similarities. Gold is primarily made into things. It is refined and alloyed and upon reaching the consumer may take the form of coins or stick-pins or any of a thousand objects. Diamonds never become anything but diamonds. Nothing is added to them. Moreover, the trade in diamonds is in the hands of a much smaller and more closely-knit group of individuals than trade in gold.

To outsiders, the functioning of the diamond market is mysterious. This is quite understandable, as it operates upon principles largely of its own evolution, with codes, conduct and terminologies very much of its personal making. Some of these have come about as the result of pressures by dynastic organizations (such as DeBeers); others are the outgrowth of generations and even centuries of tradition heaped upon tradition.

Before going into specifics it should first of all be pointed out, for benefit of those who may imagine the diamond trade as a wondrous fantasy-land populated by gnomes and munchkins, that its existence is based upon the same motivations as those of other industries: to make a profit by buying low and selling high, and to reduce operational costs as low as possible consistent with maintaining quality.

Essentially, the wholesale prices of rough diamonds are controlled, and the wholesale levels of cut stones for jewelry and investment are as well, the former by the DeBeers corporation and the latter by traders' organizations. Price control of roughs dates to the late 19th century and has become tighter in the 20th. It should not be assumed, however, that the exercise of controls in any way dampens the potential of diamonds for investment. If anything it enhances it, as these controls serve as stabilizers and greatly reduce risk of price declines that occur in most other industries from time to time.

Why should controls be set upon diamond prices?

In early times (up to about 1890, when African mining began to yield prodigious quantities of diamonds) this was neither necessary nor desirable. Today the absence of controls would almost certainly lead to confusion, delays in completion of large wholesale transactions, and wild bouncing about of prices that might excite gamblers but would do no good to the industry as a whole.

Assuming that diamonds were traded today without price regulation, they would profit or suffer much more sharply from the laws of supply and demand. In times of increased demand, the mines would work feverishly, and fresh supplies of roughs would be thrown upon the market in great quantities. After reaching circulation they might glut the trade, causing a reversal in demand and a consequent decline of prices. Mine work would need to be slowed down or halted. The livelihoods not only of miners but diamond handlers all along the line would hang by slender threads, dependent upon the daily highs and lows in trading. Fortunes would be made, and fortunes lost. The trade would be leaving itself vulnerable for the kind of crash and subsequent economic depression suffered by the U.S. in 1929. And it does not, in any manner of speaking, care to flirt with this sort of danger. It has no need to. By regulating all phases of its operations it can move along steadily, grow at a more or less prescribed pace, and not need to wonder whether its roof will soon come caving down.

It should not be presumed that controls are stiflingly rigid. They are not. So far as the wholesaling of roughs is concerned, DeBeers' policy has been in successful use for many years and is so structured that only international economic calamity can seriously disturb it. Ample witness to its strength is borne by the fact that events of the past several years — soaring oil prices, devaluation of world currencies, the 1979/80 gold fever — have not materially affected its workings. Something of much greater magnitude would be required: a depression of 1930's proportions or another World War. Even then, diamonds might pull through better than bullion.

DeBeers works its mines at a steady pace. It does not materially reduce operations in times of market stagnation, nor does it materially increase them when demand rises significantly. Rather, it meets these circumstances — which are natural and inevitable results of free trade, just like the ebb and flow of ocean tide — by advance planning. When times are less than good in terms of market consumption, as they were during the middle 1970's, it stockpiles *some* of the quantities of raw diamonds from mining. This is considered a more logical and far-sighted approach than reducing production. The more diamonds that can be mined today, the less that need to be mined tomorrow, when wages and other operating costs are likely to be higher. In a way DeBeers invests in its roughs. As diamonds are not subject to spoilage, they can be stored away for long periods if necessary and released into circulation at whatever rate the prevailing conditions dictate. As demand increases, not only freshly mined roughs are sold but some of the stockpiled "old roughs."

But what happens when demand is so strong that stockpiles become exhausted?

No cause for concern, nor cause for stepping up production. This simply means that the rough price needs to be raised, the percentage of raise calculated upon strength of demand vs. the rate at which mined roughs can be thrown on the market. DeBeers profits in this way just as it would, or possibly to a greater extent, than by expanding mining operations during periods of peak demand. The higher prices serve to level off demand. At the same time, a more or less steady flow of roughs is passing through factories throughout the world, which can proceed at a predictable, established pace of business without panic or interruption. The factories are happy, wholesalers are happy, brokers are happy, jewelry manufacturers are happy, and the ultimate customer — though he has little knowledge, usually, of what is taking place behind the scenes — *ought* to be happy, even though he may not be. He sees prices rising and he may grumble a bit over this. He fumes about "inflation." True enough, it is a form of inflation. But it is calculated, orchestrated inflation which serves ultimately to aid him, as it protects the values of any diamonds he may buy. He has the whole industry behind him as watchdogs, when he places his money into diamonds. He need not fear overnight upsets brought about by fierce trading of profiteers or big-money speculators.

The Central Selling Organization, which wholesales diamonds to major international brokers, employs the same formula of control. When demand slackens and the C.S.O. is not able to find buyers for its "parcels" (a literal parcel or box of diamonds, each wrapped in tissue, with a total value averaging between $150,000 and $400,000), it does not reduce prices. To do this would be "turncoating" the trade, and it depends upon the trade and the trade's healthiness for its own health. If the C.S.O. cut prices, for the purpose of moving its parcels, the values of diamonds already in possession of brokers and other traders, not to mention the general public, would be injured. Think in these terms: if you have an ounce of gold bought at $600, and the market declines to $500, you now are in possession of something worth $500, not the $600 you paid. The same is true of diamonds. To reduce wholesale prices would cheapen the inventories of every dealer holding diamonds, and this would not paint a pretty picture. So the C.S.O. does precisely what DeBeers does in such circumstances. It stockpiles or places aside the boxes as they are assembled. This serves a twin purpose. While keeping the level of prices firm, it also prevents an undue quantity of fresh stones from coming on the market. With less stones getting into circulation, the demand will increase if given sufficient time and if world economic conditions are not catastrophic. So, in a sense, one hand washes the other.

In times of heavy demand, the C.S.O. has the option of raising prices on its parcels. The percentage of such raises are normally from 15% to 20% at any given time. It will easily be seen that if just two such raises occur within a year, the market value of diamonds has gained considerably. It also has the alternative of enacting surcharges. These may be regarded in the category of price advances but are of short-term duration, to meet excessively strong demand that builds up without warning, and are later removed. A surcharge can be removed without having the negative effects that would result from a rolling back of basic prices. This is because the *real purpose* of the surcharge is not to make extra money, but to reduce demand down to the pre-surcharge level and thereby keep diamond prices firm. The higher the surcharge, the more it will cut buying activity, as many buyers will wait until the surcharge is reduced or removed. This is a very neat manner of controlling the market, good for all concerned (or so it has appeared).

DIAMOND BOURSES

The word "bourse" is likely to be associated by many persons with conventions and exhibitions of stamps, coins, antiques and other merchandise, where dealers sell from little stalls and tables. Diamond bourses are not brief events but are in session daily the year round (holidays and days of religious observations excepted, of course). These are large and elaborate trading centers, similar in their concept to stock exchanges but lacking the basic principle of the latter: prices based upon accumulative trading between buyers and sellers. At diamond bourses, the price is set in each transaction on a one-to-one basis.

They are, of course, extremely colorful with much haggling, wild exclamations, bustle and excitement. Diamond bourses are not for the general public. Their attendance is restricted solely to the trade, and further restricted to members who have paid sums of money and passed examinations for admittance — something like gaining a seat on the Stock Exchange. The activities and financial responsibility of members are closely monitored. When the governing board has evidence of misconduct, or reason to believe a member has over-extended himself and is in danger of defaulting on obligations, it can remove him from membership. A sort of mini-trial is held, with a verdict handed down.

These bourses are located in various parts of the world, most of them in Europe (which is nearer the geographical locale of diamond mining than is America). Antwerp in Belgium has four bourses.

Though the bourse buildings are of different sizes and layouts, the general arrangement is for long tables to be set up at right angles to the walls, going down the length of spacious halls. The buildings have high ceilings and the walls are composed chiefly of windows, which admit maximum natural light and permit examination of stones without resort to artificial illumination. This is not done for the sake of preserving old traditions but in the belief that diamonds are more satisfactorily and fairly appraised in this manner. At each table, a row of buyers sits on one side and is faced by a row of sellers on the other. There will be hundreds of each at any given time, as well as innumerable persons scurrying about the aisles. The buyer might be a dealer purchasing for his own account, or a broker acting as agent for another party. In the latter instance a different formality is observed. After examination and the usual dickering about price, the diamond is placed back into its folded paper and sealed with the potential buyer's seal, much in the fashion of old letters sealed with wax. The deal is not completed on the spot because the broker must first communicate with his client. There is a strict rule that only the potential buyer may break his own seal, as a guarantee that the stone has neither been switched in the interim or even exhibited to anyone else.

Ethics within the trade are extremely high. Most transactions are made verbally, with deals of hundreds of thousands of dollars completed without contracts or signatures. It is expected that every member dealer will be good to his word, and dealers know full well that their reputation depends upon fulfilling all agreements into which they have entered.

INVESTING IN DIAMONDS

Private investment in diamonds is already far beyond the "talked about" stage. It's become a reality for thousands of investors here and abroad, who've examined the performance record of diamonds vs. other investments and concluded that gems have an awful lot going for them.

In fact, an item-by-item survey of what diamonds have been doing, pricewise, in recent years compared to other investments leaves little room for doubt.

In the past 20 years, the average annual price-growth in gem quality diamonds has been 17½ percent. During most of those years, diamonds increased in value at least 2-3 times faster than the national inflation rate.

In 1978 the increase was a whopping 67% and another 49% was added in 1979. This, in spite of pronouncements from so-called experts that diamonds were overpriced. Prices continued skyrocketing during 1980 and reached heights by November of last year that even the most optimistic investors acknowledged to be dizzying.

What other investment has done as well, or has the prospects of continuing that kind of performance over the next 1, 5 or 10 years?

Certainly not stocks. After reaching a record 1,200 the Dow Jones averages dipped to 600 in 1973, and have, since then, bounced up and down with no clear direction. Investor dissatisfaction with stocks, during the

1970's, was one of the prime reasons for heavy investment in jewels and precious metals. It is just about impossible that the stock market — now feeling the pinch of rampant inflation, unemployment and lack of investor confidence — could match the potential of diamond over the foreseeable future.

Diamonds have a lot going for them investment-wise. They've proven to be one of comparatively few investments that go up when most others are going down, and that has to weigh heavily with the person seeking capital growth plus a reasonable degree of security. In 1973, one of the most economically unstable years since World War II, diamond prices *doubled.* And to go back further, diamonds were one of very few commodities whose price did not decline during the Great Depression of 1929-1938.

There's a tradition, historically, for people to put their money in "hard" investments during troubled times. Paper investments such as stocks, bonds and securities are not trusted; even money itself is suspect, as these things have no intrinsic value and are apt to become worthless or near-worthless. This is why the U.S. dollar fell so dramatically on international currency exchanges during the 1970's. Foreign holders of dollars decided, en masse, that they were smarter getting rid of paper notes and obtaining items of intrinsic value. Many foreign currencies tumbled as well, and some are still doing so. Though international banking organizations try to stabilize currencies, they can do nothing about the fact that money just isn't as attractive to own as it used to be.

Invariably, the value of money — U.S. or foreign — goes down, and continues going down the longer you hold it. If banks pay 5/4ths% interest, and the inflation rate is 12-15%, there's no hope of making money by holding on to money. You need something that increases in value at a quicker rate than inflation. Diamonds have established a very realiable history of doing this,and there is every reason to believe — based on market conditions — that they'll perform just as well investment-wise in the future.

For one thing, diamonds have a strong market over and above the investment demand. Even if nobody was buying diamonds for growth, prices would still rise. As the hardest substance known to mankind, diamonds are very necessary to industry, which buys up 80% of the freshly mined roughs. In machinery, scientific instruments and other devices where diamonds are used, there is no known substitute which can satisfactorily take their place. Synthetics may be able to substitute for jewel stones, where they need only please the eye; but for industry the diamond's harness is its major selling point and this has not been artifically duplicated. The odds are that it never will — or, if it is, that prices of the synthetic will be so high as to render it unattractive for industry.

Another obvious demand for diamonds comes from the jewelry market. The tradition for use of diamonds in jewelry is centuries old and shows no signs of slackening. The possibility of a decline in jewelry demand for diamonds is discussed below.

The demand for industrial and jewel diamonds is growing but the supply is diminishing — an ideal situation for investors. Presently known diamond deposits, largely in South Africa, will run dry in 30-40 years if worked *just at the present pace.* Should mining efforts be accelerated, they could become exhausted much sooner. Of course, there's a possibility that fresh mining sites will be discovered. But stop and think. If mining companies pour great amounts of money into the search for new sites, this in itself will contribute to increased diamond prices — even if such sites are found. The odds on finding a *great number of high-yield new sites quickly,* with minimal expenditure, are just above zero. If this could have been done, it already would have been!

From 1971 to 1978 prices for *rough* diamonds increased by 97% — not as significant an increase as for cut stones but noteworthy just the same. In other words they more or less doubled during that 7-year period.

So far as rough prices go, these are controlled by the DeBeers corporation of Kimberley, South Africa. Conditions influencing them are different than conditions affecting prices of cut stones. For one thing, private investors don't buy roughs. It is mostly a matter of mining cost vs. return on diamonds that have been mined. Industrial users account for most of the demand, as mentioned earlier. Only about 20% of rough diamonds are of high enough quality to become jewelry or investment stones. Therefore, industrial developments have more of a bearing on rough stones than anything which occurs in the jewelry or investment picture. This is why the increased demand by investment buyers has not, until very recently, had much influence on rough prices.

During 1977 rough prices advanced more sharply than in any year since 1973. They had remained almost stagnated during all of 1974 and 1975 and advanced modestly the following year. But at the same time, prices on cut stones were going up. Then in 1977 rough prices were raised dramatically. This trend has since continued.

DeBeers could, of course, play the Arab oil game if it chose. Having a virtual monopoly on production, it could conceivably fix whatever prices it chose, no matter how outrageous. But it does not. By pricing diamonds too high, industrial use would be discouraged. Substitutes would be sought by major industrial buyers and this might cause more harm than good in the long run. Thus, DeBeers advances its prices only when rising cost of operations or shortages in mine yield warrant.

There is irrefutable evidence that even the lower industrial-grade roughs are getting scarce, compared to 10 or just 5 years ago. The U.S. Bureau of the Mines recently recommended that the government discontinue all exports of industrial diamonds from our stockpile. This is the first time in history that such a recommendation was made.

The message is clear: need for industrial diamonds is greater in the U.S. than the pace at which they can be imported.

CUT PRICES. The market price of a one-carat "D" flawless was $2,000 in 1965. In November 1980, it was $55,000.

Part of the answer lies in increased costs of cutting, as well as handling and distribution. Every phase of its journey through which a diamond passes adds something to the price — even the insurance on registered mail parcels used to transport gems from one part of the world to another. But these are insignificant compared to increased public demand, both on the part of jewelry buyers and investors.

The fashion for wearing jewelry, downplayed by styles on the sixties and early seventies, rebounded around 1975. New jewelry buyers, who had perhaps never before purchased fine jewelry, looked upon their purchases more in terms of an investment than did their predecessors of earlier decades. They got smarter about cuts and colors and carats. Retail houses which had not previously handled fine jewelry began doing so; even Woolworth's started selling diamonds in its larger outlets. Mail-order catalogues began featuring mounted gems at prices in four figures. A near-fad developed for fine jewelry.

When investors went into the market heavily, there was no doubt that with this new "push" prices would very dramatically advance. The first wave of investors attracted more, and the geographical spread of investors increased, so that by 1980 diamonds were not only a popular investment in the U.S. and Europe but in Japan, the Near East, and South America.

Traditionally, owners of diamonds, especially fine stones bought at high prices, considered their purchases as "investments." They felt the same about their Sheffield plate and Limoges china and Eastlake furniture. They were bought chiefly to be used and admired and enjoyed, but in the belief that passage of time would only render them more valuable.

Today a much different kind of diamond investing has developed. Today's investor does not (normally) seek mounted stones. He or she does not wear diamonds. They're placed into bank vaults and allowed to remain there, untouched, to "mature." While inflation rages, while international crisis come and go, these slumbering gems are building and building in value.

The big swing to diamond investing began around 1977, influenced in great measure by rising prices of gold and silver and general economic uncertainty. As it became evident that many large investors (including banks, investment clubs and even world governments) were turning away from paper investments to materials of instrinsic value, precious gems naturally came under consideration. They offer most of the advantages of bullion and some that bullion lacks, the most significant of the latter being that world governments are less capable of influencing gem prices than bullion prices.

Every industrial nation keeps a gold reserve. The larger nations (West Germany, France, Japan, etc.) own billions of dollars worth of gold bars. When their currency falls in value on international exchanges, they can — and do — bolster it by trading in some of their gold for marks or francs or yen. This makes their currency go up and, at the same time, it causes a dip in gold prices. The U.S. and Western Europe have the ability to virtually control gold prices, if they wished to. They do not have the ability to control diamond or other gem prices. The values of diamonds and other precious gems are not tied in any way to the values of world currencies. This is definitely a "plus" for the investor, as he need not be concerned that a slump in the British pound or Italian lire or some other currency might cause an upset in the market.

To do this, he must know diamonds and he must know the market. He must know when and where to buy, and how to buy, which is explained later in this book.

RETURN ON DIAMOND INVESTMENTS. All investments entail some degree of risk; certainly all those which offer the probability of a return that keeps ahead of our inflation rate. Diamonds possess the characteristics of a sound investment, based on color:

1. Their price performance over the past 5, 10, 20 and more years.

2. The greater investor interest currently shown in them, which means heavier buying activity and resulting higher prices.

The aforementioned one-carat "D" flawless went up from $2,000 in 1965 to $40,000 in September, 1979 — an increase of 2,000%. It then hit $55,000 little more than a year later, in November 1980. Apparently at this point a great deal of investors decided to profit-take, as the value slid slightly to $50,000 in January, 1981. But this was almost certainly a temporary adjustment. It actually presented a plus for investors, as it made the one-carat "D" flawless available at what could truly be termed a bargain price.We have little doubt that by mid 1983 the price of a "D" flawless will be up to $100,000 — and that values of other investment-grade diamonds will increase proportionately.

If the present trend continues, it will not be very long before investors account for nearly 20% of gem-diamond purchases (by dollar) made in the U.S. Five years ago they accounted for less than 3% of total sales. By projecting these figures over the next five years it could well be possible that in 1986 35¢ to 45¢ of every dollar spent on jewel diamonds will be paid by investors. Incidentally, purchases by dealers are not included in this tabulation. If that should become the case, there is no reason to believe that purchasing by non-investors will decline. It should in fact increase, as diamonds — though substantially more expensive — will be that much more attractive to persons able to afford them. Therefore the future outlook definitely seems positive.

Diamonds are a less volatile investment than bullion and this, too, is appealing. They are not subject to the very sharp ups and downs of gold anc silver. There are a number of reasons for this. One is that most diamonc investors, even those spending considerable sums of money, do not look for the quick profit. They are not market-players or "overnight profiteers." They buy with the intent to hold for five years or longer. Diamonds bough by investors do not return to the market as quickly as gold and silver — which may be bought one week and sold the next. It would be safe tc assume that at least 70% of all diamonds bought by investors in the late 1970's have not yet been resold. With bullion the figure would be much much lower.

Another reason for more stabilized prices is that the diamond market is not, because of its structure, subject to the bandwagon buying and selling that occurs with bullion. Since there are no daily spot prices announced fo diamonds (except the Monday Wall Street Journal price quotation we spoke of earlier), the public as a whole is not kept constantly aware of curren values. When a large bloc of gold holdings is sold — whether it be in New York or London or elsewhere in the world — this news is flashed around th globe and gold investors become panicky. Some of them start selling, toc and soon the price has dipped low. Diamond sales are not reportec Therefore they have little immediate influence on prices. A billion dollar worth of diamonds could be sold today without totally upsetting the marke This cannot be said of bullion or most other kinds of investment.

There is less urgency in the diamond market. When a gold dealer buy $100,000 worth of bullion, he hopes to sell it — or most of it — very quickly before another substantial seller appears. If a diamond merchant pay $100,000 for gems, he isn't concerned about the length of time taken in sel ing. He may in fact deliberately withhold selling them for a while, being co fident that prices will get higher in six months or a year. It isn't that bullio traders lack confidence in gold and silver. Most of them have their own i vestment quantitites put aside, too. But the fact remains that they — r gardless their size or scope of operations or international connections - are at the mercy of the market and there's precious little they can do whe prices slip.

What could possibly happen to upset the diamond market?

If one wants to fully explore the negative angles, here is some food for thought.

1. Manmade diamonds could increase in popularity to the point of making the real thing obsolete.

This one can be discounted without too much worry. Near-perfect artificial gemstones are already on the market and have been for several years. While very successful commercially,there is not the least indication that their availability has diminished demand for genuine stones.

2. Jewelry makers might decide to make less use of diamonds as prices advance.

This is fallacious reasoning. It presupposes that, as prices rise, diamonds will get beyond the budgets of all customers except the very wealthy. This will never be the case, as the vast majority of diamonds in circulation are either too small or not of sufficient quality to command outstanding prices. They, too, will advance in price, but there is no possibility of their values ever reaching the point of discouraging their use in commercially manufactured jewelry.

3. A better investment might come along, and everyone will cash in their diamonds in a rush to buy it.

Well, possibly. But what? Just about every substance known to man has already been considered as a potential investment. Someday, perhaps, plutonium or other chemicals used in nuclear reactors will be available to investors. But they would present such risks, of storage and spoilage, that investors could hardly be expected to become enthusiastic about them.

4. If gold passes the $1,000 per ounce mark and holds steady thereafter, wouldn't this prompt many diamond holders to switch over to gold?

The fact that bullion may do better on a short-term basis is not likely to influence many gem investors, who have studied both markets and concluded that diamonds are more suitable for their purposes.

5. What if some world governments decide to build a diamond reserve and use diamonds to back their currency? Wouldn't that turn things topsyturvy?

It would be a boon to investors; such governments would first need to spend billions of dollars accumulating such reserves, and that would invariably cause diamond prices to increase.

6. Suppose a radical government takes over South African and nationalizes DeBeers — as happened in South America with Coca-Cola and American auto factories?

That *is* a possibility — not a very pretty one, but in these days of international uncertainty anything could happen. Presumably, any government, unless totally maniacal, would want to administer the DeBeers assets so they would bring the greatest possible return — which would mean continuing to run the company and mining operations in the present fashion. It would be hard to conceive of any government throwing tons of diamonds on the market, at reduced prices, for the sake of raising money in a hurry. They might succeed in raising fast money but they would be ruining the country's chief source of revenue on a long-term basis: the diamond trade.

If diamonds are beginning to sound failsafe — well, right now they seem about as close to ideal as an investment can get.

SOMETHING THE NEW INVESTOR OUGHT TO KNOW. Buying diamonds for investment is not just a matter of buying diamonds. You can buy diamonds anywhere. Walk along any busy street and you'll find jewelry shops, pawnbrokers and other merchants selling diamonds of all kinds, at a few hundred to thousand of dollars. Mail-order advertisements for diamonds appear in just about every newspaper and national magazine. Opportunities to buy diamonds are all around you. But there is a vast difference between *diamonds* and *investment diamonds,* and a great difference, too, between *investment diamonds* and *investment diamonds bought at the right price.* Unless you get top-quality investment grade and investment size stones, and buy them at the lowest possible figures, your chances of realizing a satisfactory profit are not very good.

Diamonds for investment should be at least one full carat in weight and have high clarity and color rating, as explained in detail in the chapters on these subjects. Except in rare cases, where an exceptional "buy" comes along, they should be loose rather than mounted in jewelry. And they ought to be accompanied by G.I.A. certification, to eliminate the possibility of misgrading. In terms of price, they must be bought as near to wholesale as possible. This can be achieved if you work through a broker, who will charge the wholesale price plus a commission, as we discussed earlier. Remember that when the time comes to sell, you'll be selling at wholesale, so there obviously isn't any profit to be made if you buy at retail.

DIAMOND ADS. Thanks to increased attention paid to diamonds by investment buyers over the past 1-½ years, diamond-selling ads are now regularly appearing in the press. They are not the traditional "diamonds-for-jewelry" ads but "diamonds-for-investment." Mostly they're placed by gem dealers who have set up subsidiary firms to handle investment accounts, or newly established dealers who sell exclusively to investors. There is nothing bad about this; a seller who publicly advertises is likely to have more impressive credentials than a neighborhood merchant or private seller. However, there are some things you should know before doing business with diamond brokers or investment clubs.

Most significantly, purchases made from such sources are no more secure than from oridinary dealers. Federal law prohibits these advertisers to make promises of buying back your diamonds at a certain profit within a certain period of time, or even buying them back at the price you paid. This is why you find, in the ads, such statements as:

"When the time comes to sell, we'll buy back your diamonds at the highest possible price . . . probably for a substantial profit over your cost . . ."

The word "probably" has to be included, to stay within bounds of the F.T.C. rule.

Why the rule against guaranteeing buyers a future profit?

Because it can't be done. Nor can it with gold coins, or bars, or pocket watches, or anything else. What happens when that length of time is up and prices have not measurably advanced? A dealer would be taking a loss by buying back items he sold five years earlier, if he were bound and obligated to pay a profit. He could buy back some of the material, until his cash ran out. Then what? He would be out of business, and unable to meet future repurchase requests. There can never be any such thing as a dealer "guaranteeing" to buy back something at a definite price within a definite time. Anyone who claims this is not only being foolish but going against the Federal Trade Commission. The only person who can guarantee you a profit on the resale of your investment diamonds is yourself, if you buy wisely.

DIAMOND JEWELRY FOR INVESTMENT

To many beginners, "diamond" investment means "diamond jewelry."

Just as bullion investors are not advised to buy gold jewelry, persons buying diamonds strictly for investment are cautioned against stones already set in jewelry. By and large these are not attractive investments. When jewelry is manufactured, a long chain of profits is added to the actual value of the diamond or diamonds it contains. There is a charge for workmanship, for the mounting, distribution and the like. As a result, the retail price on a ring (for example) containing a $500 market price diamond will be at least $2,000 in the jewelry store. When this kind of item is sold by the investor, he will be paid only the wholesale value of the diamond and whatever additional price the mounting is worth as bullion. Even if the diamond's market price has increased 100%, plus the ring's melt value, he would still lose roughly half his investment on the purchase price.

Diamond jewelry is handsome and valuable. It deserves to be admired, to be worn, and to be enjoyed. That is its purpose. It is not for investors. The investor must concentrate on buying superb quality loose stones. These will be a finer grade than used for jewelry. And they will be obtainable at a much lower margin of seller's profit than stones mounted in jewelry, when bought through a dependable and reliable broker.

Possible exceptions to the above would be antique jewelry of exceptional quality (19th century or earlier) or items established to have belonged to celebrated persons. This is known as "provenance jewelry." It can be faked so take care.

FULLY-OWNED DIAMONDS

A fully-owned diamond is one whose cost you have paid up in full. You don't owe a cent on it and the diamond is in your possession, not only legally but physically. (It need not be in your home, of course; a bank deposit box will do, so long as the box is registered to you.)

Not all diamond investors put their money into fully owned stones. You can run the risk of serious error by failing to do this. All manner of complications can arise with partially owned or "laid away" investments.

Let us assume that a diamond investment broker offers you a $10,000 stone. You want to buy it but can't meet the price. He may arrange for gradual payments, based on a down payment of 20% to 25% and monthly payments of 10% of the balance or something in that neighborhood. This sounds good, but explore the situation a little deeper. Until that money is paid in full, title and possession of the diamond remain with the seller. If for some reason you can't meet the payments you will be penalized a percentage of what was already paid, possibly the entire amount of the down payment. And even if you hold up your end of the bargain, there is no guarantee that everything will be sunshine and roses on the other side of the fence. The seller may go out of business or disappear.

As far as group-owned diamonds are concerned — that is, several people getting together and splitting the cost of an expensive gem — this is an even messier can of worms. A private investor should not enter into such arrangements under any conditions. In short, when you invest in diamonds you should always be buying outright, paying up the full price and taking possession. If you can't afford the full price, you can't afford to invest in that particular stone.

SPECIAL TIPS FOR DIAMOND INVESTORS

1. Review your holdings and dispose of all gems, jewelry, etc., that might have been acquired before you gained sufficient knowledge of diamonds to buy wisely. Don't feel too badly about this: you have plenty of company. Many people begin investing before they have any real knowledge of what they're buying, assuming the subject (whether coins or paintings or whatever) to be far simpler than it really is. The uninformed individual — who comprises 99.9% of the general public — trusts all appraisals, believes that jewelry can be resold for its full retail price or higher, knows about carat weight and shape but little of clarity, color or proportion of cut. He is not able to distinguish a diamond that improperly refracts light. He does not know the grading system, what the symbols mean or how they are arrived at. He only knows that such-and-such diamond is offered in a shop for $600 and he proceeds under the belief that it has an intrinsic value of $600 and will probably be worth $800 or $1,000 within a year's time. An amateur need not excuse himself for behaving like an amateur. Human beings are not born with the ability to appraise diamonds. This is an acquired skill. If he's taken the trouble to acquire the skill before buying investment diamonds, he has done far better than most. If not, it isn't a total loss. He is in possession of diamonds that, while probably not of the grade that he should be buying, are at least (hopefully) genuine diamonds that were bought at a price not too much above their true retail value. There is some salvagable value in them. By all means he should waste no time in disposing of them, swallowing some pride if need be and taking a financial loss, and transferring whatever cash is raised in this fashion to diamonds of investment quality. He will lose carats as well as money by doing this, but he will lose more by delaying such action. By holding badly purchased stones in hopes of their increase in value, he deprives himself the use of cash which could immediately be put into good stones, which will be more costly to acquire in the future. *Get rid of your unwisely purchased stones.* If you have jewelry put aside for investment purposes, it should be among the articles liquidated.

It may be possible to reduce your loss in such circumstances by reselling the stones to the dealer(s) from whom they were purchased. Since they have already handled the merchandise and are familiar with it, they may pay somewhat more than a stranger.

2. Be fussy about quality and do not seek "bargains." Your aim should be to purchase top-grade stones from a broker at the wholesale level or as fractionally above wholesale as conditions allow. As you become acquainted with diamond dealers, brokers and other merchants who trade in diamonds, you will be confronted with numerous offerings of "bargains," some of which may appear quite attractive. These should be investigated thoroughly before any commitment is made, or ignored from the outset if your expertise is not sufficient to make conclusive appraisals or the stones are not accompanied by G.I.A. testimony. In nine cases out of 10, it will be demonstrated that apparent bargains or once-in-a-lifetime opportunities are stones which are, in some way or other, not of investment quality but which the seller seeks to pass along to investors because a much higher price can be obtained in that way than selling to jewel wholesalers or others.

3. Re-certification. When the G.I.A. certification of a gem is rather old, (over 8-10 months) and states it to be FL (flawless), it can occasionally happen that a potential purchaser will ask for the diamond to be resubmitted for appraisal. While annoying and time-consuming this must be looked upon as a reasonable request, as injury could have taken place in the interval and thus would remove the stone from such classification. In instances where papers proclaim a stone to be flawless, and a prospective buyer upon examination declares to have discovered minor blemishes, there is no reason why you should accept his conclusions without making further inquiry. If you are not capable of performing an examination yourself, the logical alternative is to decline a sale at that time and resubmit the item to the G.I.A. to learn its current opinion. If the stone has been in your possession since the original certification was given, and to the best of your knowledge was carefully handled and suffered no injury, you will very likely discover that the new opinion agrees with the old and that the dealer claiming to have discovered blemishes was incorrect in his findings (whether intentionally or not you are not apt to know).

It may be more advisable to offer the stone for sale to more than just one party before going the re-certification route.

4. Be very careful of the comments made upon the G.I.A. certification when buying. Read them thoroughly and if you encounter any terminology that is not entirely understandable, check it against information provided in this book. The G.I.A. certification is your front line of defense when selling, but it can likewise be used to your disadvantage if it carries negative observations of any nature. These, whether they relate to color, girdle thickness or any point whatsoever, will be automatically seized upon by the prospective purchaser and used to make the stone appear less valuable than it actually is. You should strive to purchase stones with "clean" G.I.A. certificates. This does not mean restricting yourself exclusively to FL (flawless), as other grades are acceptable, but no stone ought to be acquired on which the G.I.A. has commented unfavorably in any regard.

5. Don't buy stones mounted in jewelry, or any other articles of adornment, under any circumstances. This may seem too elementary to merit special notice, but beginners are sometimes "steered" into purchasing jewelry by dealers who have it on hand and wish to dispose of it at a price higher than could be obtained though the usual channels. Disregard any statements made about the glowing investment potential of an article of jewelry. It is not an investment piece and its odds of bringing you a satisfactory return are just about zero, unless it is literally "stolen" at 20% or 30% of the wholesale value.

6. Don't buy *small* diamonds. Be sure the diamonds you purchase are correctly weighed and that the weight is expressed in points. Going by point weight, you should generally not buy stones weighing less than 100 points, which is the equivalent of one full carat. A stone of less than one carat, even if it misses by only a single point, is not nearly so readily salable because most investors are interested only in full carat specimens and the dealer will either hesitate to buy or offer a price well below your expectations. There is little difference in the purchasing price between a stone of 95 points and one of 105, yet the resale value is much greater. It is foolish to economize in such a fashion, by sacrificing points here and there merely to save small sums. The amount saved will be greatly magnified at the time of resale.

7. On the other hand, avoid stones that are overly large. The biggest stones suitable for ordinary investment — unless you have a great deal of capital to tie up and can wait a long period before selling — are three carats or 300 points. Stones, therefore, weighing between one and three carats are ideal for investing. They are very easily sold when the time comes as dealers and diamond brokers usually have waiting customers for stones in this range of size.

DIAMOND INVESTMENT COMPANIES

A diamond investment company or broker operates in much the same manner as a bullion broker or a broker of stocks and bonds. Essentially he buys from persons who wish to sell, and sells to people who want to buy, charging a commission to cover his expenses and allow a fair profit margin. Diamond investment companies are located throughout the world and have direct daily contact with the major buying centers. They will sell your diamonds for you on consignment, whether purchased through them or elsewhere. Under this arrangement you must hand over the gems and sign a contract, which will either state the lowest price you would be willing to accept or give the broker freedom to use his judgment. The rate of commission varies a good deal. It will usually be lower on large transactions. If your diamonds are accompanied by G.I.A. certification, the transaction is likely to be concluded much quicker. Diamond investment companies will also sometimes purchase outright, but they prefer not to do this as it means risking their own capital. When they do make a cash offer it is generally somewhat less than would be obtained if you waited for a consignment sale to be negotiated. Anyone dealing with an investment broker should, if not in need of rapid cash, choose the consignment method.

BUYING DIAMONDS AT AUCTIONS

More and more diamonds are sold at auction today than ever before, prompting the investor to speculate upon the desirability of making purchases in this way.

There are certain potential advantages and disadvantages of buying at auction. It is not a recommended approach for the beginner but the more experienced buyer may wish to explore the opportunities offered by auction buying.

The most obvious advantage is that the material is sold via bidding without pre-set prices, and therefore could sell below the price that might be established by a dealer, broker or other supply source. But unless the auction is advertised as "unreserved," which most diamond sales are not, there are pre-arranged (though unannounced) minimum levels below which the lots will not be sold. Everything sold at Parke-Bernet carries a reserve, and this is the case with many other auction houses as well. Reserves are intended to protect the owner, not the auctioneer; the auctioneer has no cash tied up in the merchandise and will not suffer even if prices are disappointing. Consignors of auction property are not, of course, permitted to establish excessively high reserves, as this would result in many lots being "bought in." The auction reserve on a diamond will generally range from slightly below wholesale value on specimens of fine quality to half (or less) wholesale on mixed lots of miscellaneous small stones.

Though reserves are not made public — to do this would, in the opinion of auctioneers, cheapen the merchandise — they are not difficult to guess when estimated prices are provided. In the Parke-Bernet catalogues, price estimates are given for nearly every lot, in the form of ranges (such as: Lot

106, $750-$1,000). If you take the two figures, add them together, then divide by two, you arrive at the median estimate. In this case it would be $875. If you then divide the median by 2, the result *will usually be* the reserve price, in this instance from $425 to $450. The lot may "open" on the floor at a price lower than the reserve, precisely at the reserve, or higher than the reserve. This depends upon the kind of bids received before the sale, by mail and phone. If no bids at all have been received on that lot, it will generally open below the reserve — say $400 for the example given. Should it fail to reach the reserve, which would be achieved with just one additional bid, it will be "bought in." But this fact is not announced by the auctioneer. The audience is not aware if the lot was bought in or sold to an absentee buyer. If presale bids have been received in excess of the reserve, the lot will generally open at the higher or next highest of these bids. It is then certain to sell as it has already passed its reserve, whether it sells to a floor bidder or to the "book."

Descriptions provided in catalogues of the larger auction houses are generally reliable but not guaranteed for accuracy. Before placing any bids it makes sense to visit the pre-sale exhibition and personally examine not only the stones themselves but the accompanying G.I.A. certificate, if such are present. You may wish to have an agent do this for you. There are a number of diamond dealers in New York who make a practice of attending all gem sales and acting as agents for prospective customers. They will thoroughly inspect all items on which you propose to bid, advising you of the quality and their opinion of the current market value — which may be different from the estimated realization published in the catalogue. They charge a fee if successful in buying the lots, ranging from 5% to 10% of the sale price. In the case of substantial purchases the fee may be scaled lower, or an arrangement may be made by which the agent agrees to take a lower commission in exchange for a guaranteed fee even if bids are not successful.

A person buying for investment will not find it profitable to pay the full "house estimate." He may sit by and watch some lots sell for double the estimate and more, and think to himself that lots bringing no higher than the full estimate must be bargains. But this is very seldom the case. The estimates, except in the case of very lightweight diamonds or stones of low grade, are approximate retail values. When an investor buys at retail he is paying too much. The stones may be alluring but very likely he could obtain specimens just as good from a broker at considerably lower cost. It should be kept in mind that many of the lots are consigned by dealers and brokers, who are selling by auction to obtain a higher price than they could otherwise achieve.

HOW YOU CAN BE CHEATED WHEN BUYING DIAMONDS

On the whole the diamond and precious gem trade is one of the more ethical. This is a tribute to the integrity of most of its members, as vast opportunities exist for all manner of cheating when transactions are made between dealers and the public.

Some of the potential tricks and "dupes" are described below. The purchaser runs greater risk of encountering these practices when dealing with small neighborhood merchants, private parties who advertise in newspapers, and, in general, tradesmen who have no real reputation to guard. They are not likely to be a problem when buying from registered brokers or the better-established jewel retailers.

For our purposes, simple overpricing is not regarded as cheating. It may reasonably be considered such, however, in the case of merchants who display no marked prices on stones and fix prices based upon their estimation of the customer's expertise or gullibility. It should be needless to warn readers against doing business with any diamond traders who do not affix marked prices to their merchandise, and to turn deaf ears to the argument that "marked prices so quickly become obsolete that we have abandoned using them." They do not become quickly obsolete. When a merchant has purchased a stone, his investment in it remains the same whether the market advances sharply or modestly. It is not, in any event, the kind of situation that prevails with gold, where prices bounce about daily. The only reason for not using marked or labeled prices is to allow their adjustment customer-by-customer, to gouge as deeply as possible from the pockets of the unwary.

The level of knowledge among diamond buyers varies from expert to about zero. There are few other kinds of merchandise upon which people who know nothing about it spend thousands of dollars. There are also few kinds of merchandise with which so much cheating can be done. A painting may be faked, but it will either be a fake or not a fake; with diamonds there are considerations ranging far beyond the mere risk of fakery. In earlier eras of diamond buying, so much advantage was taken of these opportunities, by unscrupulous traders, that the situation was referred to as "the massacre of the innocents."

MISREPRESENTATION OF BRILLIANCE. Here a stone of ordinary or subpar proportioning is shown, with the assurance that it exhibits maximum brilliance and the shaping is beyond reproach. The fact that it displays *some* brilliance, which of course even a bad cut will, is sufficient evidence to convince an uninformed customer. In these situations special lighting may be used, to squeeze as much refraction as possible from the stone. But, of course, the explanation is given that "you can't really appreciate the brilliance under shop lighting."

MISREPRESENTATION OF CARAT WEIGHT. This can be accomplished fairly easily, within a quarter or even half a carat, as the inexperienced shopper is not apt to recognize the shortage. Not one person in a hundred asks for a diamond to be weighed in his absence. Even if this is done, the merchant bent on fraud can get around the obstacle by the use of false weighing machines and similar tricks, which are very difficult to detect.

MISREPRESENTATION OF CLARITY GRADE. The devious seller will generally not make reference to the standard clarity gradings (FL, IF, VS and so forth). He assumes the customer is not familiar with them, and will enter into their discussion only if events prove otherwise. For example, he presents a stone and describes it to be "of excellent quality." This, of course, is meaningless as the clarity scale contains no such word as "excellent." If you inquire about the clarity rating, the unscrupulous dealer is likely to place his stones into a grade one or two (or possibly more) levels above those they deserve. After conversing with the customer for a while, he reaches a conclusion on just how far he can go — based on the apparent knowledge of the customer about diamonds. When he encounters someone obviously buying diamonds for the first time, and who has done no study on them, it will not be unusual for him to offer an imperfect stone as "of excellent quality." He considers himself in the driver's seat in these situations, confident that a beginner would not question his statements. And he is generally correct. Even if the potential buyer notices the imperfectness — though few look close enough — it is quickly dismissed, on grounds that diamonds must have such natural flaws. It is possible that the customer has seen diamonds of this size and cut on sale elsewhere, and looks upon this specimen as an attractive buy because the price is somewhat lower. It should, of course, be sharply lower, but the dealer has discounted merely by 10% or 15% to avoid arousal of suspicion. Often the dealer is brazen enough to invite examination under a jeweler's loupe, which he feels will instill confidence in the buyer. As amateurish as such techniques are, they have a high ratio of success. Things would be otherwise if the public did not pay such great homage to "bargains."

QUARTZ "DIAMONDS." The era of selling quartz crystals or "Herkimer diamonds" as the real thing ought to have ended long ago, but the public is not yet educated to the point of distinguishing a true diamond from a piece of this considerably less valuable substance (the average wholesale price on quartz is around $5 per pound).

REGRINDINGS. These are diamonds, usually of fairly large size, that were originally well-proportioned but have been reground on one or more surfaces to remove or reduce a blemish. Unless regrinding is carried out over the whole stone, its balance will be destroyed and much of the value lost. Detection of this kind of stone is just about impossible for a beginner. It will not refract light very well, but beginners are woefully uninformed about light refraction.

SYNTHETIC GEMS SOLD AS GENUINE. Development of high-quality synthetic diamonds within the past several years has opened the way for yet another method of cheating. Fakes have been sold as genuine diamonds for centuries, including "gems" that were nothing but ordinary glass, but the excellence of today's synthetics has greatly expanded the potential in this direction. The dealer who engages in this kind of deception is careful to display mostly genuine stones. The synthetics are brought out only when the right customers appear. Their virtues are extolled, and the "punch line" is that the diamond, though worth considerably more, can be offered at a very modest price because of special circumstances (usually explained as being left on consignment by a person who acquired it many years ago and paid a small fraction of the current value). Its selling price is generally at least one and a half times a fair sum for a synthetic of its size and quality, often more.

METHODS OF SELLING DIAMONDS

There are several methods of selling diamonds: to your best friend, through an auction, to a dealer or a broker. Selling to a broker, which we discussed previously, is to sell for the market price plus a commission. Selling to a dealer is a slightly different story.

There is no reason, other than the need to raise cash almost instantly, why an investor would sell his diamonds to a jewelry store. With so many better alternatives available, this should be regarded as the absolute "last resort." And it should be done only by persons who

1. Have average quality stones to dispose of
2. Are selling stones already mounted in jewelry.

The dealer can get all the stones he needs from his wholesaler, at very low prices. Of course, they are jewelry-quality and not investment-quality. When confronted with investment stones the jewelry dealer may or may not care to buy them. If he decides to make an effort to buy them, it will not be to use in jewelry but to pass along loose. Undoubtedly the passing along will be done to a broker, so he must calculate the price low enough to allow for the broker's profit as well as his own. Generally, jewelry store dealers will only buy this type of merchandise when it can be had far below the prevailing market. When it can't, they decline to purchase.

There are many methods used by devious jewelry shop proprietors, to drive prices down. These are so common that anyone who has attempted to sell any kind of stones in such shops, whether mounted or unmounted, is likely to be familiar with them. The dealer takes the approach that the customer is either uninformed or so desperately in need of fast cash that any story put forward will be accepted without argument. Very often this is true. When the need for "money in a hurry" arises, many people grab fo their jewelry box. Jewelry merchants encounter these unfortunate souls every day.

You may be told that your diamond is an "old mine cut" (see Glossary when in fact it isn't. The dealer may explain that the diamond is essentiall good but would require fresh cutting to be marketable. This would mean a reduction in carat as well as the expense of refaceting, so I can only pa you . . .

You may be told that the color is not what it should be, that the diamond is too yellowish.

You may be told a great deal of other things, too. "I already have boxes full of diamonds of that grade." "I can buy them for X amount of dollars pe carat right down the street." And so on.

"BUT IT WAS APPRAISED AT. . .$5,000"

The scene is repeated often. A determined-looking lady of middle years dressed in clothing that was fashionable a few decades ago, presents ring or necklace or some other article of jewelry for sale.

She watches with a dull stare as the dealer examines it.

"Well, I could offer you $1,200," the dealer announces.

Several moments of silence follow. Her face contorts. She reel backward slightly as if menaced by an attacker. Suddenly she compose herself. Her eyebrows slant. She is offended.

"But it was *appraised* at $5,000," she exclaims, with strong emphasis o the word "appraise." This, to her, is the magic word. It means she has th Almighty on her side. She has caught the dealer, she figures, in a bareface attempt to pull the wool over her eyes.

Every day this sort of thing happens, with jewelry of all kinds — bu especially with diamonds.

Why do dealers' offers fall so short of the appraised prices?

Are the dealers wrong, or the appraisers, or both?

First, let's look at the appraising business. This distinguished old profe sion is steeped in several centuries of gloried reputation. Appraisers as lot serve a worthy purpose. But the values they place upon articles consig ed for their opinions can be misleading. Most owners of jewelry believe th the appraised value bears a direct relation to the resale value. It doesn Objects are appraised at full retail and often at a slight margin above reta

Remember that the appraiser is paid, usually, by percentage. He receives anywhere from one to five percent of the appraised value, so the higher the appraised value, the higher his payment. Of course, the proud owner does not object to the difference of a few dollars in the appraisal fee. Any annoyance she might have at the additional expense is more than overcome by the joyous news that her treasured old ring — or whatever — has appreciated so markedly in value. She naturally goes away beaming, confident that the appraiser has done a first-class job. She tells her neighbors all about this terrific gentleman and they bring their jewelry for appraisal.

Do you begin to get the picture?

An appraiser who sets low values, even if they represent truly honest retail prices for the material in the condition it's in, does much less business than one who keeps his customers happy. No matter what happens later, the blame is never placed upon him. When a dealer subsequently offers to pay one-tenth or one-seventh or some other fractional amount of the appraisal, it isn't the appraiser who receives curses and accusations; it's always the dealer.

If you have jewelry or loose stones that have been appraised, throw out the appraisal and start over again. Go to an appraiser who is also a dealer or broker. Tell him that you want a clause written into the appraisal contract that obligates him to purchase your material at a specified percentage of the appraised value within 60 days of the job's completion. You will then have a meaningful appraisal. But don't count on every dealer being willing to do this.

DIAMOND OFFERS: WHY DO THEY VARY SO WIDELY?

Unlike gold and silver, whose intrinsic value can be calculated upon their fineness and weight in relation to the current daily spot price, there is no easy formula for pricing a diamond. Any particular stone might be worth $1,000 to one buyer, $1,500 to another and $2,000 to someone else. Yes, there are standards for clarity and cut and color, and a diamond can be weighed to determine its carat. But aside from the carat weight, which is an unarguable matter of fact, the other points are all a matter of individual interpretation and judgment. One person's VVS-1 diamond is another's VVS-2. The cutting that one praised is regarded as ordinary by the next. It is not easy getting two dealers to agree on the value of a diamond. And even if they do agree, they may not be prepared to pay the same price for it.

Let's explore this matter of widely varying price offers. It may not affect you at the moment, but eventually your investment diamonds are going to be sold.

First of all, you are more likely to encounter wildly differing offers if you bring your gems to different classes of buyers. The offers made by two brokers in the same city at approximately the same time (say within a week of each other) should not differ by more than 10%-20%. But if one offer is given by a broker, another by a jewelry shop, and a third by a wholesaler, you are apt to have three very unrelated figures.

Offers made from one broker to the next do not differ vastly because brokers are selling exclusively or almost exclusively to investment clients. They mark up their purchases at about the same level for resale and all have approximately the same styles and manners of doing business. A sharper than 10%-20% difference will occur if one broker is overstocked on diamonds of that particular kind, or disagrees with the grading. Whenever a broker is overstocked he will attempt to purchase at a discount to allow for the likelihood that capital will be tied up indefinitely waiting for buyers to appear. He may discount 10% from his usual buying price for a diamond of that grade and cut, or 20% or even more, depending on the state of his operations and the extent of his overstock. If he disagrees with the grading he may decline the purchase entirely or offer a considerably lower sum.

But by and large, offers made by brokers are more reliable and higher than could be obtained from any other source. You could, of course, do better by selling at auction, maybe a lot better, but that involves some uncertainty and a long wait.

Jewelry shop proprietors try to buy stones at lower than wholesale, anywhere from 12%-15% of wholesale for insignificant stones of little value to 70-80% of wholesale for more attractive gems. It is obviously pointless for a jewelry shop to pay full wholesale to a private seller, as he could obtain similar material from his ordinary supplier. And he would much rather do this, as his wholesaler extends credit.

An offer for a diamond, no matter who makes it, constitutes the worth of that stone to them at that particular time. When selling, there is no reason why you should not fully investigate the market and obtain a number of offers before reaching any decision.

DIAMOND GLOSSARY

ABRADED CULET

If the cluet facet is chipped or otherwise damaged, as the result of harsh contact with another diamond, this is known as an abraded culet.

ABRASION

This is generally taken to mean an injury to a cut diamond. Also used in reference to the natural action of water, and other elements, in shaping or smoothing gems still in the earth.

AMERICAN BRILLIANT CUT

The American Brilliant Cut, also known as the Tolkowsky Theoretical Brilliant Cut after its developer, is a method of cutting diamonds to mathematical perfection to yield greatest brilliancy and fire. This is today the most popular cut for fine stones. It is employed in Europe as well as the U.S. Sometimes shortened to "American Cut."

APPRAISAL

An estimation of the current cash value of a diamond or diamonds. Most appraisals are made for insurance purposes and in these instances should reflect replacement cost (buying the same size, cut and quality of diamond, in the same setting, at the current retail price). An estate appraisal, often referred to as appraisal for probate, valuates the diamond in terms of *what it would be likely to sell for,* if disposed of by one of the conventional methods. Obviously, the estate value will be lower than insurance value. It is important that appraisal papers describe the stone in sufficient detail for positive identification.

BAGUETTE

French for "rod." A step-cut used for rectangular stones, chiefly those of small size.

BEARDED GIRDLE
Diamond girdle which is not smooth but instead display networks of imperfections in the form of hairline fractures. Bearded girdles result from rushing the process of rounding up or shaping the stone. Sometimes called "fuzzy girdle."

BEZEL FACET
The large facets surrounding the table on the crown of a Round Brilliant cut. They are always 8 in number.

BLOCKING
Cutting the first 18 facets into a diamond — known as the "main facets" — is called blocking. The word is borrowed from the art world, where blocking in sculpture means to reduce a *block* of marble, wood, etc., to roughly the shape of the intended design.

BOURSE
An assembly of dealers, set up to buy and/or sell. There are regularly established, continuous diamond bourses sponsored by trade organizations in various parts of the world (but chiefly in Europe).

BRILLIANTEERER
An artisan who cuts and polishes the "brilliant facets," on Brilliant Cut diamonds. These are a total of 40, and are added after cutting the main bezel and pavilion facets (which is done by the blocker).

BRUTER
Workman in a diamond factory who shapes stones against a high-speed lathe. Though only "dust" is lost in this operation, it reduces carat weight more than might be imagined.

CANARY DIAMOND
Deeply colored yellow diamond, possibly with hues of green or orange. Pale yellow coloration — far more common — is detrimental to value.

CARAT
A unit of weight, by which the size of both uncut and cut diamonds is stated. A carat is equal to .200 grams. The newcomer to diamond buying should be careful not to become overly influenced by carat size that he ignores, or fails to recognize the importance of, such points as clarity, color and cut.

CARBON SPOTS
Dark particles or inclusions in a diamond, which may or may not be visible to the unaided eye. An all-purpose term; the material could be of any nature. It is frequently graphite. "Carbon" spots normally appear black to the unaided eye or under low magnification, but may prove to be another color when magnified further and examined by an individual with keen color perception. Classified as blemishes. (See Grading section.)

CENTRAL SELLING ORGANIZATION
Collective term referring to the three organizations which place freshly mined diamonds into the world wholesale market. These are: Industrial Distributors Ltd., Diamond Trading Co. Ltd., and Diamond Corporation Ltd., the last two of which are incorporated in South Africa. All were established by the DeBeers firm.

CERTIFIED GEMOLOGIST

An individual so accredited by the G.I.A. (Gemological Institute of America), after completion of its courses or by special examination.

CLARITY GRADE

The quality of a diamond in terms of its clearness or absence/presence of imperfections, expressed according to a standard scale. (See Grading section.)

CLEAVAGE

Word with many meanings in relation to diamonds, but chiefly used in reference to the dependability of crystals to divide in established directions when properly cleaved (set in a holder, marked, and divided by means of a sharp blade tapped with a mallet or other heavy instrument).

COLORED DIAMONDS

Diamonds are found in a variety of colors, generally very pale, including brown, green, pink, blue, red and yellow. When these colors are *intense* and well balanced throughout the stone, premium value is likely to be attached. But a diamond of pastel color is not as desirable as a colorless or "white."

COLOR GRADE

The color quality of a diamond, expressed according to a scale of letters representing different grades of color (see Grading Section). Crystal clear, or absolute lack of coloration, is the most desirable; these are often referred to — very confusingly — as "white" diamonds.

COLORLESS

A diamond in which no trace of coloration can be detected. The ideal state for stones intended for the Round Brilliant cut. Truly colorless diamonds are worth a permium over others, assuming they are not severely flawed.

COLOR

Color is used, normally, in reference to the degree with which a diamond deviates from being perfectly clear or uncolored. This is in the form of white cloudiness or smokiness. When actual color is present — yellow, brown, etc. — the value is sharply reduced, unless (which is rare) the coloring is so strong as to be attractive in itself.

CONCHOIDAL FRACTURE

A cut (made by a sharp blow upon a knife blade resting on a diamond) in which the initial pressure of impact radiates outward in a prescribed pattern, something like ripples created by tossing pebbles in a lake.

CRITICAL ANGLE

The greatest angle in a diamond, running from the normal surface to a surface that a ray of light may form when passing from density to lesser density. Of importance in determining the degree of light refraction and, therefore, the ultimate fire of the stone.

CROWN

The upper part of a cut diamond, above the girdle.

CRYSTAL LATTICE

The network or structure of atoms within a diamond crystal. The cleavage break is along the atomic plane of weakness. When cleaving is attempted against the plane of weakness, the break will either be uneven or crushing could result.

CULET
Small facet cut into the bottom or pavilion of a diamond. Without this facet the stone would, thanks to cutting, come to a rather sharp point at the pavilion.

DEPTH PERCENTAGE
The relationship of a diamond's height (table to culet) to its diameter at the widest part (the girdle). Good depth percentage is necessary in achieving a proper "make" or cut.

DIAMOND
A gem mineral, hardest of all mineral substances and in fact of all substances in nature. Its hardness, purity of color (in top-grade specimens), and ability to refract light render the diamond the most ideal and deisrable of gems for making into jewelry.

DIAMOND PAPER
Paper folded in a special manner (in which dealers are proficient but the beginner learns slowly), to contain loose diamonds in transit. A durable grade of paper must be used, to prevent the stone breaking through and escaping in the event of pressure or possible rough handling. Revelant information — such as weight, lot number or price — may be penciled on the outside of this packet.

DIAMOND SETTER
A skilled workman who places a finished, cut diamond into a jewelry mounting. Expertise and care are necessary, to avoid injury.

DIAMOND-WASHING CUP
Bronze cup, punched with numerous holes in the fashion of a sieve, set inside a glass jar. Used in washing diamonds (removing surface grease).

DISPERSION
The ability of diamonds to turn ordinary light entering them into brilliant colors. The principal is similar to that creating rainbows in the sky when sunlight shines after a rainshower.

DODECAHEDRON
Twelve-sided crystal.

DURABILITY
Diamonds are durable in the sense of not being easily scratched, except by other diamonds. They can, however, be crushed or broken without difficulty. Those who own diamonds should be careful not to form the very mistaken notion that, because of their hardness rating, they are impervious to harm.

EMERALD CUT
A once-popular style of rectangular or square cut, featuring steps of elongated facets.

EUROPEAN CUT
Method of cutting which varies from the American Briliant approach in

that proportions are worked out according to light falling directly from above on the crown.

EXTRA FACETS

Additional facets beyond those intended in the planning stage. Generally caused accidentally in one or more of the cutting and shaping processes, extra facets are considered defects if they occur on the crown or can be seen through the crown.

EYE-CLEAN

A diamond in which no internal imperfections can be seen with the naked eye, by a person with normal vision.

FACET

Flat surface cut into a diamond. Correct positioning and angling of facets determines whether the stone will have maximum fire.

FACE UP

A diamond set so that the table faces the observer, as in most jewelry.

FANCY DIAMOND

A colored diamond, whose color is intense enough to be a plus rather than a minus. Faintly colored stones are invariably worth less than pure colorless ones.

FEATHER

Any break in a diamond. Feathers are blemishes.

FINISH

The overall quality of a diamond in relation to the "finishing steps" in manufacture as well as overall proportioning. Fineness of polishing, girdle smoothness, and adriotness in cutting the culet are among the considerations taken into account.

FLAW

A blemish or imperfection, either on the surface of a diamond or the interior. This may be in the form of a scratch, feathering, carbon spots, etc. Bad color is not technically considered a flaw; nor is anything relating to the proportioning or cut.

FLAWLESS

The highest clarity grade for a diamond. It does not infer that tiny, minor blemishes are not visible with strong magnification. (See Grading section.)

FLUORESCENCE

The action of one kind of energy-induced radiation changing to another, thereby creating (sometimes) the apparently spontaneous appearance of color or hues. Diamonds generally show a blue flourescence, though this is not invariable.

FOUR C's

Common trade term to collectively describe the major considerations in a diamond's value: clarity, color, carat, and cut.

GEMOLOGICAL INSTITUTE OF AMERICA

A non-profit, chiefly educational organization, with headquarters in New

York and Los Angeles. It conducts courses in diamonds (grading, apprais-ing, etc.) and awards certificates of Certified Gemologist to those suc-cessfully completing these courses. In addition it operates a diamond cer-tification service. G.I.A. papers, when current, serve as the "last word" in the industry of grading. Investment diamonds should be purchased only when accompanied by G.I.A. papers. This is the only guarantee that they will be salable at the same grade purchased — assuming they incur no injury in the meantime.

GEMOLOGIST

An authority in the identification, grading, and appraisal of gems. Gemology may of course be pursued as a hobby, and the term "gemologist" is subject to use as loose as "philatelist," meaning stamp collector. A *certified* gemologist is one who has successfully completed a study course in the subject and been issued the equivalent of a diploma.

GEMOLOGY

The study of gems and gemstones: their physical properties, origins, methods of recognition, geographical distribution, uses in science and industry, and the gem trade.

GIRDLE FACETS

When used in the sense of "girdle facets," this refers to the triangular or lozenge-shaped facets in a Round Brilliant cut that touch the girdle both above and beneath it — 16 above, 16 below.

GIRDLER

Name sometimes used for employee of a diamond factory who rounds the stone (on a lathe).

GIRDLE THICKNESS

Thickness of the outermost edge of a diamond, where the crown is separated from the pavilion. It does *not* refer to diameter of the stone itself, a common misunderstanding. Girdle *height* would be more descriptive, but terms that have established a tradition of long use in the industry are not easily supplanted. In small stones, girdle thickness is greater in relation to the stone's size than in large diamonds. Variations are possible in girdle thickness without seriously influencing desirability or value. However, narrow girdles are more in preference today, as a rule.

GIRDLING

The process of rounding a stone, which is accomplished by grinding it in a lathe. Despite being an operation dependent on machinery, skill of the girdler (who holds the stone, in a dop, against the grinding surface) determines its degree of success.

GRADUATE GEMOLOGIST

An individual who has received the *Graduate in Gemology Diploma* from the Gemological Institute of America, by successfully completing one of its instructional courses.

GRAINER

Grainers are diamonds that weigh in the vicinity of full grains. Since four grains equal one carat, "grainers" weigh approximately 0.25, 0.50, and 0.75 of a carat. This could also be carried over to stones weighing more than a carat; a 1.25 carat diamond could be called a five-grainer. But this is seldom done.

HARDNESS

In gemology, the resistence of a substance to surface scratching. It does not relate in any respect to ability to escape other kinds of injury (such as crushing or breaking). Diamond is the hardest mineral substance with a rating of 10 on the Mohs scale, talc the softest (1). It is in fact at least ten times harder than the next hardest mineral, corundum. Diamonds can be scratched only by other diamonds. They can however be cut (cleaved apart) with conventional tools.

IMPERFECTION

A flaw or blemish, caused by nature or man, which may be on the outer surface or the stone's interior. Poor color or unskilled cut are not classified as imperfections, though they do, of course, play a role in value determination.

INCLUDED CRYSTAL

A small crystal imbedded or trapped within a larger crystal. Often has the appearance of an air space and is therefore mistakenly referred to as a bubble.

INCLUSION

Any substance, including fragments of diamond itself or tiny crystals visible within a diamond. These entrapped "prisoners" have influence on value, which may be greater or lesser depending on their number and size. If not too centrally situated it may be possible in cutting to remove them from a rough stone. Cuts designed to rid a stone of inclusions generally involve considerable loss of carat weight.

INTERNALLY FLAWLESS

A diamond in which no internal flaws, or only those of a very insignificant nature, can be observed at 10X magnification; but whose exterior surface displays imperfections of some kinds. Abbreviated IF. IF stones are normally polished to remove the exterior blemishes, which slightly reduces the carat weight but results in overall increase in desirability and value.

IRREGULAR GIRDLE

An irregular girdle is one whose thickness varies along different parts of its circumference. Ideally there should be little, if any, variation.

KIMBERLITE

The volcanic underground pipes in which diamonds are found in Africa.

LASER DRILLING

Drilling into a diamond by means of a laser beam, which, because of intense heat generated, can sometimes reduce or remove flaws. Used chiefly to bleach out carbon spots, in which a bleaching agent is used as an adjunct. Results are not accurately predictable, but very good success has so far been achieved by skilled operators.

LEVERIDGE GAUGE

Device invented in 1937 by A.D. Leveridge for estimating weight of diamonds, both loose and mounted. It consists of a micrometer with calipers set with a dial, on which a hand swings to indicate the reading. T user then refers to a conversion table, giving the approximate weight for a stone of its measurements. Though not 100% accurate, the Leveridge gauge has proven to be the most reliable instrument of its kind on the market.

LOUPE

A magnifying glass, either of the folding pocket variety or (more commonly) mounted in an eyepiece. Though a magnifier of any strength can be sold as a loupe, "jeweler's loupe" refers to a glass of 10X power.

MACLE

Rough diamond with a twinned crystal, the twin appearing to have been turned around at a 180 degree angle in relation to the other or parent crystal. Macles are normally flattish and lozenge shaped. Because of the enormous carat loss in fashioning a macle into a Round Brilliant, they are often (if jewelry grade) cut to fancy shapes that take advantage of nature's preshaping.

MELLEE

"Small goods." Roughs of less than two carats and cut stones under 17 points (less than 1/5th of a carat), are called mellees.

NATURAL

Small portion of deliberately unpolished surface on a jewel diamond, usually along the girdle, which appears rough in relation to neighboring surfaces. The motive in leaving naturals is to remove as little as possible in carat weight.

OFF-CENTER CULET

A cut stone in which the culet (base) is out of register with the girdle angles. When viewed through the table, the culet should be at equal distance from each opposing girdle angle. Seldom noticed by persons inexperienced in examining diamonds.

OLD EUROPEAN CUT

Style of cutting popular in the 19th century, direct predecessor to the modern Round Brilliant. Old European cuts have a smaller table than the Round Brilliant and heavier crown; overall depth is somewhat greater. Also called "old mine cut." It is sometimes possible to recut these stones into good Round Brilliants, though a considerable loss of carat weight will likely occur.

OLD MINE CUT

in general, any jewel diamond cut into an early style of Round Brilliant, prior to the Tolkowsky method of mathematical calculation, is referred to as an "old mine cut." Apparently it was believed (mistakenly) that diamonds were once cut at the mines before wholesaling. The value of old mine cuts in relation to carat weight is much less than of stones in the same grade cut to modern Round Brilliant. Recutting usually increases value, despite reducing the diamond's weight.

OVAL CUT

(1) Modern brilliant cut with elliptical girdle.
(2) Old style cut featuring narrow triangular facets.

PAPER MARKS

Surface blemishes, generally tiny scratches or nicks, resulting not from contact with *paper* but with other diamonds caried with it in the same diamond paper. Obviously, the practice of carrying loose unprotected stones in a manner that allows them to touch each other is to be avoided.

PAPERWORN

Same as Paper Marks (see above).

PAVE

Method of mounting small stones in a piece of jewel, to cover the entire field of the setting (or as much as practical) without the setting itself showing.

PAVILION

The lower portion of a cut stone, from beneath the girdle to the culet.

PAVILION ANGLE

The angle at which the pavilion facets rise up from the culet to meet the girdle. Pavilion angle greatly influences light refraction.

PAVILION DEPTH

The vertical distance from the culet to the girdle plane.

PAVILION FACETS

Facets in the pavilion or lower part of the diamond, beneath the girdle.

PEAR SHAPE

An oval cut, coming to a point at the small end of the crown, having 56 or 58 facets.

PIQUE

Term in common use in Europe, and to some extend elsewhere, referring to stones with imperfections. Modified as pique-1, pique-2 and pique-3 to indicate seriousness of imperfection, pique-1 being the least flawed. Often written as P1, P2, P3. U.S. equivalents are I-1, I-2, I-3.

PLANNER

Another name for designer. Individual in a diamond factory who decides how rough stones will be cut.

PLOTTING

A modern-day practice of recording the exact characteristics of a cut gemstone, by the use of a paper and pen. On a diagram of the stone's shape and cut (printed diagrams of the popular cuts can be had), markings are made to indicate the presence and precise location of all characteristics. These are in the form of symbols, according to a system devised by the Gemological Institute of America. For simplification, inclusions are marked in red, blemishes green, extra facets and prong mountings in black. Plotting serves not only as an aid in appraisal but identification.

POLISHED GOODS

Finished stones (cut and polished), as opposed to freshly mined roughs.

PROPORTION PERCENTAGES

A system developed by the G.I.A. in which certain percentages of value are deducted from a stone according to the degree from which it deviates from perfect proportioning. The percentages, which go as high as 15% of base value, are applied against the Table, Girdle Thickness, Crown Angles, Pavilion, Culet and Major Symmetry Faults. Table and pavilion account for the sharpest discounts, if severely misproportioned.

REFRACTION

The angling of light as it passes through a cut diamond, bounding from one wall to another. *Reflection* is the end result of refraction: the light as it exits from the stone and provides brilliance or sparkle.

SHALLOW CUT

A stone whose main pavilion facets have an angle of less than 39 degrees to the girdle plane.

SINGLE CUT

Simple style of cut employed on small stones, usually those intended to be used in mounting in conjunction with a large central stone. Single cuts are circular at the girdle.

SYMMETRY

The placement of facets on a cut stone, as well as shaping. Opposing facets — those facing each other from opposite sides of the stone — must be of the same size and shape, and placed precisely opposite, to achieve good symmetry. Deviation will result in loss of light refraciton and the stone will not be as firey.

SYNTHETIC

An imitation, commerically made gemstone, which may be very like the natural in its properties and cutting potential. Synthetics are produced in a number of grades and vary considerably in price. All are detectable, using proper equipment.

TABLE

The uppermost plane surface of a cut diamond. Like the other plane surfaces, the table is also a facet.

TAPERED BAGUETTE

Baguette shaped cut with one end smaller than the other.

TRIGON

Tiny pit-like markings found on the surface of octahedral crystals. These are "growth markings."

WHITE

Misleading term meaning colorless or clear. Derives probably from the fact that in olden times white was not recognized as a color but as the absence of color. A really white diamond (smoky or cloudy) is not nearly as desirable as clear.

ZIRCONIA, CUBIC

Synthetic material from which imitation diamonds are made. Extremely difficult to distinguish from a natural diamond, except for a very experienced appraiser or through use of special equipment (such as the Diamond Probe). It has a greater hardness than many other synthetics, but its hardness is not equal to a diamond's.